Twenty Tales on the Political Economy of Quality
©Krum Stefanov, Numen Books 2012
ISBN 978-0-9871581-6-1

Twenty Tales on the Political Economy of Quality

Krum Stefanov

TALE I

The Elixir of Life and KFC

"Change! Change! Cigarette! Cigarette! Okay... Change! Change! Cigarette! Cigarette! Okay... Change! Change! Cigarette! Cigarette! Okay!" The beggar was repeating at the very moment when he approached a middle aged man in a dark suit, sitting on a bench of a platform of Geneva's 'Cornavin' railroad station with his eyes apparently fixed in the wide open front page of what appeared to be a local newspaper.

"Hey, what are you doing here?" said the man, "Have I not seen you somewhere before? We met in Venice, back in the 18th century and as far as I remember, I saw you in a coffee house by the name of Cafè Florian, reading a book published a little earlier bearing the title '*Zadig*'."

"Yes, I was intrigued by one of the heroes of the novel, Pangloss, who happened to carry my own name, without any resemblance to me and still less to my views on the way things were going on back then, as well as now."

"I know what you talking about since I had the same problem. I did not recognize myself in the hero Cacambo, either."

"I see. But what is you real name, by the way?" Asked the man in the dark suit.

"I will not tell you. This is basically a secret, included in the secret of secrets. Furthermore, how can I be sure that Pangloss was indeed your real name back then, and not one of your several nicknames?"

"As you are so secretive - let's just call each other from now on, by these very same names since this appears to be the main point we had in common, when we met back in the 18th century."

"Okay I agree."

"Why are you begging in this place?"

"I had enough of the Elixir for extending my lifespan, but still not enough for getting access to the formula of transmutation. So this caused me tremendous problems throughout all this time as you can see."

"You have nothing to worry about. The access to the formula is available only in a particular time frame, among other things. I refrain from commenting about the rest in my turn, right now. However that may be, should you have the patience for being in my company for a few days, I will give you enough gold for a long time to come."

"That sounds great! You know what? I am somewhat hungry. So would you be kind enough to buy me a dinner at a place nearby by the name of KFC, Kentucky Fried Chicken?"

"Okay. Let's go!"

*****

PANGLOSS: The first step in the spiritual quest for Wisdom nowadays is usually to book a plane ticket for various exotic destinations, the climbing of some high mountain or at least one successful attempt to walk on foot for several days in a row. Yes - but what if it happens that such an expensive pilgrimage, unless it is paid already by some TV station as it had been the case, for example with one of these journalists, of the kind of Arnaud Desjardins or financed in a more enigmatic way as it may have been the case with the journeys of the mystic Gurdjieff throughout the steppes of Central Asia... is not the only way to the final countdown? What if we suddenly get a premonition of something ultimate to come, say in the nearby convenience store or better still in the KFC next door?

CACAMBO: Wait a minute. Are not KFC chickens actually cage chickens?

PANGLOSS: Yes - and that is why these chickens have trouble standing on their own legs and are fed with a generous daily menu of chemical substances and a bunch of antibiotics? Is there not some kind of prerequisite for at least a semblance of Wisdom such as being not just a chicken but a free range chicken? Had there been one only Wisdom this indeed would have been the case, but at this point this is out of the question since each chicken has its own Wisdom. So let's get back to the cage chicken. Here is a creature who knows the thing which in reality is the whole thing provided this whole thing is the Universe and provided the Universe is its own cage. The more cages there are the more different Wisdoms. And another thing: by being locked in a cage any chicken's Wisdom is separated from the respective Wisdom of any other chicken.

Should we assume the apparently reasonable claim that most of the time any or almost any Wisdom can be communicated, various sounds, signs and words would instantly appear and arrange themselves in the form of messages. The separation of all chicken's Wisdom in cages will form the nature of the messages. Their orientation by necessity will be self-contained, self-sufficient as hermetic as a soap bubble. A chicken who shares his cage with two other specimens of his own kind for example, would spend his entire lifespan by staring only to the chickens in his own cage without ever realizing that there are countless other chickens around him and that all the cages combined, apart from being an integral part of the Universe, are also a part of an Animal Farm owned by a Demiurge, also called a Farmer. As any subject has its own object so any message has its own content. And this content as we said it already is a self-contained whole related only to the parts in the cage and therefore unrelated to the parts of other cages. Now, should we look for the shadow of the chicken's 'cage' beyond the relatively tiny space of the Animal Farm or in the World at large, we may well end up by finding it locked in the term 'Narrative.' At a closer scrutiny its apparently self-evident content vanishes into thin air. Here is a cryptic term. When we say chicken everything is crystal clear. A chicken is a chicken which means that we have a picture of a small yellow bird imprinted immediately in our mind. Should we assume that this is so because one appears as a representation of the senses whereas the other is a notion we still miss the point. Notions have representations in the same way as any essence has an expression. Should we say, for instance, 'Justice' various representations, although less clear-cut than the one of the chicken will appear before our eyes. The same would happen with say 'Freedom' or just any other notion. Yes - that is fine, but what about the Narrative?

Here there is nothing or absolutely nothing. We are simply wandering in the dark unless we just add the preposition 'on' or say, 'about'. A Narrative is what it is if it is a Narrative on something or about something. For example, *1001 Nights* is a Narrative, among other things, on the confusion of the Awakened Sleeper, for instance or the adventures of Sinbad the Seaman or so many other things with which Sheherazade used to entertain the initially angry Prince for 1001 Nights. The same would be valid for Mao's *Little Red Book* or the figure of Socrates whom the authors of so many books like to give as an example to illustrate various fine points in Philosophy. So we may say without any hesitation that should there be a correct view, this would be the view just stated above. This is certainly so but is a view really correct if it is not an ontologically correct view?

The assumption on the primacy of the Narrative over its content is a semantic reversal of reality, where what is above appears to be below and vice versa and at the same time a methodological black hole for present day mainstream currents in the History of Ideas, since Postmodern Culture makes no distinction between the copy and the original. Had it been acknowledged that the Narrative is related to what it is narrated in the same way as a shadow is related to the body that would be at the same time a tacit acknowledgment of an invisible reality of Forms beyond the senses. Now, should we stand for the Perennial view according to which there is only one possible starting point and this starting point is the Principle of Unity, the denial of this same view by being necessarily manifested as Division, Separation will shape an inverted form of Consciousness where the Detail as the ultimate Separation, as the nucleus of the atom seems to be the Principle itself, although precisely in the name of this same optical illusion that is in the name of the denial of the Principle, the inverted Consciousness is outwardly denying what inwardly it takes to be self-evident. Because should we be consistent to the end in the denial of the Perennial view and we deny the detail as Principle or a substitute of the Principle that this detail or atom is in reality accordingly, Consciousness will fall apart, which is an absurdity, since Consciousness is Non-Duality and therefore has no parts.

Now let's get back to the chicken, to the cage chicken in particular. Our little friend has not only the privilege of being locked in a cage but instead of standing on his legs, he is actually standing on his head since now his natural position is what otherwise would have been unnatural as he is permanently turned upside down. Should we substitute the chicken's 'Cage' for 'Narrative' it would be rather reasonable to assume that as there are many cages so there are many Narratives. Yes, but cages are after all just that, that is cages, which are alike, identical. So what to do to differentiate them, to make them appear as distinctive cages?

May be the best solution to this problem, would be to paint all of them in various colors. The same will apply for the Narratives which should appear as distinctive as possible. We could conceive any Narrative provided this is a Narrative on the parts and never a Narrative on the whole. By the way, what would the Narrative on Man, for example would be, according to this view?

Man would naturally be cut into slices a little as a deep frozen broiler in a butcher's shop. So here is his head, his legs as so many other parts of his body. Among these parts is certainly also a part without which not a single body can exist as a whole. We are referring here to the digestive tube common to chickens and to men alike.

CACAMBO: …To men alike indeed! I am full already. May be we should go now? What do you think?

PANGLOSS: Okay. I will finish in a minute.

TALE II

The Digestive Tube Syndrome

Pangloss: …That is obvious indeed, since, had any creature not been equipped with a more or less operational digestive tube or a live digestive tube, there would be simply no life on this planet. As far as the Consciousness of Modernity is concerned, however the above observation appears to be far from been self-evident. On the opposite, for Modern Consciousness a body cut from the soul can still be animated, as if the various parts of a dismembered body might have had a separate existence, the body should have been alive accordingly. So is the digestive tube. Now, since the idea of a Center, of Being or of Consciousness is as impossible to be torn out of Consciousness Itself as for example to order the Sun to set once and for all and to see this order carried out in the next few minutes, Modern Consciousness by the process of its own inversion, once turned upside down assumes implicitly, whatever it might say explicitly, that the digestive tube is the center of being, the purest expression of Life or the Essence of Life. It goes without saying that as any part is a part of a whole and so is the digestive tube. To assume that it can function by itself, unrelated not only to the other parts of the body but to the body as a whole is an optical illusion. Initially this optical illusion does not seem to be an illusion at all. The breach appears only later along the way, precisely when Consciousness makes the attempt following the path of its own unconscious inversion to qualify…quantity. All that enters the digestive tube is to be measured and cut into slices according to…according to what? That is the question. Since the digestive tube now appears as the center of being it simply cannot have a reference other than itself and in such a perception there is no place for quality in a way other than refuting its own self-proclaimed ultimate starting point and take the reverse course. Therefore should we remain within the limits of what we could also refer to as The Digestive Tube Syndrome, quantity as pure inner vacuity, as the shadow of something that has been proclaimed non-existent on one hand, but whose presence, on the other hand is confusedly felt at any point will be the only possible ultimate expression of the inverted Consciousness. Now, the latter in reality refutes itself at any point by the mere fact that there is no Quantity without counting. Here it is the vacuity, the emptiness of Quantity, separated from its real content that is Quality that causes the obsession of counting. So, 1, 2, 3, 4…Count as much as you like but never ask what are you counting and even less so why are counting. Also, what really counts is to count both ways, in the outside as well as in the inside. In other words, never stay in one place either by running or by multiplying your desires, your real and moveable estate, your wallet or your collection of butterflies, of post stamps etc.

Before going any further, what is our concern at this point is to retrace the inner projections of Consciousness since everything else follows. The reason for the appearance of this particular form of Consciousness that is the Consciousness of Modernity has a Meta historical core and the historical reconstruction that it is usually put forward to explain it is a little like surfing the waves in a troubled sea. You can do any movement provided you stay on the surface. Furthermore, the tremendous expansion of the supply of information through the Internet makes it pointless to waste time on the various currents which affected in one way or another, the evolution of Modern Consciousness.

Be it in the form of enlightened self-interest or class struggle or struggle to survive or simply greed, what we characterized above as the Syndrome of the Digestive Tube made an encroachment on both private and public spheres already in the 18th century and by now there is hardly anything that is out of its reach. As you shall see later on, the particular perception of reality, the Digestive Tube Syndrome was instilled in the emerging science of Economics and has been dissolved in all spheres of life. If society is to be compared to a cup of water, the Digestive Tube Syndrome will appear as the salt poured into the water. At first the taste of salt is hardly perceptible, but gradually as time goes by the water becomes more and more salty and soon the day may come when it will be no longer possible to drink this water since the salt is making burn whoever attempts to do so. Should we look only for a brief moment to the past however, we'll be immediately stricken by the absence of this preoccupation. The conditions of life, may well have been harsher than they are today, but, nevertheless, what was still left of Traditional Science and the consciousness, however veiled, of the subtle or invisible reality, within and beyond the phenomena were preserved thorough various codes imprinted in the inherited from a remote past chain of Customs and Superstitions as well. Even in the 19th century the nationalistic pathos, the various moralistic derivatives and to some extent Romanticism were at least as relevant as the postulates of positive science and the already emerging but still marginal consciousness of Greed waiting for his time to come in the social and in the private sphere. The point here is not to evaluate the quantity of Greed in a given moment since the latter is always one and the same, since the gold seekers, the treasure hunters of the past were no less greedy than today's virtual stock market traders, but to retrace the ways it has been expressed and to see the likely outcome if it is to be given a free reign to Greed. Had it not been for a certain crypto-ontological awareness of Greed and its various side effects, there would be no legend of Faust for example, including Goethe's Faust which is only a later version of an already well-known legend throughout the Middle-Ages.

The Digestive Tube Syndrome has been able so far to exacerbate greed by gradually veiling the awareness of its expressions. The greedier you are, the less aware of greed you become. Here is the correct view today.

Cacambo: May be, but after all that I heard up to now, it still not clear to me, what is this all about. Are you talking on matters of food, on gastroenterology or some kind of abstract philosophy?

Pangloss: Our point is on salt poured into a cup of water. Water being one of the four elements, another is Air. Are you thinking of Air each time you take a breath?

Cacambo: I would say no. Breathing is coming out of itself. I mean it is taken for granted.

Pangloss: Yes and in the same way, once distilled in Modern Consciousness, the Digestive Tube Syndrome appears to be the only possible reality. There is a difference with Air, however, since, if you are to remain alive, you cannot choose to breathe or not to breathe, whereas the Consciousness of the Digestive Tube Syndrome may exist or vanish, where else, by the way than in the Air? According to your will.

TALE III

Vacuity and Movement

CACAMBO: Is your expose over?

PANGLOSS: Should we choose two key words, to express the Consciousness of the Digestive Tube, they will be: vacuity and movement. We did not say 'on one hand and/ or on the other hand', because vacuity and movement are interrelated. These are the two sides of the same coin. The more the experience of vacuity is intensified, the more we run away in the quest of substance. Had the experience of vacuity been coupled with awareness of vacuity, we would be inclined to stop the current in one way or another.

Now, should we look at the ancient past only for a brief moment, for example in the works of F. Cumont among others we'll immediately notice the now striking emphasis on ritual. The more we get back to the past, the more all-pervading the rituals appear to be in all spheres of life. Also, the further we advance to the present, the less effective these rituals become, in line with the process of Meta historical fossilization or fragmentation of what has been classified as Perennial Knowledge already in the Middle-Ages. Now, the rites and traditional science are in reality the various expressions of the awareness of the ultimate, invisible point, called much later on Principle or for example the Sun of the Neo-Platonists.

This ritualized awareness of the invisible or non-duality had been crystallized not only in the Human Psyche but also in the material sphere, which is of concern to us in the present text. Be it food, be it, Architecture or Trade, all activity, nowadays classified as 'economic' used to be rooted along metaphysical or non-material lines. Furthermore, Quality as a unique expression of the Principle of Unity is behind practically all 'economic' activity of the Ancient Past. Here we should not go any further without a description, however brief of what is actually meant by 'Quality' within this context.

Instead of going further with abstractions, we'll start with an example which at least chronologically is not that ancient. These are the figures still standing on Madrid's main square: Don Quixote and Sancho. What is of interest to us here is not really literature but one point in particular:

Should we follow their steps, we'll notice along the way not only that they are together all the time, but it appears also that in all likelihood, neither of them really wants to be the other. Sancho is what he is, that is Sancho, an individual who by no means wants to be Don Quixote, as he is no Don Quixote and does not want to be Don Quixote because as Sancho, he has a unique quality related only to what is similar to his Essence. Once more: similar but not identical. In this case, he represents the peasants of the past or the Psyche of a particular state of being or a specific ontological condition. As we said it already, what is our concern at this point is not really the literary character of Sancho, however unique it may be in its own way, but his inner self-confidence. He really has no clue what the modern term 'complex' means, invented only in the late 19th century by a German, psychologist I guess, since Sancho is perfectly alien to self-alienation. So, once again he has only one possible identity and should he move in one way or another, this is always within the boundaries of this identity that is as an extension of his own self. So were the peasants throughout the world up to the First World War. For example, the term 'landed immigrant' still valid in Canada for those with permanent residence status, used to designate individuals who on their arrival acquired free land for cultivation. So it was in Argentina, Uruguay or Brazil, where, for example, in the 19th century, Maria Leopoldina of Austria encouraged German immigration in rural areas.

Now, as already hinted earlier our intent here is not to present the main points of the debate about the traditional rural values, the question of estrangement, the mechanistic nature of modern society versus the organic unity of the past, the transmission of Folk Culture and least of all to idealize a way of life, which however different from the present is still within the sphere of what practically all traditional sources call the Kali Yuga or Iron Age. Furthermore, the subject has been treated to the point of complete exhaustion by Russian Narodniki and Intellectuals in general throughout the 19th century around their Samovars in St Petersburg, Moscow or Siberia, who attributed just everything to the peasant except a treatment of the subject at least with a degree of self-restraint, since in their eyes, the Muzhik is either, a villain, a brutal animal or just the opposite a hero of our time, of all time, a Half-God actually and there was practically nothing left for others except emulating and praising his innate, congenital wisdom. As Lenin's insistence on the proletarian nature of his regime seemed somewhat unconvincing to others, at the talks that led to the famous peace treaty of Brest-Litovsk between Soviet Russia and Imperial Germany in 1918, the Bolshevik delegation came with an illiterate Russian peasant who, they decided, had to be brought to the table of negotiations as a live embodiment of the power of the Workers and the Peasants. Our Muzhik however behaved in the old ways, since he insisted on calling everyone barin-master-much to the chagrin of his mentors.[1]

However that may be, let's get back now to core of our subject or the question of Quality versus Quantity in the conditions of pre-modern economic activity.

For the ancient peasant, craftsman or trader what now we refer to as Quality used to be:

•Inwardly, a position of equilibrium. Here is a condition of the Psyche following the inner movement of Consciousness not as an end in itself but as a mean to an end. As a result, the movement halts when appears the intuitive realization that the desired end or the substance has been reached already.

•Outwardly that same desired end or substance is always expressed in a way paved by a clockwork magical precision, despite the different economic conditions which might be similar but never identical. A pale reflection of this is the insistence of present day supporters of organic food on local produce.

One has only to see for a moment how, for example there is still prepared real traditional food in India or elsewhere to realize that 99% of all recipes are not only from the past but from the very ancient past. The only change here might be the introduction tomatoes, potatoes or corn from the New World, but this is in reality less change than a reunification of previously scattered knowledge in Agriculture. Seen from this angle the alleged creativity of present day French chefs-de–cuisine, for example is an open question.

In such an environment, there is no higher and lower Quality. There is only Quality adapted to circumstances. For example, in the last five or six millennia all food that is really suitable for humans, including some extravagant Chinese recipes, where it happens that even insects might be good for eating has barely changed. As we shall see later on this is about to happen only now with a likely devastating effect in all spheres of life.

And another thing: such an economic structure naturally excludes any arbitrary experimentation or compromises with Quality. Is there a bad harvest, for example? There will be less food. There will be simpler food but still a Quality food that is a food adapted to the circumstances of the day.

As we shall see later on, the production of food which is actually not food but only a copy of food, a cocktail of chemical substances with potentially debilitating effects on those who consume them was simply unconceivable in a traditional setting even for the Devil who at this time apparently had a deficit of imagination since he wasted his time by putting into trouble the alleged sinners into old-fashioned, inefficient furnaces.

CACAMBO: By the way, the question of vacuity is of a special concern within the context of Tibetan Buddhism to the Dalai Lama who in his own words gave a special effort to the meditation on this subject in particular.[2]

PANGLOSS: What is at stake here is the congenital vacuity of quantity.

CACAMBO: You appear to me as one of these 'philosophes' of our own time, a term which, if you still remember, at least in France, used to be the equivalent of today's adult entertainment professionals.

PANGLOSS: The attitude of Philosophy to reflection is ambiguous at best. From their very beginnings, Philosophers appear, namely with the Sophists as a distortion, as a form of estrangement from meditation. There is confusion on this point, since the very same figure denouncing them as charlatans, through his account on Socrates, not in the name of Philosophy but in the name of Tradition, Plato, has been branded as the Philosopher par excellence or the father of Philosophy to the point of asserting that all subsequent Philosophies are at last resort a commentary in one form or another of Plato's *Dialogues*. The confusion in question, by the way, currently is exacerbating, since in the eyes of modern 'Philosophes' or relativists of various kinds, Plato appears as a somewhat deranging figure who has to be silenced in one way or another since especially in the light of the on-going, process of ontological deconstruction, he appears to have the kind of vision that is transgressing the limits of the postmodern, culturally correct mind.

CACAMBO: You were talking of agriculture. Who set the quality standards of agriculture?

PANGLOSS: From Ancient China to Greece or Sumer, Agriculture used to be considered as a gift from the Gods, and indeed Agriculture a little like the Pyramids appears on the scene all of a sudden, somehow from apparently nowhere. Had not the records on the Mysteries of Eleusis,[3] related to Agriculture, been so scarce, we would certainly have known more on its origin.

CACAMBO: Are you not advocating a return to the land just like so many opponents to the way that things are going on at present?

PANGLOSS: No. Following a Buddhist legend, men in by gone ages were etheric and used to fly and it is only later on that they became solid to the point of remaining on the ground on a permanent basis. An ontological point that seems to have been forgotten or simply ignored, for example, by such figures as the Minister of Agriculture of the Third Reich R.W. Darré, who despite being himself from a wealthy merchant family based in Buenos Aires advocated literally a tightening of the peasants to the land a little as the rowers of Ancients Galleys or Galériens (fr.) used to be tied to their seats.

NOTES

[1] *Utopian Vision and Experimental Life in the Russian Revolution*, p131. Richard Stites, 1991
[2] See *The Buddhism of Tibet* by the Dalai Lama
[3] See Foucart's <u>Mysteries of Eleusis</u>, Jane E. Harrison, *The Classical Review*, Vol. 17, No. 1 (Feb., 1903), pp. 84-86, Cambridge University Press

TALE IV

The Quality of Ancient Building

CACAMBO: Why do not you come out with something more solid than your tightly packed cage chickens?

PANGLOSS: Why not, after all. Let's start with building, since the habitat of any being is also a part of the being himself. Furthermore, the ruins of the past, be it recent, ancient or very ancient are still here, either above or a little below the surface of the ground.

So, once upon a time, the whole process of Building has not been merely related but, based entirely on Cosmogony and Occult Geology. Although, there is may be no substance on our planet, apart from diamonds, more solid, more material than the huge Megaliths or the pillars of Baalbek, for example, it appears as we shall see later on, that its real nature rests on immaterial foundations. The whole process of Ancient Building, including Stonehenge, the Parthenon etc. actually did not start, with what it is called today, 'practical considerations' but with Cosmogony. The latter was thought to be perfectly consistent with present day notion of utility. There was no contradiction whatsoever between material and immaterial, since it is Cosmogony which was seen to be the ultimate source of both. Now, as so many books have been written on the Pyramids, on the Maya or Greek temples etc. and their quoted content have been repeated all over and over again in millions of pages, it would be really useless to add here one more quote, whatever our view is on the nature of these quotes and their real origin. So what? What shall we say then?

CACAMBO: You always refer to the first person plural. I do not see anyone else other than you on the horizon right now.

PANGLOSS: The 'I' is a circle because things are not what they seem to be at first glance. So the 'I' goes to the 'Other' and then comes back to itself again, but no longer alone, since now he is in the company of another.

CACAMBO: If you say nothing more on the quality of Building, there must something else you are interested in.

PANGLOSS: These are the conditions which led to the building of monuments of such a quality, resisting the passage of time. Should we look further, the question of the arrangements of the Ancient Corporation comes out of itself.

Whenever the issue of Roman Collegia or Medieval Corporations is raised, either for praising their achievements, as in Italy in the 1920s or the opposite, for vilifying them in the name of Modernity, the term 'Hierarchy' has been inevitably the first point to start with. So, in the name of concision we'll bypass it here. There are two things worth mentioning at this point, however:

In the first place this is the system of Rights and Obligations within the Guilds. The hierarchy did not suppress the principle of autonomy on which rested any Guild. Each trader in the Hanseatic League for example, despite the various constrictions that his membership in the Guild implied, did remain what he was in the first place, when he became a member of the Guild: a trader. The evolution from independence to the gradual loss of it by a likely process of bureaucratization that nowadays is thought to be natural simply did not take place in the ancient Guild. The autonomy of the individual member remained effective right to the end, when the Napoleon Code formally suppressed the Guilds. And this is valid even for the East India Company which on this matter at least was not the precursor of modern corporate bureaucracy. So, once again, the Guilds are not the precursors of the Corporation. It is quite the opposite: The Guilds in reality preserved a degree of freedom for the individual member in all spheres of activity such as the ownership of the tools of production or his rights and obligations, whereas the Corporation right from its early beginnings in the middle of the 19th century following the Limited Liability Act of 1855 in the UK appears as an abstraction, as a ghost entity, divided by the dichotomy between its nominal outer form and its real inner form, where the former in the last resort is nothing more than a cover-up, a Trojan horse for the latter.

By the way, the KFC chickens are competing with the Beeves of Mc Donald's ever since the 1950s. They say, any Mc Donald's sandwich is made out of no less than 100 different animals, whose diverse bodily components had been somehow pressed by the food processing industry in a way as to form a single solid substance by the name of hamburger. By the way the employees of many Mc Donald's restaurants, as we had the occasion to notice recently, seem very affable. Sometimes various leaflets might be seen on the tables concerning the latest promotions and job offers of the famous fast food chain. So, the following might be read, in the leaflets destined to the job seekers in particular: 'Mr or Mrs Merit has been so efficient at the work place lately that only at the age of twenty and something, He (She) has been appointed as a manager of a whole MC Donald's restaurant etc. The message is clear: whoever you are, wherever you are, whatever you do, provided you do what we want you to do, you can raise and raise up the top of the pyramid and from up there you'll get a panoramic view on everything, including your own rapid escalade.' So the twenty and something candidate would say to himself (herself): 'That's fine. I only have to work harder to be noticed and getting a better position. What does he (she) believes in for good? He or She believes in his (her) ability to fulfill his (her) obligations toward his (her) employer and in return He (She) expects to have rights, such as for example, the right to remain on his or her job, the right to move up the professional ladder, the right to receive a decent pay for the given effort. Believe it or not, soon comes the day when a bubble bursts somewhere along the global line and the restaurant is closed, as a result. Our employee is out in the street now, and the explanation he (she) is given for this sudden, unexpected turn of events is no more relevant for his (her) condition than the latest weather forecast. He (she) realizes that he (she) had obligations such as to wake up early for work, to be honest and polite with the clients etc. which have been of little or no help at all to keep him or her on the job. It happens that He (She) has been on the mercy of an invisible hand which operates separately from the fulfillment of his (her) obligations. A hand that is invisible to others but visible to itself. So, our employee, once fired, comes back one more time to the restaurant and demands French fries and a Cheese Burger. Still under the effect of his resignation, he has no appetite at this point. One minute, two, three… ten minutes already and his (her) meal is still untouched in the plastic plate. And then, at last, he (she) decides to go into action. So He (She) is stretching out his (her) arm toward the small plastic bag with the French Fries. Something is wrong. He (She) tries one more time. No way. He (She) cannot eat these Fries. Suddenly, in a flash he (she) sees all that he (she) has been doing in this place: the burgers, the fries, the sundaes, the cokes, the clients, the faces of the clients are just moving before his (her) eyes right now, faster and faster. He (she) realizes that throughout the months since he (she) has been on the job he (she) had time for everything excepting for waiting the few minutes that are required so that a Mc Donald's Hamburger and French Fries becomes…cold. Once the dizziness caused by the acceleration of all movements around the corner is gone, our employee discovers something he had no time to discover before: a cold hamburger and a cold French fry have no taste or worse still they have a bad taste. So what else the fired employee may say to himself other than something like: 'This is not what it seemed to be?'

As for Ancient Corporation, it used to be what it seemed to be. On the place of the above referred invisible hand, there was a visible sanctification of the rights and obligations of its members. There was an oath of loyalty to the Guild as the feudal Vassals and Lords had oaths toward one another. The likely objection that, all this is in name only or that the façades of the Temples and the Cathedrals that the Guilds were erecting were actually cracked by corruption and oppression if true, might be so to a little extent. And there is no better record for attesting the very plausible effectiveness of the system of rights and obligations within the Guilds than the remains of Ancient Temples throughout the Mediterranean and the Cathedrals still standing on the skyline. Had it not been for the outmost care and precision, these monuments would not have been built in their present form since all this does not work with mere compulsion.

CACAMBO: So, what then? Are not the Guilds nothing short of perfection?

PANGLOSS: No. The Guild, as so many other things in the pre-modern world, was in a state of fossilization,[1] since as we shall see later on the knowledge was not transmitted as modern knowledge is, through inventions, new discoveries etc. but through the authority of Tradition. Knowledge was given once, in a Pre-Historical Age, and all the rest appears as a descending curve, as involution following a process of Meta historical, so to speak cognitive fragmentation. The once given knowledge was falling apart throughout the centuries. If there were some outbursts of change, as the evolution from the relatively crude Romanesque style of the High Middle Ages to the sudden appearance of the Cathedrals or the conception of a different type of architecture during the Renaissance or the gradual transformation of the Louvre or the Hofburg in Vienna, for example from Medieval Castles into Palaces, that is not creativity as the modern Consciousness is inclined to assume but a reintegration of old, previously hidden sources, even to the otherwise secretive Guilds. For example, the first depictions of Classical architecture emerged in Italy during the early 15th century when a copy of *De Architectura* by the first century Roman architect Vitruvius, was suddenly unearthed in Rome.[2]

CACAMBO: What else attracts the attention when the question of Ancient Crafts is raised?

PANGLOSS: That is the amazing ability of Ancient Corporations to keep secret their technology as it is the case in Architecture and also other crafts. Who knows today how a Stradivarius or Purple, already available for sale by the Phoenicians in High Antiquity, used to be made? Furthermore whereas in late Roman Antiquity, for example, by the 6th century almost nothing had remained of the other Ancient Institutions, already suppressed by the advent of Monotheism, Building Crafts somehow survived this Cultural, but also Economic Metamorphosis.[3] And what is more, in the chaos of Late Antiquity, the members of these Crafts were still able to build such a masterpiece of Architecture as the Hagia Sophia in Constantinople, whose huge Dome is a still an unsurpassed achievement in building, comparable in sophistication only to the earlier Seven Wonders of the World. A few centuries later appears another enigmatic phenomenon: Gothic Architecture.

CACAMBO: Who really built the Cathedrals and how were they built?

PANGLOSS: This question has been debated from all possible angles, including the most extravagant ones, only to add further in the general confusion on the matter. The hypothesis that there was indeed a real cohesion on all levels between the Ancient Building crafts, dating from the highest Antiquity and therefore a chain of continuity with the Ancient Mysteries of Egypt and Greece is coming out of itself, provided we are not walking with a huge parrot of the Ara type, on our shoulder all the time, repeating, its endless words: 'No evidence, no evidence!'

It would be really intriguing to know how would it be possible to deny something or to ignore it simply, because there is still no way to see the Workings of Ancient Craftsmen, with the same undisputable clarity as the last dialogue of the soap bubble type, between the heroes of a new TV serial or the latest scoop on a flat screen TV. The thing is that the know-how for the fabrication of the Crystal Ball of the Legend has yet to be rediscovered. It goes without saying that should we be fair to ourselves, we should acknowledge in the first place, that it might have been better indeed to have such a Crystal Ball and thus to make things really crystal clear to anyone under the Sun, but this is not the case and it may not be the case in the foreseeable future. To our regret if life is indeed a puzzle it is still an unresolved puzzle. So as a result we would better remind ourselves that we have heads on our shoulders and that a head unless it is chopped off by the Guillotine, abolished only in the 1980s in an impressive display of Humanism by the then French President, F. Mitterrand,[4] is designed among other things to reflect on the Four Elements. Otherwise, we'll always be turning in circle and we'll always be finding out that the only evidence is the lack of evidence. Already in the 19th century, the real thing was thought to be just anywhere, including, should we follow the French intuitivist philosopher Bergson, in the tiny legs of any insect, except in a human's brain.

Now, once more: As a social and economic phenomenon, within the Ancient Crafts there was a chain of continuity on all levels, be it cognitive, spiritual or social. So solid and effective was this chain of continuity that even the chaotic economic conditions of the Late Roman Antiquity were not able to break it. As it has been mentioned already sophisticated building continued in Byzantium, but also in the Middle East and Spain and reappeared in the West with the Cathedrals. Although the Italians during the Renaissance disliked Gothic Architecture, this does not exclude continuity in the building process and the organization, but rather indicates the basic autonomy of different Guilds, despite the essentially universal nature of the transmission of knowledge. Also, it is worth mentioning that the building of Cathedrals ceased all at once in the 16th century, not only in Italy, but also in the North where the Gothic Style appeared in the first place. Here is a sudden and simultaneous halt everywhere that is not easy to explain given the turmoil of the 16th century and the Protestant Reformation. Furthermore, the well documented insistence of Medieval Guilds on the After Life, may be due less to the influence of the Church than simply being a reflection of the former link between the Crafts with the Greek Mysteries and the Temple Culture of Egypt, where the Craft used to be only the visible expression of an Invisible Essence, not nominally as it happened later on, but effectively i.e. in a way affecting the way the building process was carried out.

This chain of continuity was shaken only after the 16[th]century[5] before being finally crashed not even in the 19th century, but only after WWII with the emergence of something really without any precedent such as the KFC type modern Architecture. Any traveler going to Europe will notice that practically anything that is worth looking at in Paris, Vienna or St Petersburg was built before the 20th century. In the outskirts of this same city of Geneva, a place with the otherwise enviable reputation of being an international hot spot for keeping in stock, piles of fiat money, we had the occasion to see brand new apartment blocks, for example, Le Lignon, on the Ch. De Chateau Bloch, made out of pre-fabricated elements, precisely of the KFC type with a length of no less than one third or even half a mile, without balconies and with a height of each floor of no more than, if not exactly a chicken's cage, so only a little taller, may be half the height of older buildings, dating from the 19th and the early 20th century. So if we are able to witness such a phenomenon in Switzerland, what about other places such as Moscow or Bombay or Paris or Sao Paolo?

And another thing, related to the modern conception of the motivation behind any form of economic activity. Should we follow in its inner logic the modern methodological framework on the Economy, we'll simply be unable to explain not only the functioning, but the mere existence of Ancient Crafts.

Yes. How would it be possible indeed for such a supposedly oppressive hierarchical structure as the Ancient Roman Collegia or the Medieval Guild to erect these extremely sophisticated monuments, Temples, Cathedrals, Palaces, Theatres which simply have no equivalent in the modern world and what is more, completing their work often in extremely unfavorable political and social conditions? Should we stick to the epistemological dogmas of present day economic science, such as the key tenet of greed, being the driving force of economic activity, there would be simply no way of providing a rational answer to this question.

CACAMBO: Why then your hierarchy type structure did not work in the modern conditions of the now defunct command economy of the USSR?

PANGLOSS: They were somewhat in the position of the Monarch from St-Exupéry's 'The Little Prince', who is sitting on his throne and giving commands to the Sun to rise and set, except that in our case there was nothing to rise neither to set, since in the few decades when this 'Command Economy' existed, the Soviets were able to produce weapons, but unable to supply on a regular basis even the nearby convenience store with a loaf of bread or a piece of cheese of the lowest quality. Therefore, the claim that the chain of continuity of Ancient Crafts throughout the centuries, used to be based on a mere compulsion is nothing less than an utterly groundless claim. There is something else at stake which present day methods are unable to account for.

Cacambo: What is the difference?

Pangloss: In the quality of the arrangements or in a different conditioning of the Psyche, despite the outer resemblance between ancient guild and modern central planning, since both are based on hierarchy. Greed and what is called nowadays, the competitive instinct, though certainly present in a degree appear to have been contained in one way or another. At last resort, Compulsion is a brute force antithetical to the devotion to quality that characterizes the legacy of Ancient Corporations and Guilds. Greed as well as its negative expression, anger is in reality a chaotic, blind life force, suitable for the Cyclops throwing stones at Odysseus in Greek Mythology but unsuitable for the preservation of a unified structure, represented by the various Guilds and lasting for millennia.

Furthermore, the guilds were in a position of at least relative independence, which is not easy to explain, unless we take for granted that in these days nothing really mattered to the representatives of political power, whoever these representatives may have been, than the collection of taxes which, by the way, rarely exceeded 10%.

As we have seen it, with Traditional Agriculture, which appears to be first of all, not an amount of something but something of an amount that is a quality whose expressions naturally stretch further within the social organism than the configuration of the digestive tube, so the Ancient Building Crafts operated along the same lines. As an expression of non-economic or extra economic motives Quality, within all spheres of the Ancient Economy had a well delineated limits. Beyond these implicitly sacred limits, economic activity was simply unconceivable.

So was Building. Beyond a certain threshold of quality, of substance, of rationality and common sense Ancient Craftsmen simply were not building anything.[6] At last resort, however, the Guilds were out of the touch with the new conditions and their ultimately fossilized structure was reduced to ashes by the leveling effect of Quantity. Yet nothing in reality can vanish in the air completely. With Guilds, it is the same. The day when you'll go to the nearby Wal Mart store and present to the cashier an item by the name of '100% pure Quantity' will never come, since Quantity can emancipate itself from its essence Quality, whatever this Quality might be, as the attempt for such a metamorphosis by the tailors who made New Clothes for the Emperor shows, in words only and never in deeds.

NOTES

[1]By 'Fossilization' here is meant a process of oblivion setting in motion a process of inertia. Should we affirm the primacy of Consciousness over its visible expressions, the question of

Knowledge can no longer be derived from its opposite end or solid matter. Seeking life in solid matter is no more likely than imagining the conception of a child from the accidental collision of two stones set in motion, for example by an earthquake. The transmission of Knowledge does not appear to be a straight line but a V curve despite the fact that the further we go look at the past the more enigmatic and sophisticated ancient monuments become. By the Middle Egyptian Kingdom, the Pyramids seemed probably much older to the then Egyptians than the Roman Coliseum seems to present day tourists. Otherwise, the sudden appearance, abrupt end and also reappearance of various modes of building cannot be retraced. The Cathedrals for example, emerged all at once in the 12th and by the 16th century their building came to a halt. Also, the above V curve or rather V curves do not exist by themselves more than the waves exist in themselves apart from the sea where they arise. Now, this tendency of separating the waves from the sea manifests itself ever since the linear perception of time has veiled the Perennial view of the Cycles.

For Joachim de Fiore or Hegel, Civilization is a bullet projected indefinitely in the air whereas for G. Vico or Spengler this same bullet is definitely projected since it will inevitably fall on the ground at some point. However, although the Guilds did not disappear somehow of themselves but were suppressed by decree, their fossilization, either economic, technological or social is a fact in line with the legend of the Ages of Humanity. Seen from this angle, the evolution is a step within a circle and therefore any so to speak, vision of a kind of cognitive Catastrophe appears to be groundless.

Fossilization possibly means also that the knowledge inherited from the ancient past, as a transmitted knowledge had a tendency not only of waning over time but also of being encapsulated within the Guild and hence not diffused for other possible applications. For example, the building of such sophisticated monuments as the Cathedrals or later on various Palaces did not help to eradicate the lack of hygiene and the bad sanitary conditions persisting up to 20th century in European cities. By the way bathing was considered dangerous for the health and a likely cause of pest by the heirs of Hippocrates as far as the 19th century, when Napoleon I and Josephine set the new standards of hygiene by taking frequent baths. Also, Napoleon's insistence on the utility of vaccinating all his soldiers is another sign that a new epoch was coming out.

[2]In the Middle-Ages there were only scattered fragments of *De Arcitectura*. It is the scholar Leon Battista Alberti who rediscovered the Manuscript in the early 15th century. In order to establish the text of the first printed edition (Rome, 1486) Sulpizio da Veroli had to collate several manuscripts since neither of them contained the full text, and he relied on the manuscript of the Escurial (dated from the XI century.)

[3]By the 6th century the population of Rome had dwindled from possibly several millions to less than 50, 000. Urban Culture had to wait for more than 1000 years to resurface again in its present day form. There has been a controversy over the population of Ancient Rome as it is still not clear how many people really inhabited the average Roman Domus (House) and Insulae or a Building of several floors, for example in the ancient port of Ostia (a type of building taken from the Punic Carthage, where there was such high buildings.) Also, the usually advanced view holding that the Insulae were of very low quality is flatly contradicted by the discovery, somewhere in the 20th century that the foundations of a building in Rome, in proximity to the

Forum were actually the same as those of ancient ruins, and thus attesting that this building had been inhabited all the way from Antiquity to the 20th century seemingly without interruption.

[4] The Guillotine appears as the first live show of Modernity, although still only a show since there was still no Show Business at that point. Among the reportedly 40,000 executions following the French Revolution, the beheading of aristocrats in particular on public places used to be highly appreciated especially by old and often homeless women or Clochardes (fr.).

[5] Modernity proved to be inimical to Ancient Guilds right from its early beginning during the Protestant Reformation and therefore almost three centuries before, J.J. Rousseau, A. Smith and the Code Napoleon, when Guilds were suppressed altogether. That may be related to the heavy emphasis of Medieval Corporations on rewards in the afterlife and probably with the Protestant hostility to anything that even remotely resembles the sale of Indulgences.

[6] The Guilds, had no concern for the building of houses in the villages, for example where the peasants or at least most of them were building their often wooden huts themselves. However exotic such a fact might seem today, this is well in line with the conception of organic unity of the pre-industrial economy and also with the Meta historical perspective brought by the universal Legend of the Ages of Humanity, since the prevalence of physical effort over other sources of energy, together with the almost permanent state of war are the characteristic signs of the Iron Age or Kali Yuga. The peasants had their own clothing and local customs often coming out from the very ancient past but also their own houses suitable to their way of life. So a high standard of living for them was not a jump away of these conditions but an extension of these same conditions, such as a good harvest for example etc. Had most of the peasants been like the wife of the fisherman in the tale of the Golden Fish, who at some point, being no longer happy with a new house asked the Fish for a palace, it would be really impossible to imagine how they were able, often despite strongly adverse conditions, to preserve folk tales, legends and customs coming out from time immemorial. Also, far from contradicting the key assertion on Quality in the first place as a psychic disposition, a metaphysical awareness and then as a material expression, being the very foundation of pre-industrial economic activity, this fact reaffirms it once more. There was indeed something very concrete, very practical and yet beyond profit and beyond compulsion which today being no longer a real life force is taken into consideration only in the ambiguous vocabulary of legal action: integrity. The Ancient Building Guilds, as we shall see later on, on many occasions in the section devoted to the Modern Economy, simply were not willing to trespass a certain threshold of Quality which in these days did not permit them to build palaces for the peasants. Furthermore, the building of a peasant house by the owner himself was the norm, being within the traditional limits of organic unity in the economic and the social sphere.

TALE V

The Liverpool Syndrome or Lucy in the Sky of Diamonds

CACAMBO: Would in not be better if we get out of this place and go for a walk along the Lake?

PANGLOSS: Okay. Let's go.

CACAMBO: You have discussed so many things up to now and yet still not did not make it clear, what is your main point?

PANGLOSS: Every story or 'narrative' as it is correct to say these days, has a beginning and an end, since it goes without saying that what is in the first place ultimately goes to its opposite end or in the last place. As for the present story, this time, we'll start by relating the beginning to the end in just two words: These are: 'The Liverpool Syndrome'.

CACAMBO: Is this the main intrigue of your story?

PANGLOSS: Not yet. What is at stake here is the present day global economy, from the point of view of quality. Our approach is a synthetic approach and therefore anything in such a view may be related to anything else, where the only limit is the intuition for a sufficient reason.

CACAMBO: Is not there a long way to go from what you call the Syndrome of... whatever, to the economy?

PANGLOSS: May be not as much as it may seem at first glance.

CACAMBO: So, what is your...syndrome all about? Is not Liverpool a port in the north of England, so often cited by the sources on the history of the British Economy or else as the place where the Beatles met for the first time back in 1961?

PANGLOSS: No, it is not, since Liverpool is also the name of a British Prime Minister who proclaimed at the turn of the 19th century that the steam engine counted more for the UK than the victory over Napoleon.[1] Here is an extraordinary statement and to comprehend today how extraordinary it is indeed, there is may be no better than imagining Alexander the Great for example, shouting at his soldiers that the victory over the Persians is due to a new breed of mosquito or the Roman Emperors erecting Arches where, instead of relating their exploits, they just praise the craftsmen supplying their armor made out of a new type of iron. By the way, when the question why Modernity and Industrialization occurred precisely in our own time, the late 18th century and not much earlier, is raised, various conventional sources on the History of Technology cite the supposedly high level of economic development in the city of Alexandria or else, the Roman Emperor Diocletian who refused the offer of a craftsman with a new invention by replying that many workers would lose their jobs and thus revealing, according to modern observers, his essentially unenlightened attitude toward technology and the question of economic efficiency. So, as we said it already, the statement of Lord Liverpool is extraordinary since it betrays that something really unique was taking place, at that point, starting with the UK. But how come, that the steam engine may have anything to do with a mosquito, as stated above? Yes, it may, but just anything and therefore by no means everything. It goes without saying that the effect of the steam engine on economic activity and society in general is really different from that of a mosquito, be it a new breed of mosquito. On the other side, there is indeed one common point. This is the question of the attention toward steam as a source of energy. Steam was known in Alexandria but apparently no one really cared about it since the attention was diverted elsewhere. The possible applications of steam power did not seem more relevant for the then society than the likely effect of a mosquito on the problem of Imperial Succession in Ancient Rome.

So, does it not follow from all this, somehow out of itself that those on power in the Ancient World, be it Emperors or Kings or Tyrants or Feudal Lords etc. simply were not giving a damn about Science and Technology?

Definitely not since Ancient Rulers did care about Science at least as much as today's Politicians care about Atomic Energy or the latest generation of Fighter Jets. By the way, had it not been for the seemingly open minded attitude toward Science of the patron of Archimedes, the Tyrant of Syracuse, he would not have been able to display his mirrors before the Roman Legions besieging the city. Going further in this vein, we should make it clear what we mean by Science when referring to the ancient past, since broadly speaking everything related in one way or another to any form of spiritual consistency, including the Arcane core of practically all rituals may appear to be within the scope of Science.[2] In its narrow expression, however, Ancient Science may be characterized as the use of this same spiritual consistency for an immediate effect on the Elements. This is Astrology and Divination but also the Transmutation of the Elements and the Elixir of Life, where there is less room for ambiguity. Whereas Divination rests basically on the expectation for something to happen and therefore retreats in the horizon of the future, both Transmutation and the Elixir of Life are achieved right now or are not achieved in the sense that their process of achievement cannot start in the present and unfold toward their final outcome in the future as it is the case with Divination. An attempt for Transmutation is either successful or it is not since any visit to the nearby money-lender's shop will be a sufficient reason to realize that there is no such thing as a little golden necklace. The evaluation of gold is a question of mixture not a question of consistency. Alchemy is omnipresent since the beginning of recorded History throughout the World. Although its objects of Experimentation are both the Elixir of Life and Transmutation there is enough evidence to assume that the attention that had been paid to Transmutation gradually increased over time at the expense of the Elixir of Life. It is no coincidence that it is the Arabs who brought the first Alchemical texts to early medieval Europe. As traders they certainly had a special concern for Transmutation. When in the last decades before the fall of Constantinople various manuscripts made their appearance in the West,[3] the interest for Alchemy far from receding actually increased to the point of obsession[4] comparable only to the Tulip mania that devastated Holland in the 17th century but on a much higher scale. Now, any psychological sophistry[5] on Alchemy is a misleading verbiage since the mobiles behind Transmutation are self-evident.

This is simply the old version of any modern quick buck scheme. Once you achieve Transmutation, you do not have to bother with a perilous journey, for example from Lima to Seville on the board of one of the countless Galleons now resting on the bottom of the Atlantic ocean, since the door of your house will open up as Sesame once did and your garage will turn out to be like Ali Baba's cavern. Yet there is a difference. Modern quick buck schemes as we shall see in the next parts of the present essay are essentially pyramid shaped piles of paper, like the one of John Law and his 'Compagnie des Indes Orientales', whereas Transmutation appears as the repetition of the same magical scenario for thousands of years. Before getting to the point on the actual nature of this scenario and its apparently conflicting two sides, we should point out that there is nothing really special in Transmutation. Here is one among many other expressions of the firm and practically universal ancient conviction, according to which behind the veil of appearances or Maya is the all-pervading interconnected Cosmic Whole. Following the perception of Non-Duality, in the last resort, nothing can really stand by itself and the only possible representation of Time and Causality is the Circle. Since all parts are contained within the whole, there is nothing left other than the assumption that All is in All. Therefore, the more we know about any drop of the ocean, the more we'll know about the ocean itself. Also, Substance far from being an inert mass is exactly the opposite, a flow of energy, the all-pervading primeval Ether or Akasha.

Now, the awareness of the energy animating all bodies, including those that do not seem animated by anything, may lead to its conscious transfer from one body to another or from one point to another. Here is the foundation of Transmutation. Here is also a point as we shall see later on, where Transmutation is in agreement with such modern figures, as Leibniz or Tesla. And yet, is not there something definitely odd about the millennia old repetition of an operation such as Transmutation which at least in the History recorded by conventional sources never really took place? How come that so many apparently learned people throughout the world spent their life time in the futile effort for a 'Tour de Magie' leading simply to nowhere? Earlier on we said that Alchemy has two conflicting sides. As Evil is the lack of Good and Darkness the lack of Light, so is the Dark side versus the Bright side of Alchemy. Transmutation is no less real than the electric charge of a thunder in the sky. Its epistemological basis is anchored in the Metaphysical insight or magical lucidity or Non-Duality and therefore the possibility for such an operation to occur seems as certain as the rising of the Sun. Yet something in potency is one thing and something in act is another. Between what may happen on Principle and what happens in Practice, there is an abyss. So unshakeable was the conviction of countless Alchemists, according to which, the code allowing the Principle to be put into Practice may be found at any time that the attempts for Transmutation continued for several millenniums and outlived many different Cultures. But how come that the Principle of Unity or Non-Duality, assumed to be all pervading, all present should be put into practice at all? Had not His expressions have always been here and therefore all the talk of setting in motion Aristotle's Unmoved Mover appears as a mere verbiage? Now, there are essentially two answers to the above question, the one is on relative and absolute truth, developed to its core by the Buddhist Two Truths Doctrine, which is besides our subject and the other deals with the unfolding of Three Dimensional Time. The lack of correspondence or the discrepancy between Visible and Invisible forms or the Essence and its Expressions is only apparent since ultimately the chain of Causes and Effects restores the broken equilibrium. Here is Proclus' fascinating description (New Elements of Theology) of the tendency of the Principle to revert upon itself and hence the definitely Metaphysical foundation of all the bizarre for the modern mind setting, superstitions on retribution, on the ultimate effect of any act and on a deeper level, of Karma. By the way, what is the actual message of the Medieval Legend of Faust, if not, that there is a price to be paid for the sinking deep down the Elements and that this price just as the bill in any restaurant, is paid at the end of, in our case, at the end of the whole thing or the whole spectacle. The modern Status Quo style, fascination with such figures as Sade, for example speaks for itself, since Sade is ultimately an extravagant figure under the spell of blindness and there is hardly a more crystal clear reflection of the impressive display of superficiality to which Post Modern Culture has sunk. Further on, it is no coincidence, for example, that in Tibet as repository of Arcane Knowledge, the only legitimate Succession is the Spiritual Succession since the Dalai Lama biologically may come just from anywhere, including a poor peasant family. Now, as far as our point on Transmutation is concerned, since all the components of a seaside view, for example, such as boats, birds etc. appear less and less distinct in the last moments before the setting of the Sun, so the code for Transmutation seemed less and less evident due to the obscurity of this particular moment of the Cosmic, Meta Historical day. On the surface occult knowledge has been condemned, for example by the Bien-Pensant James Webb (The Occult Establishment) referring to occultism as the thrash of knowledge. Yet a little below, the usual fascination with the hidden treasures of the ancient past was no less present in the modern age than before. When an author of the kind of G. Meyrink refers to the 'Rusty Key of Occult Knowledge' he is in line with a chain that in reality was never completely broken.

Yet the attempts of inserting the Key into the lock of the door for which it had been made, proved to be unsuccessful since, as it has been said already, in recorded history, there is no really tangible proof for an act of Transmutation. The endless repetition of the same operation, the fruitless effort for something that does not appear to be really in sight charged the Primeval Ether or the World Soul with a rising tide of negative electricity. At some point, the tension caused a shock, an explosion and it became increasingly evident that a new way had to be found for achieving Transmutation. At the surface it seemed that it would be possible to shift the epistemological poles from what it is below to what it is above and vice versa from it is above to what it is below. It is this impression which later on fixed the methodological framework of Positive Science. Transmutation, they said, now, was finally achieved. However, as it has been mentioned already, whereas the old Transmutation used to start from the Principle of Non-Duality and end with its expressions, now it seemed that a new Transmutation had come out, turned to the opposite side, like a reversed triangle. Here is Empiricism. As a negation of the Principle the latter appeared to be a New Principle.

Steam seemed as good as the Elixir of Life. Any mixture of the Old Four Elements, now, could be moved from one point to another in no time, a little as the flying carpet of the legend. And what is more, later on, thanks to such figures as Descartes, among others, the speed of Trains or Steamboats or simply Progress could be weighted or measured or quantified or trimmed as the trees in a French garden. 'Steam', they said, 'is only the beginning', since the possible applications of this new Elixir of Life, had apparently no limits. Yet, the essence of steam was seen either as a projection of the senses or a geometrical form, a figure, a pure abstraction. So, the void thus created, had to be filled with a substance, whose nature, just like the nature of any line on the horizon was to escape, the moment you approach it, somewhat as the ghost boat of the Flying Dutchman. Further on, whereas the Old Elixir of Life had to be absorbed just once, as in the legend of Alexander's half-sister Thessalonike, in its new version, it was now to be taken in ever greater quantity since between sand and mirages in the desert, thirst is the only guiding line. The ever shifting mirage scene, at some point in the 19th century, as the speeches of Lord Liverpool attest, turned into outright euphoria. The Earth and the whole Universe for that matter appeared as huge mechanical clock pointing to a vast Sky of Diamonds. And what is more, all that seemed for millennia a self-evident truth, such as the simple assertion that the Sun is rising and setting every day, suddenly became a matter of controversy. The expansion of Steam transmuted also the human Psyche and along with it transformed the surrounding social and material landscape to the point of no return. 'Unique' became the new key word for 'Sesame open up!' As what happened before the Flood was not much of a concern to those who lived up to see the things after the Flood, so what happened before Transmutation was not really counting any longer or else it counted but as a burden that one had to relieve oneself of as quickly as possible.

So why then paying attention at all to the attempts for the Transmutation of the old school, aiming at the limitless supply of something that later on has been characterized as a 'Barbaric Relic' and whose record is one of a systematic failure lasting for centuries? Since, everything now seems to be unique should not the story of the new Transmutation could start just as any story by: Once upon a time… steam came up… and they, in our case, the one or two billion individuals composing the Humanity of the early 19th century, lived happily ever after? Furthermore, had not the impression that the miracle of steam was been made possible thanks the reversed epistemological triangle, become a hardened certitude?

Should we take all of the above questions as potential knots, the initial step in the attempt to untie the first of these knots, would be to assert once more the key presumption according to which the reason for this failure is by no means to be found in the epistemological foundation of Arcane Knowledge, since there is no possible cognition and therefore no possible Scientific Knowledge outside the consciousness of Non-Duality or the awareness or the intuitive perception of the Spirit. The preoccupation of Alchemy with gold and longevity and the emergence of a picturesque assortment of figures that in Venice used to be called, Ciarlatani is one among so many other illustrations of the Meta Historical process of fragmentation of Knowledge. By the way, it is these scattered fragments from the mythical Elixir of Life, which made possible Ayurvedic medicine or traditional Chinese medicine, initially based on Taoism and its countless attempts to supply various Chinese emperors with a substance keeping them alive indefinitely. Now, the theoretical possibility for a practical expression of the One in the many or the potential of the Spirit to affect Matter is self-evident since it is based on reflection, not on induction and least of all in vested authority. If Transmutation is to be achieved, this would not happen by changing the epistemology but by following the Principle of Non-Duality as the only possible source of genuine Knowledge beyond which the cognitive value of the search, be it experimentation or thinking is simply nil. And this implies to shift the attention from the inertia, the formalism and the superstition of the past and to make an effective and not merely a nominal effort for insight. However, Transmutation is one or is nothing as there is simply no place for two Transmutations.

But was not steam the result of another, a new Transmutation? No. Steam was not discovered as a source of energy by the reversed epistemological triangle of the New Science. Steam is based on the old Metaphysical worldview. Here is the same worldview that made possible the analogical correspondence of magic and rituals at the very beginning, still present in the form of fossilized fragments in the customs of any Amazonian tribe, but expressed in such a way as to become effective. The impulse which led to the discovery of Steam came from the correspondence between Leibniz and Papin[6] where the former provided the theoretical basis and the latter its practical application. As we mentioned it already earlier, the living dynamic force that Leibniz saw behind the phenomena is another expression of the Perennial conception of the primordial Ether. His doctrine of the Monad is at last resort a modern replica of the key Metaphysical point, presented in the *Corpus Hermeticum* and elsewhere that All is in All. Also, it is worth noting here, that the process of fragmentation of Arcane Knowledge that was already going on in the Old Egyptian Kingdom, apart from being reflected in the persistent effort of the Alchemists to recollect something that had been lost a long time ago, as for example it is hinted in the *Epic of Gilgamesh*, is also evident in the primitive state of ancient mechanics, relying on the passive effects of pulleys and levers etc.

Now, it is precisely those that have been presented later on, as being at the forefront of the New Science, such as Newton or Savery who actually continued this trend of inertia where bodies are similar to billiard balls with the notable difference however, that whereas the inertia of ancient mechanics used to be more or less unconscious, the result of the gradual loss of the ability for recollection, here is an inertia erected as a doctrine. Once denied, the Soul had to be replaced by something since motion is possible either by itself or by another and once you deny the Soul as a life force, there is nothing else left to explain motion than the force of inertia with all the absurdities accompanying such a conception as a space devoid of matter or a gravity with a rather uncertain origin etc. Here is an apparent paradox with far reaching results. On one hand, the steam engine, as hinted already, is a departure from the senile, fossilized inertia of the traditional preoccupation with Gold and the Elixir of Life and on another hand, as a technological breakthrough, it is another illustration of the metaphysical essence of the cognitive process in general, perfectly consistent with Arcane Knowledge. However, the real nature of this leap forward has been usurped by the pseudo- scientific verbiage of Empiricism, both in its obscurantist Hobbes style chaotic naturalism and the geometrical formalism of Descartes. So what it follows from all this is that Pseudo Science posed as Science and vice versa, genuine Science appeared in the eyes of mainstream public opinion as the thrash of Knowledge. A whole Culture of deception has been created producing one hoax after another already for a fourth century in a row. In reality there is no such thing as positive Science. There is only a negative opposite double of real Science with its devastating results on Society and as we shall see later on Modern Economy.

Here is a the highly toxic combination of the LSD effect initially coming from the technological breakthrough achieved by the use of steam power on one hand and the unleashing of the self-destructive impulses of the human Psyche on the other hand. The volcano irrupting out of these impulses coagulated in the projection of a world in reverse, centered on the dogmas of Empiricism. Now, what is the effect of all this on the Modern Economy?

In the first place, this is the appearance of a unique mind setting characterized by the fetishism of Quantity. Also, the initial euphoria caused by steam at some point turned into an outright cult of greed, into the sanctification of the impulses that are the same in Man as in all other living organisms starting from the unicellular microbes and up to any reptile in the still non cleared parts of the Amazonian jungle. It goes without saying that such a leveling down would not have been consistent if it had not been combined with the methodical and grotesque attempts for intellectual and emotional self-mutilation. The supreme wisdom for the souls under the spell of modern, post-modern etc. pseudo culture is somehow to fly away from the human condition, to get asleep and to wake up one day as, why not a rat, for example? By the way, somewhere in India, there is temple, where it is believed that rats had been humans before and as a result, being considered sacred, the rats come in great numbers to get food from the priests of the temple. So patience would definitely be a virtue in such a context since, an eventual wish for being a rat may indeed be fulfilled but by no means in this life, only in the next.

The result of this mind setting on the economic activity is what has been called lately: privatization of profit and socialization of losses. On a deeper level here is a congenital aversion to real responsibility and to reality in general.

The LSD type hallucination and the euphoria initiated by steam in the 19th century together with the cult of greed paved the way, as we shall see in the next parts of our essay, to the present virtualization of economic activity and to the illusion that the gap between the nominal and the effective dimension of reality can go on forever.

Should there be a formula for the Modern Economy, it would be the following: Modern Economy= ME, Dynamic=D Quality=Q Quantity=Q1, where the dynamic of the modern economy is expressed as the attempt to reduce any Quality into Quantity by extending the substance of Quality on the ever shifting horizon of a permanent future through its own representations.

Therefore, $ME=D=Q—Q1$.

CACAMBO: Are not your points a kind of substitute to counting, which you seem to dislike, I guess? Copies are what they are precisely because you can count them. I am somewhat confused on this point because you seem to dislike the very notion of counting. Yet I do not see how would it be possible to evaluate economic activity, once we bypass figures?

PANGLOSS: There is nothing to bypass. Figures used to represent quality and substance or the principle of sufficient reason. The Pythagorean numbers appear to be a resonance of an antediluvian time, when both the physical and the metaphysical dimensions were united in a single science. However that may be, even in their present use, as units of accounting, figures may still have a positive and a negative expression, as we said it already before.

NOTES

[1] The inscription upon Watt's statue in Westminster Abbey, written by Lord Brougham, (This was set up by public subscription initiated at a public meeting, presided over by the Prime Minister, Lord Liverpool, on 18th June, 1824) is as follows:

> Not To Perpetuate A Name Which Must Endure While The Peaceful Arts Flourish But To Show That Mankind Have Learned To Honour Those Who Best Deserve Their Gratitude The King His Ministers And Many Of The Nobles And Commoners Of The Realm Raised This Monument To James Watt Who Directing The Force Of An Original Genius Early Exercised In Philosophic Research To The Improvement Of The Steam Engine Enlarged The Resources Of His Country Increased The Power Of Man And Rose To An Eminent Place Among The Most Illustrious Followers Of Science And The Real Benefactors Of The World. Born At Greenock 1736 Died At Heathfield In Staffordshire 1819.

[2] ...or Magic since the modern interpretation of Magic as a mere Belief does not seem to be more valid than, say, the claim that the existence of electricity is matter of conviction. The performance of an effective Magical Act is a scientific accomplishment, not less scientific than the use of the internal combustion engine or electricity, which in conditions of the Dark Age, however may still be accomplished but only in its virtual, symbolic expression.

[3] The texts of Plato or the *Corpus Hermeticum*, for example appeared only in the 15th century in the decades prior and shortly after the fall of Constantinople and hence their diffusion by such figures as G.G. Pletho or M. Ficino etc. Yet the intriguing question on the transmission of Ideas and Arcane Knowledge coming out of itself from all this is seldom raised. Was Plato really unknown in the Middle-Ages? How come that these same Byzantines who from Constantine on, (also, Theodosius and especially Justinian; the Byzantines were calling themselves, Rumei or Romans up to 1453) practically destroyed the ancient heritage, somehow did also the opposite, i.e. preserved at least a part of this heritage? Also, why the Venetians, who maintained close contacts with the Byzantines for centuries did not really pay attention to Plato and the University of Padua remained a stronghold of Aristotelians well after the 15th century?

[4] The concern for Transmutation of Rudolf II, for example or Newton (in 1936 some of his

writings on Alchemy were bought in a London Auction House by the economist Keynes.) or Boyle or Tycho Brache is well documented by modern sources on the subject.

[5]Without its metaphysical foundation, Psychology is something like a ghost in the search of his body, a little as a soul in Hades, whose last touch with the real world is the coin in his mouth for the passage of the Styx in the boat of Haron.

[6]Leibniz, Papin and the Steam Engine, Philippe Valenti, *Fusion Magazine* December, 1979.

TALE VI

The Standard of Living: 1929-2010

CACAMBO: As I see the yachts in this lake of Geneva are so small, they are definitely no match to their counterparts, for example in Monaco.

PANGLOSS: There are empty yachts in Monaco, anchored there for years.

CACAMBO: Why?

PANGLOSS: The attention is diverted now to the places of the Dubai variety where present day concrete pyramids are mushrooming one after another by the day.

CACAMBO: What is this building right there?

PANGLOSS: 'Le Palais des Nations', which used to be the headquarters of 'The League of Nations'.

CACAMBO: How come it used to be? What is it now?

PANGLOSS: As I see, you do not seem to know that 'The League of Nations' was disbanded in 1945 and replaced by the United Nations.

CACAMBO: I came to this city of Geneva because I was told this is the center of the modern world, the point where all local points converge into a single global whole.

PANGLOSS: You said you were wandering up and down, ever since our own time in the 18th century. So, how is it that you missed the point by more than 50 years with the UN?

CACAMBO: Have I not told you already I overslept myself, at some point and actually woke up only recently?

PANGLOSS: There are also so many other places from where all that is entangled in the knot of Modernity is clearly visible. One of them is the city of New York, across the Atlantic Ocean, where the UN is located.

CACAMBO: So let's go there!

PANGLOSS: Why not? Can you be ready by tomorrow?

CACAMBO: Yes, for sure.

PANGLOSS: Fine, let's still walk now a little further since, I have not finished yet, my point on the epistemological limits of present day views on the way economic activity is carried out.

CACAMBO: Okay.

PANGLOSS: The digestive tube or what we may call, the KFC syndrome, combined with the toxic, mirage like effect of what we saw as the Liverpool Syndrome, reflect a form of Consciousness with an all pervading effect on all spheres of social life, including economic activity. Now, it happens that the nature of this Consciousness is such, that the stronger is its effect the less it is perceived by its objects or by the subjects, objectifying it in its physical dimension.

CACAMBO: You present the whole thing as something given. What is the specific origin of this Consciousness?

PANGLOSS: There are basically two possible answers either it sprang from the one or from the many.

CACAMBO: What do you mean?

PANGLOSS: Any form of universal Consciousness, as we will see in more detail, arises in individual Consciousness in the first place and is dissolved in the form of universal Consciousness only later on. The sudden emergence of one and the same thing in the heads of millions of people out of thin air or else, a thing which had not being instilled from somewhere but just from anywhere appears to be an absurdity. Should such a reality be possible even for a fraction of a second, this would by necessity require also to tear down the whole chain of causality, the interconnectedness of all the phenomena and thus to scrap the Cosmos altogether. When the Sun is rising every day most people except the blind and those in coma realize that this is indeed so and they take it for granted that the Sun would not be the Sun if it had not rays that affect them and also affecting anything else. Therefore, the spontaneous arousal of a Collective Unconscious is as possible as a rising of a Sun without rays. Present day insistence on Quantity, in the form of accounting and statistics seems to be a reversed mirror, an optical illusion. Also, to assume that this is not an illusion after all, since something so massive, so all pervading cannot be an illusion somehow by its sheer volume would be the same as to assume that if all the individuals, composing present day Humanity decide one day to order the Sun to stop bothering them any longer and start looking to the sky and yelling: Do not rise! Do not rise! The Sun will indeed obey them and will simply stop rising. Had we not been taking for granted that reality exists in potency and in act and therefore assuming the smooth, spontaneous transition from the one to the other in practice whatever we profess about this same transition in theory, hardly anything that appears before our eyes would be the same. For example, should you follow the tenets of the inductive, empiricist approach to its core, once you leave your car in the nearby parking lot you'd better never come back since once parked the car will pass from a car in act to a car in potency and in the quantitative method there is simply no place for such a transition. Again, should you turn the key of your car the engine will start running and once this takes place, the empiricist methodology will record it with the outmost precision and so at this point everything will be just fine. However, shall you follow this same methodology to its core you'll not be able to stop the car at will since the only thing you are provided with is nothing else but what is before your eyes right now, at this very moment. As your attention will be taken by the counting of the seconds or indeed minutes during which the engine of your car has been running, at some point you may no longer remember how to stop the car. Worse still, as an integral empiricist or expert on statistics or economist this same method that you profess to be the truth and nothing but the truth, will not allow you to do so, since what counts is to count and or in other words to record only what is in act by implicitly denying the validity of what is in potency. Therefore, should you not resign yourself at some point to be less catholic than the Pope at least for a time, the engine will stop but by itself and not by your own efforts with all the consequences that all this implies for your car and indeed for your own well-being in general.

Now, at the very moment when we acknowledge that something in act is one side of the coin and something in potency its other side, just as inspiration is as relevant to breathing as expiration or the essence to its expressions, we may well profess empiricism in words but not in deeds. However, should we cease professing one thing and doing another, we'll become aware of this contradiction by necessity and the question of a different methodological framework will come out of itself.

The frozen KFC cage chicken will suddenly resurrect. The cycle of economic activity will be transmuted from an endless serial line of figures, of accounting units into a vibrating Life force evolving within a Universe where the free fall of dead, inert bodies in the dark abyss of nothingness will be nothing more than a remote souvenir of a bad dream. In such a Universe there will be an incessant movement from the Essence to its manifestations or from the One to the many and from the many to the One. We may call this Perennial Economics or Economics of Quality. In such a methodological framework there will be two criteria for the assessment of economic activity: Quality and Equilibrium. Now, since these criteria are at last resort, reflections of Consciousness the question of their presence and respectively absence in a given object will come back to their source i.e. Consciousness. As in a domino, each part will go to its natural place. Quantity will still be relevant but only in relation to its essence i.e. Quality. There will still be separate areas of investigation or expertise or spheres of activity along the cognitive process but as parts tending toward a whole since there is no such thing as a part of nothing. There will still be a pursuit of Happiness but without the ultimately false dichotomy between collectivism versus individualism. There will be also something which today is in its last stage before being virtualized altogether: personal responsibility, real private property and genuine liberty. The present mental setting of blind attraction versus repulsion toward trade and finance, reflected for example in the 1986 movie, 'Wall Street' will appear from this perspective as a sterile dichotomy. Here is a creature mutilating itself by attempting to stop his own bloodstream. The seemingly endless spider web of modern finance with its 'derivatives', modern trade with its ever growing list of items that have been making several tours of the globe, before landing on the shelves of the nearby discount store or modern agriculture, with its dead end OGM seeds or the ever diminishing scope of present day economic information, preoccupied by the configuration of its own shadow reflect in the first place a broken ontological equilibrium. The criticism of such an environment with the tools that made it possible in the first place is a dead end street and so is its mere condemnation on moral grounds.

Following the above presented epistemological outlines, the goods produced by present day economy will look like the new garments from the Emperor's new clothes, wardrobe.

Now, let's start with the Emperor's new redingote for example, described by the tailors to its outmost detail within the tangible setting of thin air. So, how would it be possible to transcribe the term 'redingote' in the realm of modern economic terminology?

One of its likely representations might be, why not for example, standard of living?

As an image of a world of plenty, the concept of 'standard of living' is nothing new under the Sun. What makes it really new is the implicit rejection of anything that might retain the drift to the ever shifting line of an endless horizon, filled with those objects, which otherwise appear in Consciousness only in the moments of abject privation from the basic necessities required to preserve one's physical existence. The standard of living, they say, is either expanding or it is not. There is simply no middle way.

Now, why not going a step further now and pay more attention to the term 'physical' by applying all that has been presented theoretically in the previous parts in its concrete, practical expression?

Let's assume now that his clothing takes a real form, i.e. becomes real clothing. So the Emperor looks happy with his new redingote, he is watching its golden buttons all the time, he is walking all over the place with it and he is waving to his subjects expecting their unconditional approval. At some point however, the tailors come back with a new redingote and they succeed in convincing the Monarch that he will look still better if he just puts on his shoulders another, a second redingote. And then, he puts a third, a fourth one. He is wearing a whole wardrobe now and under the heavy weight of all these redingotes he has trouble moving and is barely standing on his feet. So, at some point he falls on the ground just any Christmas tree would fall if it has nowhere to lean on.

Should we assume that the highest number of redingotes which the Emperor can bear before falling are, say, seven, the moment when the tailors convinced him once again that he would be better off if he puts another, arguably last redingote, the seventh in a row, would have been simultaneously the point indicating that this is the beginning of the end, since it is precisely this seventh redingote that will make him vacillate and ultimately fall on the ground of his palace. The redingotes are in reality no other than AD or Aggregate Demand. We could call them also, AQ or Aggregate Quantity since the finality of the Modern Economy is no other than the quantification of its own movement. And so is the concept of Standard of living both in words and in deeds. The highest point of the AD coincides with the highest standard of living since the latter is on the microeconomic level what the former is on the macroeconomic level. Now, this same seventh redingote, from above, which caused the fall or indeed the collapse of the Emperor, will be recorded by modern economic science as nothing more than the last consecutive, incremental rise of AD or the standard of living. In other words, should we follow the quantitative methodological framework in a really consistent way any concern for the eventual fall of the Emperor will be dismissed as a mere hypothetical supposition, since according to immediate sense perception he is still standing on his feet and therefore the cause and effect link between the weight of all his seven redingotes and his fall will be bypassed, although once this takes place, the fall will be indeed recorded since it is already before your eyes right now or within the scope of the quantitative or statistical or empiricist or indeed positive approach. Should we try to find a reliable way to represent how the fall of the Emperor is taking place, we have to look beyond quantity and therefore beyond the epistemology of current economic science.

Following the inner bond uniting Quality to the Psyche, what is generally seen as being in 'purely economic terms', will cease to appear so, since in reality there is no such thing as purely economic thing. Reality is no ham that could be cut into slices. At last resort any Quantity is the imprint of a given Quality, where Quantity is no more than the effect of the cause that is taken into consideration.

CACAMBO: There was no such thing as standard of living in our own time. People were either rich or poor and that is it.

PANGLOSS: We'll take the figures on the standard of living in the reference books or the magazines on the shelves of any bookshop throughout the world and interpret the available information in the light of both Quality and Quantity. Since what has been characterized as the First Industrial Revolution ended abruptly with the stock market crash of October 1929, we'll use some data on the living conditions of this period and compare them to the present day situation.

Below are quoted the retail prices of various goods in the US in the 1920s and up to 1931:

> 1. Bread 1 lb. 10¢ 1925 New York
> 2. Bread 1 lb. 10¢ 1929 Chicago
> 3. Beef Rib Roast1 lb 39¢ 1926 New York
> 4. Chicken lb. 42¢ 1929 New York
> 5. Cheese I lb. 38¢ 1926 New York
> 6. Oranges 1 Doz.57¢ 1925[1]

How much things cost in 1931:

- Average cost of new house $6,790.00
- Average wages per year $1,850.00
- Cost of a gallon of gas 10 cents
- Average cost for house rent $18.00 per month
- A loaf of bread 8 cents
- A lb. of hamburger meat 11 cents
- Alarm Ccock $3.50
- New car average price $640.00[2]

By the way, in the second half of the 1920s the price of a Ford T car dropped to $290, the equivalent to $3258 today.[3]

According to the US Index of Composite Wages the average US worker's monthly wage in 1930 was around $104 and what is more, the salaries of most Americans were equal to their disposable income.[4]

How does all these data compare to present day 2010 prices?

In February 2010, a 20 ounce loaf of bread in the US cost $2.49.[5] The retail price of beef in the third quarter of 2008 was $4.46 per pound.[6]

- Average cost new car (2008) $27,958
- Average cost cents per kilowatt hour electricity (Jan 2009) 11.03 cents
- A loaf of bread (2009) $2.79
- A lb. of bacon (2009) $2.99
- A lb. of potatoes (2009) $0.32
- Dozen eggs (2009) $1.89
- College tuition state (2009) $6,585
- First class stamp (2009) $0.42[7]

Now, as the nature of our subject is such that there is no way to bypass numbers, we'll have to mention at this point that numbers, in Plato's *Dialogues* or in the School of the Pythagoreans, used to represent Quality in the first place and not mere Quantity. Being extensions of geometrical figures numbers from the perspective of Descartes, are units and from there is paved, so to speak the ontological way to modern accounting.[8] Here is a measure of the curves, triangles, squares etc. from the spatial perspective available to the senses. At this point the divorce with the idea of substance and hence quality is no less than complete.[9] So the resulting estrangement with reality naturally follows and it is precisely from this source that is springing the material or economic, a posteriori expression of this same estrangement and definitely not the other way round, as it is the case with use of this concept by Marx, since the elements or any solid matter in reality is by definition powerless to affect the essence, that made it possible in the first place. To fly away from the idea of essence in such a way is a little like an impressionist painting where various faces in a state of deep alienation seem to reflect all the time on their own nature and the probability that they might, somehow be mistaken by taking themselves for humans whereas they are actually confused ghosts, flowing relentlessly within the remaining pockets of empty space in a world filled with solid matter. Further on, since any quality or any substance has its sufficient reason in a combination of 'Pythagorean' numbers, it follows from here that a given quality may be reproduced in its entirety almost at will and better still at any point in time and hence the validity of Alchemy. It is from here that is coming out the key argument of reversible time, accessible evoked by mystics, yogis, psychics etc. and also the notion of Resurrection.[10]

NOTES

[1]www.thepeoplehistory.com.

[2]Ibid.

[3]Martin W. Sandler, *Driving around the USA: Automobiles in American Life*, Oxford University Press, 2003, p.21.

[4]www.lewrockwell.com, *The Plague of Self-Delusion* by Tim Case.

[5]www.thepeoplehistory.

[6]Chris Hurt, *Cattle Business is Back*, www.Farms.com.

[7]www.thepeoplehistory.com.

[8]Numbers had been used in the ancient past as units of accounting, (Some of the cuneiform tablets unearthed in the Middle East are exactly this, units of accounting of ancient granaries.) but they also had another function. The awareness of this function had been either lost or denied. Numbers used to represent also qualities, of substance unfolding within the Cosmos, not the Cosmos of ghostlike numbers but the real, manifested, Cosmos.

[9]Present day Numerology is a pale reflection of the idea of cosmic substance that used to be associated with any combination of numbers. Here is a vision of based on the perception or the intellective intuition of the Primeval Essence behind all manifested reality, of which Alchemy is another expression. Also, the principle of computer networks as a way to transmit data appears to be a modern application of the same idea, revealing among other things that had it not been for the tendency of modern technology to transgress its alleged empirical, positivist foundation all the time, there would simply no such thing as technology at all. The awareness of the correspondence between numbers and their respective substance or quality had been lost and as a result, to the modern mind came out the idea that this correspondence might somehow be arbitrary, a distorted perception, revealing the ever expanding fragmentation of Knowledge, being a key feature of the Iron Age of the legend. Another indication of this is for example, F. de Saussure's theory on Linguistics. (Le significant et le signifié or the signifier and the signified) which affected all spheres of Culture, starting from Philology, Anthropology, the study of Myths and Symbols etc. Here is the spark, initiating the on-going global semantic revolution culminating in the credo of structuralism with its 'narrative', propagated by an army of 'technicians of the discourse'. In the growing spider web type complexity of the modern world, the crudity of outright empiricism had to be veiled somehow by the attempt to reduce the process of reflection to a mere 'Techne' and thus to exploit intellectual activity and at the same time, obstructing the way of its natural propensity for free reflection, which modern philosophy denied altogether: the Thing in itself or 'Intelligible Essence'.

[10]The idea of Resurrection had been dismissed by Modernity not only on the grounds of the materialistic denial of the existence of the Soul, but also as an apparently flat contradiction to common sense, since the point of death and the point of Resurrection are seen to be a mere spatial and temporal extension of the ever changing configuration of the physical body, whereas the certainty for the probability of such an occurrence to actually take place rests on the metaphysical insight on the eternal recurrence. From this point of view Resurrection is a Reconstitution, not a reconstruction of the remains of the body. Now, should we look at all this from the point of view of materialism, namely Atomism in the way, it has been already formulated in Ancient India or by Democritus, the endless recurrence has to happen to its outmost detail, exactly as any numerical combination on a Black Jack for example, sooner or later, has to take place, even if we have to wait for this combination to appear for eons. The rabbit from 'Alice in Wonderland' having tea and always repeating the same gestures with the same words would appear from this perspective as the ideal representation of the Eternal Recurrence in an accelerated time frame. It

is only because there is no such thing as an indivisible material whole that the Eternal Recurrence is unfolding in its Essence and in its Essence only, since the details are its infinite expressions and therefore are contained within the perfect, indivisible whole that the Essence is.

TALE VII

The Bread of 2012

Cacambo: This was my first voyage on an airplane and I am still dizzy now. You have been right after all. This place New York seems to be the center of the world. Everything is so big. As you can see, these buildings are not built according to the Cosmogony you were referring to and yet they are so massive, so imposing.

Pangloss: Ancient temples are built according to the quality of numbers whereas modern skyscrapers are built according to the numbers of quality. The space in these buildings is a closed space, since it is confined to the intrinsic limits of the form at the expense of its content.

Cacambo: Okay. Look at all these cars and lights everywhere!

Pangloss: I have been here before. The place we are walking right now is called Time Square. You seem to assume that all this movement is the prelude to the point where 'Tout est pour le mieux dans meilleur des mondes possibles.' (Everything is for the best in the best of all possible worlds').

Cacambo: Definitely. And yet, sometimes I find myself in trouble since I wonder if the whole thing will keep going on like this in the future. Will it be growing bigger and bigger forever and ever?

Pangloss: Of course not. And that is precisely why what you just said about the best of all possible worlds is indeed so.

Cacambo: Listen to me my friend: you did not seem to take notice at our previous meeting that the best may turn to the worst in no time. How is that you forgot what happened to the Pangloss from the novel, in the place by the name of Paraguay?! Don't you understand that these are only words! You have the useless propensity of doubting the obvious, this same obvious that is before your eyes right now! You see, you hear, you touch. So what then? You just make your way ahead and you see what happens next!

Pangloss: You watch but you do not really appear see what is before your eyes at this very moment. As for your questions, I'll answer to you but not now, only after I have showed you what will happen next. So would you be so kind as to be patient for once my dear friend?

Cacambo: How can you say I do not see?! I see everything of course. I mean I see all these figures above and not only I see, but also I touch and I count, I measure. And what I counted at this point is that in a matter of a few years the figures were just growing and growing.

Pangloss: Would you just put your glasses and look at these figures once more? You will notice that both earnings and prices went up several times and since 1929. By the way do you like flowers, for example, tulips?

Cacambo: I just put my glasses. So would you put your flowers aside for now? Also, before asking me anything, could you at least specify, how much and how many... I mean how many units of course, you counted out of...just out of any number you can imagine. You do not seem to understand that, all that really counts is counting.

Pangloss: As I see from all these figures, a monthly salary in the 1920s used to buy more than 1000 breads and in 2009 less than 900 if we take the approximate figure for a monthly salary in today's US to be, say, about $30,000 a year. Furthermore, should we subtract the difference between gross and disposable salary, the above figure will be substantially lower. And there is more to come.

Cacambo: I had enough already. Who lives on bread alone? How can you be so blind to all the light that is just everywhere? Did you not notice that everything is moving so fast! Don't you remember the carriages, the wooden ships and the horses of our own time?

Pangloss: We'll get there later on. You promised to be patient for once, right? By the way did it happen to you to taste the bread of 2012?

Cacambo: No...I mean...yes. But this is...this is just taste. And what is such a subjective impression as taste in comparison with the objective status of accounting? The figures displayed on any of these...mirrors...

Pangloss: Computer screens.

Cacambo: Okay then...screens yes... there are more figures on any these screens than in all the archives of our own time and probably even in 1929.

Pangloss: Wait a second. You do not see that the endless line of figures displayed on these screens every day, proves in the most irrefutable way that the part of agriculture in the price of today's bread is much smaller than before, since the inputs up to the price of the final output on the shelf of any supermarket are composed of a growing number of processed and most of the time, non-agricultural ingredients.

CACAMBO: We'll talk about the price later on. At this point, why not take a look at the way bread is produced? In 1929, the percentage of agriculture in the total employment in the US was a least 20% whereas today it is may be less than 2%. Furthermore, back in 1929, food processing used to be carried out at home by women who then as now made at least half of the overall population. This same food processing is made at this point, many times faster with only a small fraction of the working age population, as the vast majority of women, nowadays, do not bake bread any longer since they work in offices from nine to five. In 2007, the US Agri-Food industry provided only 1.5 million jobs out of a total population of more than 300 million.[1] So, could you just tell me my friend, by how much the timeframe for the production of bread has been reduced since 1929? Is it ten times, twenty times or more than hundred times?!

PANGLOSS: May be even more than hundred times.

CACAMBO: And so what then? Is not everything still going up and up?!

PANGLOSS: The higher the quantity, the lower its common denominator. As a gift from the best in the best of all possible worlds, when Giants and Dragons were still roaming the Earth, real bread was composed for millennia of water, salt and water combined with yeast. The taste of 2012's bread derives its objective foundation in high speed mills where the produced flour is mixed with water, with soya flour, hydrogenated fats, baking aids, ascorbic acid and yeast.

CACAMBO: Is what you refer as the bread of 2012, the bread in the US alone or the bread throughout the world?

PANGLOSS: It could be both, although at this point, the quality of the industrial bread elsewhere, as for example in the granary of the Old World, Egypt, the granary of the New World Argentina, or the one in the Middle Ages and up to 1913, the Ukraine and also other parts of Eastern Europe, might be lower than in the US since in all these places, quantity is the first priority. Now, lets' take a look, one by one, at all of the above:

> 1) *Water:* When the wheat is milled in these high speed still mills,[2] the flour as a result is able to absorb more water and that is why the consistency of modern bread is at least 50% lower than the one of the old bread.
> 2) *Soya flour:* Soy is safe for consumption only in small amounts, not as daily food. Furthermore, soya flour contains hexanes obtained by the refining of

crude oil.[3]

3)*Hydrogenated fats:* these are literally "plastics", which do not have the same properties as natural fats. Tissues made with the "false" fat cannot function properly, as thousands of enzymes can't bind to them, giving rise to a host of disease states.[4]

4)*Ascorbic acid:* here is a synthetic vitamin depleting your body of other nutrients, which among other things, is also used to make appear the meat that can be found on the shelves of the supermarkets, red. It is the same as, for example, to make a somewhat dried grass by the Sun greener by dying it in green.[5]

NOTES

[1]www.competitivealternatives.com - KPMG *Guide to International Business location 2010 edition.*

[2]The industrial production of bread in the US appears to be kept as a professional secret, but it is not so in the U.K. where records on the Chorleywood Industrial Bread Making Process, introduced in 1961 are widely available. (See,www.allotment.org.uk Wednesday, 09.February 2011 Allotment Dairy).

[3]Auteur(s)/Author(s) Khetarpaul, Neelam (1); Raj, bala grewal (1); Goyal, Rajni (1); GARG Renu (1); Affiliation(s) du ou des auteurs/Author(s) Affiliation(s) Department of Foods & Nutrition, CCS Haryana Agricultural University, Hisar 125004, INDE See also, *The Dark side of America's Favorite Health Food Revealed* Posted Jul 08 2009 9:20pm www.wholesoystory.com.

[4]Hydrogenated fats: www.becomehealthynow.com - Friday February 4, 2011. *The danger of hydrogenated of partially hydrogenated fats*, Submitted by Dr Garry Far.

[5]*Synthetic vs. Natural Vitamins* By Dr.Ben Kim - DrBenKim.com.

TALE VIII

The Price of Cars

Cacambo: Your point reminds that I have not eaten anything ever since we left the plane. So why not we just enter a place where I could simply bypass bread, since present day standard of living is allowing us to replace bread with steaks, with French fries and with so many other tightly packed items full of nutritional consistency?

Pangloss: Okay. Let's go. There is a car for me, parked around the corner.

Once outdoors, they cross a jammed N.Y. street and get into the car.

Cacambo: My dear friend, you seem to be completely out of touch with… I mean, just with everything! How can you drive such an antique, lemon car in the early 21st century? Didn't you steal it from a museum, did you?

Pangloss: No. Here is collection car by the name of Ford T which by the way is anything but cheap these days. Would you be so kind as take a seat and wait a minute while I start the engine.

Cacambo: What happened? Did you lose the ignition key or something?

Pangloss: Not at all. This model had been manufactured prior 1919, when there was still no electric starter[1] and as a result I have to execute the following operation: I'll pull the tall lever-the one jutting from the floor next to the steering column –all the way back to engage neutral and the parking brake. Then I'll push the timing lever all the way up to retard the timing and move the throttle down a few clicks. Next, I'll move to the front of the car and close the choke by pulling a wire ring that pokes from the bottom of the radiator cover. So at this point I'll be ready to crank.[2]

Cacambo: As I see, from all that you are about to do, we are definitely living now in the best of the best of all possible worlds! Is not all the progress that has been made since 1929 simply embodied in the few seconds that are required to start the engine of any new car with a simple ignition key?

Pangloss: Would you just let me crank for a while!

CACAMBO: I would appreciate if you just speed up the whole process of cranking, which at this point as I see, has caused a huge jam all over the place! Look at all these Yellow Cab drivers standing right there and watching us! Obviously, they have never seen such a spectacle in their lifetime, other than in their souvenirs of black and white movies of the Laurel and Hardy variety, from their early childhood! They must think you are a ghost or something!

PANGLOSS: Here we are! The engine is running already!

CACAMBO: Could you tell me how many gallons of gasoline you'll have to spill out into the tank of this antique to drive me up to the next KFC restaurant? As I see from all these billboards with car commercials scattered all over the place, each new car is better than the previous one and as a result, I wonder how many times a 2012 car is more fuel efficient than your lemon from...

PANGLOSS: ...From 1908, when the first Ford T such this one was introduced. As for the fuel efficiency, the answer, my friend, is none! Ford T went at 25 miles per gallon. As of 2004 for example, the average fuel economy of cars and trucks was 24.6 miles per gallon.[3]

CACAMBO: Maybe, but at least you cannot deny that your antique is no match to any modern car as far as the comfort is concerned.

PANGLOSS: Ford T had tufted leather seats whereas most modern cars of the same class are equipped with vinyl seats.

CACAMBO: And so what?

PANGLOSS: Do you know what a new car smell is?

CACAMBO: What the hell is this all about? Where are you getting at?

PANGLOSS: I will tell you: 'new car smell' is a concoction of tens or hundreds of chemicals that off-gas from different car parts. One of the materials that play a big role is vinyl, also known as PVC or polyvinyl chloride. Vinyl contains a chemical that off-gases and causes 'fogging' on the inside of the windshield. A lot of vinyl is to be found in vehicles with leather seats, which often have a very strong 'new car smell'. While the front of the seats are usually real leather, in most cases the sides and back of the seats are made of vinyl. Consumers can't tell, because the vinyl industry has done a great job of making it look exactly like leather. Vinyl is one of the worst types of plastic. It's been strongly linked to fertility problems and cancer. It's important for consumers to know that when they buy leather seats, they are actually buying a whole lot of vinyl.[4]

Cacambo: Would you stop this nonsense! How can you prove that this is indeed so?

Pangloss: I'll get there later on. Now, let me just say that we have a crystal clear correspondence between all layers of reality at this point. There is the ontological level, the psychological, the social and the economic. So, in the first place, here is the original 'thing in itself' or 'leather' and its copy 'vinyl' acting as a Plastic Maya, a substitute and therefore, as a timeless, eternal second best. One step further is the key principle of Delusion and Self-Delusion: I have a sufficient reason to suspect the authenticity of the leather on my seats, but why should I pay so much attention to something looking just like the original? After all, is not the only original that I see from the windscreen of my 2012 car a constantly shifting original, an original in transition, just like the representation of my own self on the ever present horizon of the future? And last but not least, here is the Principle of Modern Economics in full action, where the ever present doomed attempt to reduce Quality to Quantity takes the deceptive form of an endless serial of the representations of this same Quality. The present day ghost like scene of fleeting images speeding in a multilayered quantum type space, back in 1929, was only a dream my friend!

Cacambo: How come that vinyl is what you said it is?

Pangloss: Listen, whatever you do and whatever you think, reality is a puzzle, a domino. It happens that for one reason something might be described the outmost detail and buried or say, censured and then unearthed and presented for another reason elsewhere. The thing is that the context may shift but the content does not. So, is vinyl, which is a copy of leather as well as the sources on the whole shift from one to the other.

Cacambo: You are giving me a headache. So much talking and driving along these towers with their never shifting shadows and you still did not say a word about speed. Any 2012 car can make 120-30 miles per hour in a few seconds while your lemon has trouble driving up any slope! By the way do not count on me for pushing this old wreck!

Pangloss: The top speed of Ford T is 45 miles per hour.[5] Provided that the speed limit in the US of 2012 is between 65 and 75 mile per hour, on the board of Ford T, you simply have no chance of getting a speeding ticket any time soon.

Cacambo: Look! Whatever you say, your lemon is no match to any modern car! It does not even run as a car but as a donkey carriage. You have been driving for only a few minutes and I have trouble with my back already!

Pangloss: I definitely agree with you at this point my dear friend! Ford T does not run as smoothly as any modern car, except may be the car that lately has been posing as its 2012 equivalent: the Tata Nano. Now, would you just let me go on, somewhat further, on this key point?

Cacambo: Go ahead, but be short, because we passed by a number of fast-food outlets and my patience is running out!

Pangloss: Sorry, but I am confronted with another problem of 2012 car traffic: we have not been lucky enough so far to find out a parking lot! As for my point, it is the following: Modern cars run more smoothly than a Ford T. That is fine, but why should I miss the opportunity that this point is giving me, for evaluating something that right now, in 2012, is the top priority of just anyone under the Sun?

Cacambo: What?

Pangloss: I'll tell you. My point is about cost. What has been the cost of the only advantage that modern cars have over the Ford T that is smooth running? Here we can make a distinction between three qualitatively different types of costs:

1) The Human cost
2) The Social cost
3) The Economic cost

Pangloss: If there is to be a principle of sufficient reason, why then there should not be a principle of sufficient quality? There is a point in the Universal Reason where cars are good enough as they are.

Cacambo: Is not the Universal Reason in reality your own Reason? You are substituting your own judgment to the judgment of the countless participants in the market. Is not the preference of millions of consumers and producers more relevant than your own, so to speak preference?

Pangloss: The number of the thing in itself is never more than one.

Cacambo: Let's go back to cars. You did not say anything about car prices yet?

Pangloss: As we saw it already, the nature and the number of car components as well as the way it is produced on the assembly line change all the time and therefore represent the variables, entering in the constitution of modern cars. Now, let's also assume that there are indeed Akashic records somewhere in the Universe and that the Platonic Forms are one of the variables of these records. Therefore, there should be a layer in Consciousness, where stands the idea of the ultimate or universal car. Now, provided that the average human on our planet is neither Lilliputian nor a Giant, the urban space is congested and any car's performance is related to its weight and length, we do not see how a stretched limousine would match the criteria for our universal car. Also, it goes without saying that a renewable source of energy, the solar or the wind being only two among others, would be the only rational alternative and therefore, the engine of such a vehicle will not be propelled by oil. Further on, there will be definitely no flagman at the front of our universal car to comply with the regulations of speed limit as it has been the case in the UK up to the end of the 19th century.[6] By the way had there been no such thing as sufficient reason, the courts, for example and with them, all contractual agreements of whatever nature and therefore all forms of organized social life, will simply stop functioning since any lawsuit, would be an occasion for taking into consideration just everything under the Sun, including the number of the technicians of the discourse and other deconstruction experts, dancing on the top of a needle.

CACAMBO: And so what? Did not a figure of our own time by the name of Jean-Jacques Rousseau, say that the state of nature is the best in the best of all possible worlds?

PANGLOSS: The awareness of the sufficient reason is as much part of the state of nature as its absence. Therefore, in its quality of universal car, our car will not deviate from its own nature or intrinsic quality in a single iota.

CACAMBO: Yes, except that apart from being in your head, such a car is nowhere to be seen.

PANGLOSS: The deviation from the sufficient quality is the absolute proof for its existence. A philosopher once stated that, the Principle has a tendency to revert upon itself.[7] You cannot alter a given quality or a particular essence, because, if there was no such quality in the first place, there would be nothing to be altered. Again, had there been no truth in itself, we would not hear, for example, a single lie on this planet, since the possibility to distort something rests on the presumption that, this same something has to exist in the first place, otherwise there would be nothing to be distorted.

CACAMBO: I see a fast food outlet of the Mc Donald's type over there. Let's go.

PANGLOSS: Okay.

CACAMBO: By the way, what is the quality of a hamburger, according to your theory?

PANGLOSS: The original hamburger is a based on an old recipe from the city of Hamburg in Germany, whereas modern hamburgers are its representations, reproduced in billions of copies all over the world. Here is another example of a quality, of an original reduced by the industrial matrix to its shadow, i.e. to the status of a copy, somewhat like the little Venice or the fake Pyramids of Las Vegas.

CACAMBO: Okay. Fine. And what would be the price of your universal car?

PANGLOSS: Do you remember that in back our own time there was still genuine polemical disputes between the tenants of different points of view and not only in matters of detail, as it is nowadays, but in matters of principle? Even medieval inquisitors found it appropriate to engage in such disputes with their opponents, for example the Cathars. Today, the flow of Consciousness is wrapped within essentially two types of soap bubbles: the bubble of estrangement and the bubble of relativism. The thing is that when you stop confronting reality in its own terms, the willingness for arguing vanishes also. However that may be, as far as the car prices are concerned, there is the following picture: Once the starting point of economic activity is shifted from quality to its representations or from the original to its copies or from quality to quantity, cars have to change all the time and this is carried out by the exponential growth of car inputs such as plastics, electronics etc. As the expansion of quantity by necessity is related to speed, the time required for the production of these car outputs is reduced. Now, modern presentation of this same phenomenon, by the name of Labor theory of value, came to call it, progress or higher productivity or lower cost or higher profit.

CACAMBO: How does quality affect price?

PANGLOSS: Quality cannot be quantified in itself. Once again: quality can be represented, but cannot be quantified in the same way as a copy will never be the essence of its original. The intrinsic quality of cars has no price, since an essence cannot be transferred neither divided in itself a little as my best friends, the Monads, which have no parts. Now, our Universal Car, discussed earlier, is the sufficient reason or the embodiment of quality or the essence of cars. From there, the way to the representation of this same quality and therefore its quantification, is paved. At this point and at this point only appears price. The latter is an expression of the movement toward the essence or the sufficient reason for a given quality, in our case, cars or for the deviation from this same quality. There is no single price of cars in reality. There are four prices: the immediate and the ultimate price or the price for the car's buyer and the price for society and for the environment as well as a positive and a negative price. The positive price can either immediate or ultimate whereas the negative price cannot be immediate. It can only be ultimate, since no buyer would pay to an Alfa Romeo dealer for refusing to buy his car.

CACAMBO: What are the four prices of modern cars?

PANGLOSS: Modern cars are a deviation from our Universal car and this movement is accelerating by the day. The ultimate negative price of these cars, however, contrary to their quality can be measured in monetary terms. One has just to calculate the cost of the ever growing car inputs, whose negative effect both to society, to the environment and to the car' buyer with its toxic 'new car smell' staff and its absurd insistence on speed is self-evident. And there is worse still: one has to calculate the cost of using a non-renewable source of energy such as oil. Furthermore, the labor value theory is only half of the truth of car prices since as already the theologians of Salamanca had pointed out in their time, price is at last resort an expression of scarcity not just labor. What will happen to the price of modern cars with their hundreds of components based on oil, such as, the now, seemingly cheap plastics, when at some point the oil price will skyrocket? Further on, supposing that due to an oil crisis, someone decides to revert back to crude Ford T type cars so that the price might be made affordable to the impoverished consumers of the future, it may turn that the cost of production of such cars with their seats of tufted leather, if we refer back to the original, will turn to be more expensive than in 1929, since thanks to decades of negative evolution of ultimate car prices, the basis for the manufacturing of such cars is no longer in place for a long time.

CACAMBO: And how about the immediate car price?

PANGLOSS: Car prices in part due to their relation with modern Psyche are as inelastic as those of salt for example and as a result relative to the average income, prices of new cars are at best the same, if not higher than in 1929.

CACAMBO: Are not cars are solid matter, after all?

PANGLOSS: Cars are a status symbol. A change of car is perceived as a change of identity, although Socrates in a Bentley is no more Socrates than Socrates in a WW Beatle. May be 90% of today's immediate car price is simultaneously a part, although a tiny part, of its negative long term ultimate price. Had it not been for the never ending chain of components from where countless additional producers make a profit, the price of a car with somewhat better characteristics than the Fort T in all probability would not exceed $1500-2000 in today's prices, as this had been shown by such relatively simple cars of the 'Logan' variety, produced by Renault in Romania or Tata in India.

CACAMBO: Is there at least one positive element in modern cars? By the way, have you not heard that modern car buyers seem to dislike the Tata Nano?

PANGLOSS: You distort my point. I am not suggesting a conversion to simple 'Caisses'(fr.) neither am I making an apology of technical primitivism. The smooth running of many modern cars will be a part of our Universal Car, where the immediate price, due to the suppression of today's oligopolistic, inelastic prices, will be lower and where the ultimate price will be positive.

NOTES

[1] www.popuplar mechanics.com, October 1, 2009, *Ford Model T Test Drive: Behind the Wheel of America's Most Important Car on its 100th Birthday.*

[2] Ibid.

[3] www.current.com, Model T has the same fuel economy as modern cars. April 12, 2008.

[4] www.cartalk.com. *Interview with Geoffrey Gearheart,* www.healthycar.org. Also www. healthystuff.org 16 sept 2010, www.ecomall.com. www.edition.cnn.com. *Don't inhale that new car smell,* July 31, 2008.

[5] www.popularmechanics.com, October 1, 2009.

[6] The 1865 locomotive act required all road locomotives, which included automobiles, to travel at a maximum of 4 mph (6 km/h) in the country and 2 mph (3 km/h) in towns and have a crew of three, one of whom should carry a red flag walking 60 yards (55 m) ahead of each vehicle. The 1896 Act removed the need for the crew of three and raised the speed to 14 mph (23 km/h). *Privatized Infrastructure: the Role of Government,* Thomas Telford.

[7] See *Elements of Theology,* Proclus.

TALE IX

The Woodstock Syndrome

Pangloss and Cacambo are back to the Ford T. The roof of the antique car is open since, both the driver and the passenger, on the front seat, apparently enjoy being exposed to the hot summer wind that is lifting in the air, scattered papers and empty Coca Cola cans, falling back on the sidewalks, almost empty of passers-by at this late afternoon hour. Cacambo is looking in all directions to the various configurations of the 2012 NY urban landscape.

CACAMBO: The food here is no different from the one in the place we left. The cage chicken you spoke about before seem to be the same everywhere. I am definitely full at this point and yet I still had no desert. May be we could go somewhere for example, for an ice cream?

PANGLOSS: Should we come back in time only few decades ago on this same spot where we are right now, we may see the passengers on a car like this who, went for a drive along the same way and with the same purpose, that is, to look for ice cream on a hot summer day.

CACAMBO: And so what?

PANGLOSS: These are the heroes of the Great Gatsby.[1]

CACAMBO: May be but how did it come that they embarked on a Ford T? It should have been at least a Panhard et Levassor or better still a Hispano-Suiza or even a Bugatti.

PANGLOSS: Okay I agree with you on this point. By the way, in the epistemology of the new science, whose criteria had been set a little before our own time, there is no place for the principle of analogy and the notion of objective validity has been encapsulated in a cage, precisely of the like of the KFC chickens. Once the mind is cleared from its natural propensity for making allusions in the way for an overall synthesis, the very idea of quality is obscured, so to speak out of itself. This is to remind you that we are treating our subject on the modern economy by following the tenet that all is in all. By the way, The Great Gatsby is somewhat like Ali Baba: he had been able to make his fortune in secrecy since as stated in the novel nobody knew where did his money come from.

CACAMBO: Look at this over there! Did you see the neon sign by the name of Babe Land Sex Toys Shop? What is this all about?

PANGLOSS: Here is the Wood Stock syndrome.

CACAMBO: What?

PANGLOSS: Yes, what apparently happened in the social arrangements at that point is similar to what had been going on in the economy. The world is a theatre and here is an attempt to turn the roles in the play, upside down.

CACAMBO: Is not your subject irrelevant to the question of the World Economy? I still remember what happened to you and to Paquette.[2] And yet, as I notice at this point, you still cling to your dogma of optimism.

PANGLOSS: Have I not told you already the Pangloss in the 18th century novel, in reality is not me? Yet the optimism you refer to is no dogma. It is a principle.

CACAMBO: Why do not you just stop for an ice cream before going any further?

PANGLOSS: We'll stop when I find a parking lot.

CACAMBO: Great! By the way what is this theatre thing all about?

PANGLOSS: Would the theatre still be theatre if it were not a play? A piece of theatre is always a play, no matter its content, since had there been no play there would be simply no theatre at all. Now, as a representation of real life, any theatre play is performed in all directions, in the sense that there is constant movement a little like the uncertainty principle of modern quantum physics. Some actors are heading north, some to the south, some stand still whereas others are agitated and so on. The thing is that there is no point in time when two creatures are alike or identical either in act or in potency.

CACAMBO: And so what? Why are you paying attention to something that appears to be self-evident?

PANGLOSS: The actors in ancient Greek theatre, used to carry masks, not of their own persona or soul or essence but the persona of the heroes that these same actors used to represent. So, during the play an actor used to speak, behave, think in a way that is in accordance with the persona represented by the mask on his face. However, once the play was over, the actor used to put down his mask and get back to his own persona. Now, would it possible that the mask and the corresponding mindset going with it during the play somehow affected or changed or metamorphosed the actor?

Cacambo: Yes, any good actor is affected by the roles he plays.

Pangloss: Is not the actor, by the mere act of putting down his mask, reverting to his real face or real self? To claim that the mask changed his self or identity is the same as to claim that the mask is no longer a mask, since now it has become a face, has turned into something that is no longer itself or a mask or a representation of something other than itself or a copy but its opposite, a real face or an original. Again, if it happens, that one single stone, among billions of other stones, suddenly starts speaking English or Gujarati for example its stone like essence would be irrevocably altered in the sense that this same stone would no longer be a stone. Furthermore, even if the actor, distracted as he might be by his theatrical performance, decides that he is in reality affected by the play, he forgets that before being affected by anything, he has to be something in himself in the first place, that is, he has to be a persona in himself or has to have an essence or a form or a soul. The so called chain of causality is in reality like a pack of cards, displayed on a huge table or the Universe where the Vedic Gods play dice games, and where each card possess its own essence, since the Cosmic Egg is no formless mass that can at will be reduced to ashes. Now, in the original theatre or society at large of which the Greek theatre is only a copy, things are far from being crystal clear in a way that they might be in their theatrical or symbolic representation. More specifically, there is clarity only in proportion to the degree of dispersion of the individual consciousness within the spider web spin by the four elements during each cosmic cycle.

Cacambo: Great! You spoke so much and yet you did not make it clear when you'll get back to our subject, the 2012 World Economy.

Pangloss: As you will see later on there is a sufficient reason to treat our subject from this angle and therefore, I have nowhere to get back since I have been all over the place all the time. Reality is, basically no piece of ham that can be cut into thin slices. As for your ice cream, I have real trouble finding out an authentic pastry shop. So, I suggest you to go back to another Mc Donald's, since over there we can find something by the name of Sundae which is a kind of postmodern ice cream.

Cacambo: We might have stayed at the Mc Donald's we have been already. By the way, was not what you refer to as the Woodstock Syndrome, the starting point for the so called gender revolution?

Pangloss: The Meta historical process of inversion of the roles in the social theatre has accelerated and the confusion between identity and equality is a constant feature of present day world as a result. The Wood stock syndrome is in reality only one among several steps in the path toward the ultimately impossible attempt to level down the elements and their at last resort, invisible configuration. Once again, the thing is that since you cannot destroy an entity that simply cannot be destroyed, like it or not, you set, a dynamic of inversion and therefore of confusion, although this same dynamic is perfectly contained, within the cycle of manifestation. Most of the time, today's actors are not aware of the way their own faces look like, neither are they aware of the form of their masks. In the Venice of our time, there was also confusion concerning this same gender kind of thing, but by far lesser extent, since the forms inherited from the ancient past were still there, such as for example the division of courtesans in two classes, the cortigiana onesta or cortigiana di lume[3] although they had their own brand of masks and their own kind of theatre: the Carnival. The still on-going message of Modernity has been set in our own time, and the basic content of this message states something like this: Anyone under the Sun, is to be like anyone else and therefore is to make the ultimately impossible attempt of achieving perfect sameness or perfect leveling to the ground one's self, unless this same self is already filled with the only acceptable postmodern filling: the filling of confusion, envy and resentment, so that it could be made heavy and never fly away to the sky. In the sphere of 'gender' there is a growing confusion, since, according to the postmodern correct gender line, there are two options left for modern day females: either to estrange themselves from their own nature by imitating males, preferably mechanically minded or monkey like males or else, aligning themselves to the archetype of the cortigiana de lume of our own time. And on the opposite end, males are to abdicate in their turn from their own real self. This consciousness of inversion of gender is followed by an inversion of quality in the sphere of economics, as we will see later on in detail, where the original is reduced to the endless series of its representations or copies. Once again, if both males and females have a built-in essence or a soul, each male and respectively each female is simultaneously a unique individual, a crystallization of the principle of polarity and an emanation of the principle of unity or non-duality. Now, if for some reason a fraction of them makes the attempt to depart from their built-in configuration, there would be two likely results: either the essence or the configuration will be changed for good or else, the sterile denial of one's self will remain the only other alternative. If the latter turns out to be the valid option, a consciousness of frustration and self-delusion will naturally follow, since this is a failed attempt for a metamorphosis that did not take place. Now, those who persist in the denial of their own self would end up with self-delusion as their only real friend and respectively self-awareness as their worst enemy. The more a given female for example, is repressing her own femininity by assuming femininity to be something coming from the outside, following the tenets of gender correctness, the less empowered she is on the ontological level, although initially this may not seem so on the outer level, where the play on the stage of the social theatre is going on, with all the actors disguised behind their masks.

Modern view of eroticism is another version of the denial of the soul, a key point on which materialism and atomism have always rested. Now, the reversal of roles starts with the embryo in the womb.

CACAMBO: Is not dark out there? My dear friend, are you not just sinking into obscurity?

PANGLOSS: Any living being has a natural disposition to move from darkness to light, including the legendary Lotus and that is why freedom of movement is the first sign of life. Therefore, the vitality of any child is in direct proportion to his determination for getting on the loose. Real personality, including sexuality goes with the emancipation from the womb. Yes. Those who make such a claim attempt to persuade the others that space is somehow not three dimensional and as a result of this you cannot move both ways form the top to bottom as well as from bottom to top, but only one way from top to bottom or from north to south, following the entropy of dead souls. So, what has always been self-evident indeed, or that the embryo has free will either to raise or to degrade himself, seen from this point of view appears differently. The unwillingness of the embryo to leave the womb, leads, once he is no longer there, but out in the open, to the desire for reversing upon one's self or the kind of relations Oedipus had with his mother with the notable difference, however, that in the Greek legend, this happens somehow by chance whereas here, it is a method, a predetermined move. And what it follows form such a reverse path, is the surrender to desire, since desire is dependency on the womb and therefore on the four elements. In the perception still prevailing in our own time, going back to the enigmatic founding fathers of ancient cultures, desire is to be contained. Life used to be seen as the effort to stop the flow of desire and hence the key notion of equilibrium, defined as the point where intersect the two opposite currents of life or desire versus freedom from desire.

CACAMBO: Wait a second. I remember having read somewhere about a thing by the name of neurosis.

PANGLOSS: Yes. This is the result of the reverse path, where freedom is associated with the same kind of relief a smoker is experiencing by postponing once again the moment he will quit smoking for good, by lighting another, supposedly last cigarette. From economic point of view as we shall see later on, the claim that neurosis is to be treated with self-indulgence is simply a way for the supplier to create his own demand.

CACAMBO: Is not the containment of desire a suppression of pleasure altogether?

PANGLOSS: If you just stop talking right now, say, exactly for twelve minutes, would not such an act be motivated by something other than your natural response to the circumstances of your immediate surroundings?

CACAMBO: Yes.

PANGLOSS: How is your silence during all these twelve minutes to be qualified if you think that whenever you perform this same act there will be raining somewhere in the southern hemisphere?

CACAMBO: Superstition.

PANGLOSS: And how is it, if you indeed cause rain in a remote spot by observing silence for twelve minutes and you know why this is happening?

CACAMBO: Superstition.

PANGLOSS: Superstition or Magic? The act of observing silence for twelve minutes is a ritual. The difference between such a ritual taken as random and other rituals is that the latter are established and transmitted from past experience or tradition, on the presumption that they are effective, whereas the former, is conceived arbitrarily. Yet, any act performed in a way as to counter the chain of immediate causes and effects to which consciousness reacts, is a ritual. Now, the effort conscious or not to perform a ritual has its source in the belief that such a momentary exit from the immediacy of necessity and the corresponding set of emotions going with it, leads to another dimension beyond the limits of the physical and this dimension is in reality the soul. The soul being without parts is associated with something in itself and therefore with simplicity or perfection and hence, the presumption, that everything is connected to everything else. Therefore, to affect any part of the whole, be it a by observing silence for twelve minutes, is to affect all parts simultaneously and through them the precise part corresponding through the law of sympathy to the part that is affected in the first place, since perfect equilibrium is the ultimate outcome of the Cosmic domino. Any ritual has a degree of transcendence in it otherwise it would not be ritual at all. And transcendence is the effort to go beyond something, including pleasure and various other emotions which obstruct the way to the soul. The further we go back in time, the more, ritual sexual activity becomes explicit. Do you see an object better when you see only a part of it or the whole of it? Now, the only way to see the whole of something is transcendence and lucidity. The ultimate erotic act is a magical act, where lucidity puts into effect the natural law of polarity similarly to conductors transmitting a high charge of electricity.[4]

CACAMBO: And where is the freedom of choice in all this?

PANGLOSS: Some of the players are inclined by nature to put a high value on the family and may have only a limited sexual drive. Others, on the opposite, have a psycho-physical natural endowment for eroticism. In today's environment both of them are oppressed, since on one hand professional eroticism is regarded with contempt, or outlawed, for example in Sweden, and hence affecting the consciousness of those who are engaged in it and on the hand a woman staying at home is seen as an old-fashioned, immature specimen. The mutilation of women reached an all-time high, may be in the early days of the Soviet Union, when women working in steel mills and hot blast furnaces were shown as the example to follow. Men in such an environment are incited to stop making a distinction between a matron and a courtesan, since modern women are expected to deny both of these conditions. So what had been a nightmare to St Augustine, who used to be in favor of prostitution for fear that otherwise adultery would be too widespread, nowadays, is a reality. Furthermore, women being incited to emancipate themselves from their own essence by becoming more masculine tend to confuse men as well, who respectively are incited to somehow abdicate from their own masculinity. The ultimate result is mistrust, alienation and confusion. Once the last remnants of the traditional family are shuttered, the way to the anticipated integral promiscuity of the 'Brave New World' type, naturally leads to the present obsession with sexuality.

CACAMBO: And what about the Brave New World of the past when during the Saeculum obscurum Pornocracy reigned supreme?[5]

PANGLOSS: The tide once was rising and then receding ever since the highest antiquity. Today the very expansion of quantity is making that what used to be a phenomenon confined to relatively narrow limits, now reappears on much larger scale. So the ontological tension and the confusion that we have described so far, has been exploited and actually worsened by a huge network and a complex set of activities that we have called the Viagra Economy.

CACAMBO: You made vague allusions on the likely effect of the Woodstock Syndrome on the economy, but nothing specific so far.

PANGLOSS: The inversion of the natural law referred to as the Woodstock Syndrome is not the cause of the changes that took place in the economy. It is a reflection of a specific condition of the modern Psyche, which is the source of these same economic changes. Being a relic going back to the time of Cato the Elder, the family has been deconstructed following, so to speak, J. Bentham's dissection of pleasure into units of utility. Once atomized to a degree that was still unconceivable only a few decades ago, the postmodern individual or economic agent had nothing left other than the short term outlook, which is the most fertile ground for speculation and gradual deconstructive virtualization of economic activity, as we will see more closely later on.

NOTES

[1]F. Scott Fitzerald, '*The Great Gatsby*'.
[2]In Voltaire's novel '*Candide*', Pangloss had an affair with the chambermaid Paquette who gives him syphilis.

[3]See Rosenthal, Margaret F., "Veronica Franco's *Terze Rime* (1575): The Venetian Courtesan's Defense" *Renaissance Quarterly* 42:2 (Summer 1989) 227-257.

[4]See *Metaphysics of Sex*, J. Evola (1958).

[5]Liudprand of Cremona. *The Complete Works of Liudprand of Cremona*, Paolo Squatriti, ed. and trans. Washington, D.C.: Catholic University of America Press, 2007. Also, Di Carpegna Falconieri, Tommaso (2008), *Marozia*, in *Dizionario biografico degli italiani*, 70, pp. 681–685.

TALE X

The Viagra Economy

CACAMBO: Look, I checked what this Viagra kind of thing is all about and I what I found out is that the progress achieved by modern pharmacology is no less than amazing. The herbs of our own time are no match to these wonderful synthetic pills. Take the Andean Mountain Herb: it is no more or less effective than any other food ingredient contributing to general health[1] and there is much worse, such as Yohimbine, whose side effects include panic attacks, kidney failures, hallucinations and aforementioned death.[2] Many other so-called aphrodisiacs are dangerous—either to the consumer or the endangered species supplying the ingredient. For example, Spanish fly is ground-up blister beetle containing a caustic acid-like juice called cantharidin that causes burning or swelling sensation in the urinary tract misconducted as sexual stimulation.[3]

PANGLOSS: What you say is true, but since you seem to be in a hurry, it is only half true. The herbs you are talking about do may indeed not be really effective due to the Meta historical fragmentation of knowledge ever since the Deluge, a process, those in contact with the sources going back to prehistory such as Plato were well aware of, and hence his insistence on recollection. So is the elixir of life, we have already spoken already. Countless generations of alchemists have tried in vain to reproduce this once real substance, since the key for the way to produce it, was lost millennia ago. By the way, there is a number of Chinese Emperors whose death was likely due to elixir poisoning.[4]

CACAMBO: Could you just tell me my friend where does your assurance regarding the ancient past come from? Are you not one of those enlightened mystics of the Edgar Cayce or Christia Sylf variety who happen to know what Atlantis did look like through the experience of direct visions, but cannot see what is going on under the counter of the nearby grocery store?

PANGLOSS: Since nothing comes out of nothing and hence anything follows from anything else, all things or phenomena are composite and therefore perishable. Vacuity is their ultimate substance. Yet vacuity having no parts is also simplicity and simplicity is also non-duality, which is all-pervading since duality and its derivative, multiplicity is reduced to unity. By the way, that is why concepts such as the multiple universe of the so called quantum physics is a sheer absurdity, designed to bring confusion in credulous minds exactly in the same way as the lifeless, fragmented, alienated universe of the Nouveau Roman has been presented as literature or the cut newspaper collage as art. Now, since unity or non-duality is the ultimate substance, it is no contradiction to assume that this substance must have an expression throughout the Universe. Hence comes out the notion of cosmic energy. Once consciousness is aware of such an all pervading life force, there are only two possible manifestations of this same awareness: a symbolic or a nominal and an effective or a practical manifestation. The nominal manifestation is right here in the myths of just any culture and the more or less vague souvenir of its practical manifestation is also right here in the quest for the elixir. And still further, the way for recollecting such a forgotten knowledge is also right here. According to legend the ancient Rishis recovered all that had been apparently lost precisely through meditation, being by definition the very opposite end of empirical observation or computation.[5]

CACAMBO: Okay. Fine. And yet I still do not see where the recovered staff is?

PANGLOSS: You seem to be rather tired and may be already hungry again. I'll park the car in a moment, since we have an appointment with someone. Recollection is lucidity or insight or intuition. Had not the war of currents[6] been won by Tesla, as we see in more detail later on, electricity would still be a dream or at best a mere curiosity and all that would have been known about it would be its symbolic or nominal manifestation, confined to the souvenir of the legendary Etruscan king of Rome, Numa Pompilius or to the representations of Zeus on ancient Greek vases.[7] The difference between ancient alchemy and the perception of an all pervading life force which is behind Tesla's discoveries, many of them still not declassified, is a difference in degree, not a difference in kind.[8]

CACAMBO: Are you not going too far on this point?

PANGLOSS: No. Commercial electricity is unthinkable without the Alternating current.

CACAMBO: Has it not been said already that Viagra is one of those synthetic wonders, dissipating self-doubt from the mind of any male, by allowing him to play the role of a modern day replica of Priapus?

PANGLOSS: Is it possible to know what a theatre play is all without seeing its end, in the last act?

CACAMBO: You just said that the herbs of the past are ineffective, right? There is something I do not really get here. Why do not you enlighten me why should you recollect anything at all? You'd better make the effort of inventing something from scratch, such as these Viagra pills.

PANGLOSS: Everything comes from everything else, and therefore nothing can be lost, but only forgotten. Following this, at last resort, there is no such thing as creation. By the way, the US Patent and Trademark Office partially rejected the patent on Pfizer's little blue impotence pill after deciding a chemical ingredient in the herb Horny Goat Weed is similar type of enzyme inhibitor found in Viagra.[9]

CACAMBO: Are you kidding? The active ingredient of Viagra, Sildenfil is eighty times more effective at inhibiting PDES than icariin, which is generic compound of Horny Goat Weed.[10]

PANGLOSS: Mario Dell'Agli from the University of Milan and his team extracted icariin from the plants, and produced six modified versions of it, which they also tested on PDE five. The most efficient of these, compound five, "works as well as Viagra." says Dell'Agli. A drug made out of compound five could also cause fewer side effects than Viagra.[11]

CACAMBO: Yes, but what is the difference? Is not the one as good as the other?

PANGLOSS: The modern economy is running after its own shadow, since economic activity is confined to the destructive impulse of reducing quality to its own representations. Once the awareness of this process comes out in one way or another, this is the sign that the whole economic cycle is near its completion. Before mass industrialization, prescription drugs were herbs. For example, white willow bark is the origin of Aspirin. The knowledge of growing, harvesting and using herbs was passed on from generation to generation until factories took over the mass production of prescription drugs. The high volume demand for these drugs drove the manufacturers to shorten the time to produce and distribute them to market. As a result today's drugs are made from the chemical constituents of herbs but no longer the actual plants themselves.[12] Viagra and Icarin are related to their respective sources as a copy is related to its original.

CACAMBO: How about these copies being more effective than their originals?

PANGLOSS: Our world is the best in the best of all possible worlds, precisely because there is no copy that it will ever surpass its original. Herbs work in conjunction with the symptoms to resolve the root causes of imbalances in the body and eliminate illness over the long term. They work with the body's immune system to help it do its job of natural healing. In some cases, herbs help relieve the symptoms while the healing is taking place. More often, they work "behind the scenes" quietly assisting the body's natural processes. After a course of herb therapy, the disease is gone, the body's imbalances are cured, and you forget you were ever sick. Prescription drugs work to suppress symptoms but leave the disease intact where it can become more serious and eventually chronic.[13] And here there is no coincidence. Had not been the original closer to the essence than its copy, it would not be an original at all.

CACAMBO: I mentioned icarin, but you still did not made it clear from where the original of Viagra did come about.

PANGLOSS: How about the Sacred Blue Lily of the Nile? According to recent chemical analysis at the Egyptian section of Manchester Museum, the Blue Lily contained phosphodiestres, the active ingredient of Viagra.[14]

CACAMBO: Why do you speak in the past tense?

PANGLOSS: The Sacred Blue Lily of the Nile (Many mistakenly call it Blue Lotus because that is how it is referred to in India) was found scattered over Tutankhamen's body when the Pharaoh's tomb was opened in 1922. Many historians thought it was a purely symbolic flower, but there is mounting evidence that strongly points to ancient Egyptians using it to induce an ecstatic state, stimulation, and/or hallucinations, as well as being widely used as a general remedy against illness and shown widely in Egyptian art.[15] The full knowledge of the Blue Lily is gone since it had apparently disappeared already in Antiquity. When the Romans conquered Egypt they introduced new breeds of fish into the Nile, which poisoned and wiped out the Sacred Blue Lily.[16]

CACAMBO: But is not Viagra still effective although a copy?

PANGLOSS: As a synthetic drug Viagra is another reduction of quality to its representations, where the relation to the whole i.e. the human organism is deliberately ignored at the expense of the parts or the immediate effect. Ancient plants had a limited capacity for mass production since their cultivation rested on the environment, on precise spatial and temporal conditions intrinsically related to their quality. The propensity for a quantitative expansion creates by its very nature the conditions for abuse. Since it has been in circulation for only a few years the long term side effects are still unknown. It is no coincidence that today the cultivation of herbs is in danger because of deforestation and the expansion of synthetic drugs.[17]

CACAMBO: Are not modern drugs at least less expensive than herbs?

PANGLOSS: By no means. It is precisely the opposite. The price of modern drugs is skyrocketing since the patents on whom rests their production are based on exclusivity and hence on monopolistic prices. Now, would you be so kind as to go out because our friend will be waiting for us in a few minutes in front of a nearby Tiffany store.

CACAMBO: You did not tell me who is this?

Pangloss: This is the Great Cophta alias count Caliostro.

NOTES

[1]www.so-stadium-status.com *Do natural aphrodisiacs work?* 12 04 2011 Christopher Wanjek.

[2]Ibid.

[3]Ibid.

[4]See Joseph Needham, a British historian of Chinese Science compiled a list of Chinese Emperors apparently poisoned by false elixirs.

[5]See *Sri Aurobindo on Rishis*, Integral Yoga.

[6]Modern alternating current (AC) electric power systems are based on N. Tesla's patents.

[7]See *Pliny-book II* Ch. 55.

[8]www.greenoptimistic.com "*Tesla's Free Energy Inventions suppressed*", January 29.2008 Interview: The Electrical Genius of Nikola Tesla and Tesla's Electromagnetic Healing Devices - On Jan. 31, 2010, Tom Valone, Ph.D., was interviewed on 21st Century Radio, reviewing the then latest issue 89 of Infinite Energy magazine, which was devoted to the subject of Nikola Tesla.

[9]*What Do Viagra & Horny Goat Weed have in common?* 17 Feb. 2010 Ed. Silverman. www.phramalot.com.

[10]"*Horny Goat Weed can be better than Viagra.*" 26 Sept. 2008 by Catherine Brahic www.newscientist.com.

[11]Ibid.

[12]www.applecottagefoods.com, also "*Comparison of Synthetic drugs and Plant Medicines.*" May 24 2010 www.naturesphrama.org.

[13]Ibid.

[14]From *The Times* November 21, 2009 Howard Marks discovers the Viagra of old Egypt.

[15]www.entheology.org.

[16]Howard Marks discovers the Viagra of old Egypt Nov. 21, 2009 *The Times*.

[17]*Deforestation, a Major threat to development of several herbs,* Dr Venkitaraman Feb 3, 2010. www.my.yoga-vidya.org.

TALE XI

The Alchemy of Modern Finance

PANGLOSS: Hello! How are you doing today my friend? I am pleased to meet you!

CALIOSTRO: If some are more equal than others, then time is to be shorter for some than others! I am pleased to meet you too!

CACAMBO: You may have interesting things to say since we last met back in the 18th century. So I will invite you for dinner at a place nearby where the food still resembles what we used to have in our own time.

CALIOSTRO: What dinner? Clearly, you do not seem to realize that we are different. I am only an astral projection or a ghost as they say and therefore I do not eat whatsoever.

PANGLOSS: But were you not in possession of the Elixir of Life, as so many souls throughout Europe came to believe?[1]

CALIOSTRO: I was not in possession of anything not even my own identity, except what is inside this small silk bundle that I hold in my left hand right now.

CACAMBO: So, what is this?

CALIOSTRO: A small diamond from the Queen's Necklace[2] and one ounce of fake gold.

CACAMBO: Let me see.

CALIOSTRO: Wait a second. I have to untie the elastic band of the bundle.

PANGLOSS: As an astral projection, you can fly and therefore you basically have no travel expenses and what is more, you can become invisible on request. So you may have seen various, otherwise inaccessible places. Where do you come from right now?

CALIOSTRO: I have been to a place nearby by the name of Jekyll Island.[3]

PANGLOSS: What did you do there?

CALIOSTRO: I made an unsuccessful attempt of selling my gold to the inhabitants of the place.

CACAMBO: They realized your gold is a fake and they just threw you out, right?

CALIOSTRO: No, my friend. They did not even bother to look at my gold, since they say they do not need gold, for the time being, at least.

CACAMBO: Is it because they have all the gold in the world?

CALIOSTRO: They do not care about my gold since they said they possess the know-how of transmutation.

CACAMBO: So the whole island must be like the kingdom of the Prester John or the Eldorado, covered with gold.

CALIOSTRO: No. I did not see gold anywhere.

PANGLOSS: What did you see then?

CALIOSTRO: I saw a pyramid shaped volcano throwing his ashes on a huge printing press which in turn is transmuting the whole thing into tiny green sheets of paper or greenbacks, as they say.

PANGLOSS: By the way, when you just untied your bundle with the diamond you put the elastic band in your pocket, right?

CALIOSTRO: Yes, and so what?

PANGLOSS: Could you give it to me for a second?

CALIOSTRO: Why?

PANGLOSS: Because this same elastic band counts more than all the diamonds for example from Sierra Leone and from Antwerp combined.

CALIOSTRO: Here you go.

PANGLOSS: Each incremental or rather infinitesimal movement of the band affects the lives of countless humans scattered around the four corners of the world.

CACAMBO: What are you getting at?

PANGLOSS: My dear friend, would you be so kind, as to just pull this band.

CACAMBO: Since you did not tell me what this is all about, you'd better pull it yourself.

PANGLOSS: Okay. Fine. So as you see, I am just pulling it, right?

CACAMBO: If you pull a little further, it will snap.

PANGLOSS: Great! Now, what if I just pull and pull but the elastic simply does not snap?

CACAMBO: There is no way it will not snap. The resistance of the band has its limits however elastic it is.

PANGLOSS: So, the more you pull the less likely is that the band will not snap at some point, right?

CACAMBO: Listen, is not all this self-evident? Why do not we just pass to a more serious matter? Furthermore, thanks to the progress of modern chemistry, it may well be possible that a kind of a super elastic band will be invented in the future and so, the elasticity of this band will just go on and on.

PANGLOSS: To assume that an elastic band will never snap is to ignore the universal Law of Equilibrium and accordingly this is to assume that an action will never cause a reaction, which at one time or another, by the virtue of this same law, will be in equal proportion to the action that has been initiated in the first place. Such an opinion also has to deny the very existence of the notion by the name of 'breaking point', since the latter is precisely the point of equilibrium where the two opposing forces, in our case the built-in propensity for resistance of the elastic versus the pressure applied to it, negate each other. Furthermore, by the virtue of another law, this time, the Principle of Sufficient Reason, an elastic band has a very precise potential for elasticity. Otherwise, this same elastic band would not be an elastic band but something else, and this something else would have its own sufficient reason and so on ad infinitum.

CALIOSTRO: Is not you concern for the elastic band somehow related to the volcano on Jekyll Island?

PANGLOSS: The volcano you are talking about was already active prior to WWI although its first clearly visible eruption took place in 1931, then in 1934 and later on in 1971 and more recently in 2008.

CALIOSTRO: Did not the whole thing start in our own time?

PANGLOSS: Yes it did, in a place by the name of Venice, which in its own way, sought to emulate for centuries the Roman Empire.

CACAMBO: Did not Sir J. Law spend his last years gambling in Venice?[4]

PANGLOSS: The first casino, the Ridotto of Venice which opened in 1638[5] is the matrix for all later versions of this activity. So, as you see, there was still no Monaco or Deauville at the time of Sir J. Law.

CALIOSTRO: Was not the Banco de Rialto a public institution?

PANGLOSS: In 1587 the Banco della Piazza di Rialto is opened in Venice as a state initiative. Its purpose it to carry out the important function of holding merchants' funds on safe deposit, and enabling financial transactions in Venice and elsewhere to be made without the physical transfer of coins.[6]

CACAMBO: Who cares if it is public or private? The thing is who's who or who gets the money!

PANGLOSS: Yes, my dear friend, the question is who is who indeed, but as I see, you do not make a distinction between one individual and all other individuals, in the sense that apart from being the sum of separate entities, individuals are also a whole, in the same way as all plurality is ultimately reduced to the basic duality between subject and object or the I and the other.

CALIOSTRO: Had it not been the Queen's Necklace, essentially an individual or a private reflection in a universal or a public mirror, my name would have been forgotten for good, a long time ago.

PANGLOSS: At the beginning that which is above used to be as visible or transparent as that which is below. In ancient Japan, there was the Emperor's Mirror, reflecting the basically ritual activity of the sovereign with the utmost attention to detail.

CACAMBO: Sight nowadays exists only in relation to movement.

PANGLOSS: Have you ever seen something by the name of nothing to move in any place of the Universe, apart from the equations of scientifically correct Physics, covering classroom blackboards with white chalk? However that may be, let's go further with our subject, for now, on the question of financial transparency. From time immemorial the power to coin belonged only to the King.[7] This is the Royal Monopoly of Minting.[8] So the degree of transparency in this sphere was gravitating around the absolute. And what is more the transparency was a sine qua non condition of power, either political or economic. Even the recall or the recoinage cycles and the premium of the royally authenticated coinage over the value of its metallic content[9] or the seigniorage or the debasement of coinage was carried out in the open since there was no other way nor was there willingness for such a way, had this other way been possible, to execute these operations otherwise or covertly.

CALIOSTRO: Nowadays it is exactly the opposite. Is this so out of preference or out of compulsion?

PANGLOSS: It is a natural outcome of the shift away from the original to its representations, copies or substitutes. Once you take this direction, the turning point, when your next move is to hide the original whatever this original may be, gold or silver or a commodity or even paper money in its physical expression, will coming out of itself. The so called, 'Money Creation', ever since the hay day of the bank of Amsterdam in the 17th century is literally creation, since it comes from nothing or from thin air or from self-delusion.[10] The Bank of Amsterdam literally 'created' money for over a hundred years without being discovered.[11] Hence, the natural propensity of modern finance for going private, where checks and balances function basically on two levels, the formal public level and respectively, the informal private level.

CACAMBO: Is not money creation a prerequisite for wealth creation?

PANGLOSS: It is a prerequisite for perpetual debt as we will see later on.

CACAMBO: You said that the value of coinage back in our own time used to be self-evident since any goldsmith would had been able to weigh precious metals and check on the spot, the difference between the metallic content and the face value of coinage. Nowadays, things appear to be different, don't they?

PANGLOSS: Do you see this $10 bill in my hand?

CALIOSTRO: Yes. How can you determine the real value of a $10 bill?

PANGLOSS: Since in its quality of fiat money, this bill is not covered by gold or silver, its value is directly related to the goods or the fraction of goods that you can buy at this very moment.

CACAMBO: So, what is the problem then? Money is still money, with or without the mediation of this useless 'barbaric relic'[12] by the name of gold.

PANGLOSS: The scale of the problem is so vast that you cannot see it right now, my friend.

CACAMBO: Great! Could you tell me in the meantime what a $10 bill can buy in this gigantic city of New-York?

PANGLOSS: There is on one hand, say, the relative purchasing power relevant only to the consumption goods that a $10 bill can buy and which may be determined, right away in the nearby convenience store, and on the other hand, the total purchasing power, as an infinitesimal fraction of the Aggregate Money Supply related to all available goods and services in circulation, not only right here but throughout the world.

NOTES

[1]Iain McCalman: *The Seven Ordeals of Count Cagliostro*, 2004: Flamingo (Australia) and Random House (UK); published in the USA as *The Last Alchemist*, HarperCollins.

[2]Fraser, Antonia (2001). *Marie Antoinette, The Journey*. Anchor. ISBN 0-7538-1305-X ; Alexander Lernet-Holenia: *Das Halsband der Königin* (The Queen's Necklace, Paul Zsolnay Verlag, Hamburg/Vienna, 1962, historical study on the affair of the diamond necklace).

[3]*Secrets of the Federal Reserve*, 1952. Reprinted John McLaughlin, 1983, 208 pages, (ISBN 0-9656492-1-0 Eustache Mullins, Ezra Pound).

[4]*John Law, The Father of Paper Money* by Robert Minton (Association Press, 1975) treats Law's financial innovations that led to modern paper money See, J. law and the Mississippi Bubble by Jon Moen, also, Peter Garber, "Famous First Bubbles," in *Speculative Bubbles, Speculative Attacks, and Policy Switching*, Robert Flood and Peter Garber, eds. (MIT Press: Cambridge MA, 1994).

[5]*The Revolutionary Ridotto The World's First Public Casino,* 1638-1774 David G. Schwartz, Ph.D. Center for Gaming Research University of Nevada Las Vegas.

[6]*Money and Banking in Medieval and Renaissance Venice* Lane, Frederic Chapin, 1900-, Mueller, Reinhold C. Year: c1985. Publisher: Johns Hopkins University Press. © The Johns Hopkins University Press.

[7]p 168, Davies, Glyn. *A History of Money from Ancient Times to the Present Day*, 3rd ed. Cardiff: University of Wales Press, 2002. 720 pages. Paperback: ISBN 0 7083 1717 0. Hardback: ISBN 0 7083 1773 1.

[8]Ibid.

[9]Ibid.

[10]John Kenneth Galbraith, *Money: Whence it Came, Where it Went*, Houghton Mifflin Company, Boston, 1975, p. 18-19.

[11]Rupert J. Ederer, *The Evolution of Money*, Public Affairs Press, 1964, p. 118-119.

[12]See J.M. Keynes, on *Gold*.

TALE XII

Fiat Money and Science

Cacambo: ...This sounds so vague. Why do not you just make it clear what is really at stake in this 'goods and services' thing?

Pangloss: Yes. The confusion you have noticed is intrinsically instilled in the very nature of the term 'goods', since the statistical or quantitative approach of modern accounting that is behind the computation of the GNP figures, does not make any distinction between good and bad. Now, to claim that this is in the name of objectivity is the same as to strip the minus and plus sign altogether, from the mathematics textbook for any elementary school.

Cacambo: We have been walking for so long. I am tired and hungry. You said we'll have dinner somewhere.

Pangloss: We are heading toward to the Waldorf Astoria. We'll be there in a minute. It is the next block.

When, already in front of the main entrance, Cacambo is watching the façade of the building and at some point raises his head to the sky.

Cacambo: What a tall house! I have trouble seeing the roof. In our own time, only Churches used to be of a comparable height. I see a spire up there. So, this must be a Church whereas you said you are going to a restaurant. I am confused.

Pangloss: I am confused too my friend. This is not the Waldorf Astoria I knew. The building is much taller and this inscription Waldorf Astoria is gone and as I see right now, it has been replaced by all these letters.

Cacambo: Empire State.[1]

Caliostro: We still could go somewhere else, couldn't we?

Pangloss: Yes. There is another place I remember from my last stay in the city. This is the New Yorker Hotel.

They keep on walking and later on enter one of the Hotel's restaurants.

PANGLOSS: I hardly recognize this place. This time the building is the same as the one I had seen the last time I came, but everything inside is different.[2]

CALIOSTRO: I wonder what I am going to do right now. You'll have a dinner whereas I'll have to stay idle, just watching, something which will remind me that before becoming a ghost I definitely used to have a good appetite. Maybe I should make myself invisible.

PANGLOSS: Better not. The waiter or any other figure for that matter, may notice that we are talking to someone who does not seem to be here, since the place you occupy will appear as an empty space.

CACAMBO: And so what?

PANGLOSS: I have no time to argue with you on this point. Caliostro, as for you, I'll order, say a cup of green tea so that you may have something other the mere white cover of the table in front of you.

CALIOSTRO: Why do not you also order some hors d' oeuvre or a pastry? I just saw a picture from the past of this place. Here is an old man feeding pigeons in a suite of this same hotel.[3]

PANGLOSS: We are in a land that has been called for generations a land of opportunity. The old man you claim to have seen was one of those who knew the language of birds.[4]

CACAMBO: Listen, the waiter is coming. Why do not you just have a look at the menu?

CALIOSTRO: I see.

PANGLOSS: The thing is that what happened in the end is a missed opportunity for all lands. The man in question had a direct insight into the core of reality.[5]

CACAMBO: Would not Tesla have been called a mystic, a poet?

PANGLOSS: Do you remember Jules Verne?

CACAMBO: Why?

PANGLOSS: Here is an author devoted to the idea of Progress and, say, to the technical aspect of this idea in particular who wrote about a trip to the Moon on a balloon.

Cacambo: I'll order a Chateaubriand and a Chocolate Mousse.

Pangloss: Caliostro, your tea has been served already. So, we may exclude for the time being, our wise friend Cacambo from the points we are making on all these things, since at the sight of food he is rather distracted.

Caliostro: I'll be raising my cup of tea from time to time to make think that I am drinking it and before leaving I'll make one of those tricks of mine, allowing me to pour the content of the cup into this vase of flowers in the middle of the table without being seen, from any malevolent observer eventually present at the place.

Pangloss: As I see, you'll appear a little as the enchanted white rabbit from '*Alice in Wonderland*', who is always raising his cup of tea and then is sitting again on his chair.

Caliostro: What does the Jules Verne's balloon have in common with your last point?

Pangloss: Had it not been claimed from all sides that the Soul would not have been a Soul if it were heavier than the body?

Caliostro: Yes, and so what?

Pangloss: So following from this the Soul being definitely lighter than the body should have a natural propensity for elevating itself, leaving the body on a temporary or a permanent basis and erring throughout the Cosmos, right?

Caliostro: Yes, but I still do not get it why you should pay attention to such an obvious point.

Pangloss: Now if someone, be it a ghost or a reptile or a centaur or a pigtailed devil or the village idiot clothed in the Emperor's New Clothes, decides to make a consistent effort so that you may forget that you have a soul, what would he do?

Caliostro: He will pour in your cup of tea, why not a sleeping tablet?

Pangloss: Fine, this is your Caliostro style, but does not everyone have his own style? So, how about a trip on a balloon? One might just put the Soul in one of those huge balloons coming out right from the book of Jules Verne or from the whole of the 19th century for that matter and send it straight to the Moon. Thus evacuated from the body, the Soul will be still the Soul, since there is no such thing as a living body without a Soul. However, being hidden from the inner sight of Consciousness, in this way, the Soul will leave the body without any protection from the blind impulses of desire or from the illusion that there is no Soul and therefore the body in such as a condition of the Psyche, will appear to be the starting point of everything or the Essence of Life.

CALIOSTRO: Are you not flatly contradicting yourself by talking on one hand of the flight of the Soul from the Body and on the other hand, by claiming that there is no living body without a Soul?

PANGLOSS: By no means. Your sleeping pills and Jules Verne's balloon do not really cut the Soul from the Body. As I told you already, these pills only attempt to do so by making you forget of the existence of the Soul by creating a false perception of the body. Now, this same false perception has two possible expressions: the first is to deny the Soul altogether as the professor from the University of Padua by the name of Cesare Cremonini did. He died in 1631 and on his grave was said to have been written at his own request: *Hic jacet Cremoninus totus.*[6] The second perception is to assume that there is a Soul indeed but that this Soul has somehow left you for a far distant realm beyond everything that really counts in our own bodily, down-to-earth existence. Thus, you have two options left: either displacing your Soul behind a thick, but highly transparent mirror and lamenting yourself of the sheer impossibility to do anything other than watching its beauty or the other option, being a negation or else a reaction to the false perception of the Soul that is making it an inaccessible and therefore a useless image. The reaction in question is another false perception based, this time on the confusion between the Soul and the body. Once you take your body for a Soul or for your own essence, you'll submit to the forces of blind desire or to the vegetative Soul enslaved by this same body and therefore to the dependency that this false perception is causing in all kinds of ways, since you'll be drifting away from unity into multiplicity. So, seen from this angle, falsehood will appear as truth, weakness as force, slavery as freedom. And last: Science will appear from its opposite end, since a massive, false Science will come out, resting on the cultivation of systematic blindness or methodical ignorance. However, the Soul in itself is no more altered by this same false perception than the Sun's rays would be altered on your opinion of their existence or for that matter electricity by your knowledge of it. When they said Tesla is a poet, they in reality were aiming at discrediting him as a scientist. This did not prevent them however from stealing his knowledge on electricity or his patents leading to the invention of the radio, the radar etc. The false pseudo-science is exploiting in practice this same Principle of unity or the Spirit which it denies in theory.

CALIOSTRO: What is the missed opportunity you talked about earlier?

PANGLOSS: Had it not been for Tesla's patents and the correspondence between Leibniz with this French doctor by the name of Papin, there would be no such thing as technical progress today, since for the epistemological framework of early modern and present day correct Science, there is hardly anything less scientific, than this same intuition that led to the steam engine and the alternating current AC electric power systems. Here is in reality a sign of a new epoch. As for the Antediluvian Science of previous cycles, the latter is shrouded in mysterious, cryptic legends and what it had remained of this pre-historical knowledge is either mere scattered fragments or fossilized superstitions. It is symptomatic that Tesla did not rely on drawings in the first place, since he had visions leading his intuition to the essence, not merely nominally as it is the case with philosophy, but effectively by transcending all layers of reality. Now, his later discoveries related to the concept of free cosmic energy contrary to the earlier ones were met with hostility since there is no profit to be made out of anything that is free.

CACAMBO: I finished my dinner at last. The Chocolate Mousse was really great. Yet this did not prevent me from hearing at least part of what you said. I have two questions on your latest point: first, are you not attempting to introduce a kind of personality cult with this figure by the name of Tesla? He seems to be so special, so unique. Furthermore, you seem to forget that this trip to the Moon you are talking about has been done after all, already in 1969, but not on a balloon.

PANGLOSS: You are definitely wrong my friend. The legacy of Tesla or rather the part of it that has been available to the public is on the opposite end of this rather extravagant, if not outwardly ridiculous concept of the genius. Truth does not belong to anyone since being what it is, i.e. truth, it does represent the Universality of the Spirit and therefore it is forever accessible to those who make a real effort to see, whereas the apparent uniqueness of the so called genius is the very embodiment of falsehood, since here there is nothing else but egocentric self-alienation. As for the trip to the Moon, provided that this trip ever reached its ultimate destination, today's 2012 technology is no longer able to replicate such a trip, since the blue prints of the Saturn V rocket have been lost.[7] May be the figure behind this rocket, Von Braun, simply took away with him the ultimate know-how, on which the assembly of the different parts of the rocket had been made. Furthermore, Tesla's insight is based on the Cosmic Energy or the Ether or the Akasha. Compared to this Principle of propulsion, the Saturn V rocket is like a plastic bucket of sea water versus the water of all the sea.

CACAMBO: You started with modern finance and now you simply changed the subject in the most arbitrary manner.

PANGLOSS: You are wrong once more. Present day Finance is organically related to the subtle reality of Consciousness and therefore to the prevailing spiritual condition of Modern Psyche. Furthermore, the missed opportunity of free energy I just mentioned, as we shall see later on, is intimately related to the present day grotesque expansion of fiat money, since, as we shall see later on, Oil is traded and denominated only in US dollars. The very nature of money, is universal whereas the developments that led to the suppression of the last remnants of the gold standard back in 1971, apart from being without any precedent in recorded human history, are exactly the opposite:

undoubtedly, one of the most arbitrary acts ever, that makes, the most ruthless of the Ancient Greek Tyrants, appear, in comparison, as a child from the kinder garden.

CALIOSTRO: You spoke about the value of a $20 bill and you did not go any further.

PANGLOSS: Yes. That is precisely what I am about to do now: go into detail concerning this key issue of Modern Finance.

CACAMBO: What is going on? There is no electricity. We are in the dark. There seems to be a power cut.

PANGLOSS: No my friend. It is the whole Universe which just stopped at this point.

CALIOSTRO: What do you mean?

PANGLOSS: In the world of Classical Mechanics, there is the still unresolved question of the origin of motion, since the free fall of bodies has to stop at some point and the Universe has to be periodically set up as a huge mechanical clock. Right now, we seem to be passing through one of those periodical tune ups of the whole thing, unless the Creator has forgot his key or is fallen asleep.

CACAMBO: The electricity has come back. No! No! Have you seen this crack up there on the ceiling? The wall…the wall is crumbling! Let's go out!

PANGLOSS: Yes, indeed. This time it is space itself which is just curving and that is why the wall may just tumble at some point.

CALIOSTRO: What did you say? Space is no Night Club Acrobat to be curved!

PANGLOSS: Yes. And yet, should you start from the shadow of quality that quantity is in reality, you may indeed curve various equations in your own unique way and end up with something like this. Now, let's just go out and later on I'll go into detail with the $20 bill.

NOTES

[1] The Waldorf Astoria at the original location was demolished for the erection of the Empire State Building. Around the time of World War I, Nikola Tesla lived in the earlier Waldorf-Astoria.
[2] Opened in 1930, the New Yorker slowly lost profitability and closed its doors in April 1972 and then re-opened on June 1994, History of the New Yorker Hotel in Manhattan Official site

[3]The inventor Nikola Tesla spent the last ten years of his life in near-seclusion in Suite 3327 of the New Yorker (where he also died), largely devoting his time to feeding pigeons while occasionally meeting dignitaries. 'Cooing for a strange genius' Bloomberg News, 2008-05-11.

[4]In mythology, medieval literature and occultism, the language of the birds is postulated as a mystical, perfect divine language, green language, adamic language, enochian language, angelic language or a mythical or magical language used by birds to communicate with the initiated. In Indo-European religion, the behavior of birds has long been used for the purposes of divination by augurs. Marzluff, John M.; Tony Angell (2007). *In the Company of Crows and Ravens*. New Haven and London: Yale University Press. pp. 284–287. ISBN 0-3001-2255-1. McDougall, Len (2004). The *Encyclopedia of Tracks and Scats*. Globe Pequot. p. 296. ISBN 1-5922-8070-6. Tipton, Diane (2006-07-06). "*Raven Myths May Be Real*". Montana Fish, Wildlife & Parks. http://fwp.mt.gov/news/article_4663.aspx. Retrieved 2008-02-08.

[5]*Lost Science*, Ch 4, See also *Secrets of Cold War Technology*, Gerry Vassilatos.

[6]Latin for "Here lies all of Cremonini" As it has been shown by recent scholarly sources on the intellectual History of Europe, Empiricism, both in Science and Philosophy has originated not in England but in the Republic of Venice: Bacon was brought into contact with Sarpi by William Cavendish, shortly after Cavendish's protege Thomas Hobbes began to serve as Bacon's personal secretary. Cavendish was in regular contact with Sarpi, and there are indications that Hobbes' appointment may have been arranged at the suggestion of Sarpi or his aide Micanzio. In 1616 Cavendish personally initiated the correspondence between Sarpi and Bacon, which then lasted for many years. In the course of their relationship, Bacon sent many of his works, including his Essays, to Sarpi for critique. Micanzio actually became Bacon's official literary agent in Venice, helping to spread his fame there, and another Sarpi ally, Marco Antonio de Dominis, also aided Bacon by translating his Essays into Italian. Bacon's famous philosophical method of induction, where understanding proceeds from the senses to the intellect, is taken entirely from Sarpi, as is easily demonstrated by comparing it with Sarpi's Pensieri #146, written many years earlier. Bacon was, in fact the perfect agent for spreading Sarpi's method of empiricism into England, and his philosophical influence continued to grow in the years following his death in 1626, culminating in the founding of the Oxford Group (Invisible College) in the 1640s, the forerunner of the British Royal Society. Thomas Hobbes and William Cavendish – the story of Thomas Hobbes and the Cavendish family will be told later in this work. For now I will just say that the Cavendish family were unquestionably the closest personal allies that Sarpi had in England. William Cavendish, the Second Earl of Devonshire, accompanied Thomas Hobbes on a trip to Venice in 1614, where they both met with Paolo Sarpi and his associates. Following this trip Cavendish maintained a 13 year correspondence with Sarpi and his secretary Micanzio, from 1615 to 1628. Seventy-seven of Sarpi's letters from this correspondence still exist, all translated from the Italian into English by Thomas Hobbes. It was thought for many years that Micanzio wrote the letters, but it is now proven that, until the time of his death in 1623, Sarpi himself was the author. It was also this same Cavendish who was a founding Director of the Virginia Company, and a member of the group which seized control of the Company in 1619. His allies at the Company, and in Parliament, included Southampton, Edwin Sandys, John Danvers, and several others. During his tenure as a Director of the Virginia Company, Cavendish gave one of his shares to Hobbes, allowing Hobbes to attend Directors' meetings. Thomas Hobbes

later became active in the Micanzio-run Paris-based Mersenne Circle, which was to become a center for the propagation of Galileo's works, and a hotbed for empiricist science. It was during the Mersenne Circle period that Hobbes would write The Leviathan and De Cive, his recipes for oligarchical rule. *News Networks in 17th Century Britain and Europe,* by Joan Raymond, Routledge Press, 2006 See Appendix 1 *Paolo Sarpi: Between Renaissance and Enlightenment,* by David Wooten, Cambridge, 1983. See Chapter 6, Ibid. This is confirmed in a letter written by the then British Ambassador to Venice, Dudly Carleton. *News Networks in 17th Century Britain and Europe,* by Joan Raymond, Routledge Press, 2006.

[7] *Thunder In A Bottle: The Non-Use of the Mighty F-1 Engine* by Dwayne A. Day, Monday, March 27, 2006 www.thespacereview.com.

TALE XIII

The Statue of Liberty

Once back to the Ford T, Pangloss drives his two companions to the South Bank, where they leave the car and embark on a boat to the Liberty Island. Our three heroes take a seat at a table of the Statue of Liberty Crown Café.

PANGLOSS: I definitely have to go on further with our subject on the Finance, since the whole thing is disappearing literally before our eyes. So there is no time to lose. Each second counts, may be as much as a decade in the pre-modern past.

CACAMBO: What? Money disappearing? This is might indeed be the case with your own money, but by no means with the World Aggregate Money Supply.

PANGLOSS: The latter might be represented both in visible and invisible terms.

CALIOSTRO: Where does, the distinction you just made, come from?

PANGLOSS: In visible terms money is just omnipresent, since all the restrictions to the flood of fiat currency have been lifted. Today there is no portion in the public sphere, however small, which is not literally covered with banknotes and/or their never-ending scriptural representations. In invisible terms, there is the consciousness of money or the quantitative approach or the ever growing tendency to count for its own sake or for the sake of blindness or for the sake of blind greed of for the sake of the exponential growth of the vegetative Soul or the dogma or the ghost like illusion of Pure Quantity. And yet, as you shall see later on in detail, too much money and it should be noted, that there is no such thing as too little here, as there is only too much... So, too much money leads to the ultimate fixing of its price or its real price that is always at last resort, equal to zero. Therefore the only relevant economic question today is by how much, this too much is growing and when it will vanish in the air or when, so to speak the party will be over.

CACAMBO: Is not the public getting richer and richer? Is not the wealth in 2012 a Manna literally falling from the Sky or from outer space or from Helicopters?[1]

CALIOSTRO: I have trouble speaking to these 21st century people, since they have no clue what Alchemy is all about or what a real Diamond Necklace does look like. Wherever I go, the first question I am asked is inevitably: is it expensive or cheap or by how much this is more or less expensive than that and vice versa etc. Most of the time, they do not give a damn about the quality, for example, of the things they pick up from the shelves of these...so called supermarkets, since they pay attention to the price, at the expense of its expression or the thing they buy for that price. The correct consumer today is the price responsive consumer. In our own time, the food in each place had a unique local quality, since they had no planes to transport one and the same product to the four corners of the world, neither had they refrigerators or food additives. So, travelers like me, could spend hours in a row to describe the unique characteristics of local agriculture or local cuisine or local, just anything for that matter. And again, it was simply unconceivable, for the public attending, say, the Opera House in my native city of Palermo to count the loges occupied before the curtain has been lifted, let alone, equating their view on the value of the spectacle and the performance of the singers to the profit derived from the selling of tickets. Although, this, what they say, Iron Age, in reality started millennia ago, when humans had no more direct knowledge on the Mystery of the Elements and had been leveled down to the last plane of reality or the physical plane and had to devour each other like brute animals, wondering in the dark of Tamas,[2] in our 18th century, which in Meta historical terms is only a few hours ago, the thing that counted before and for that matter, after the lifting of the curtain of the Opera House, used to be who was seating next to whom, both in visible and invisible terms. So that is why the quality of the monocles that the members of the public used to carry with them really mattered in, say, the final countdown of the whole spectacle.

CACAMBO: That is great, my friend! I am glad to hear all this, since now I have an occasion to pour some of my assets in the Public Relations Industry and in all this Baccarat or the Election Machinery with its never ending quest for fiat money. I'll hire some of these highly trained experts on the grammatically correct discourse, and your assertion will be analytically deconstructed and then reconstructed to the point of no recognition. According to our dear law of entropy, quality is always destroyed under the sheer weight of quantity. Had it not been for the all-prevailing wish of each member of the public, to be more equal than others, the stocks of equality traded on the socio-political stock market will be delisted in no time.

PANGLOSS: There is no such law of entropy, since at last resort as we saw it the New Yorker Hotel, electricity came back and it is an illusion to assume that a figure from outside turned a cosmic key to make it come back. This was nothing more than a temporary power cut, since beyond electricity, there is the ever and the all present Energy or Ether coming out from the Cosmos. Furthermore, those who want to be more equal than others are not all, but only the Monads that had lost their sense of equilibrium.

Cacambo: Listen, whatever you may say, we are right now under the rule of the masses with their mass kind of attitude toward everything.[3]

Pangloss: My dear friend, once upon a time, there used to be the city of Rome with its famous Coliseum, whose ruins, if you do not mind, are still with us today. This mass kind of thing that you are talking about right now had been carried out on the arenas of the Coliseum and the Circus, for almost a millennium. Countless Thraeces or Essedarii or Retiarii fought each other or Bestiarii,[4] who fought against lions, and eventually various other wild beasts, so that the mass or the crowd or the plebe might be kept happy. Better still, at some point even an Emperor, Commodus or Caracalla fought in the arena and still many others, including Nero, were taking very seriously the preferences of the crowd or the mass on the final issue of the fights, although in theory it was the Emperor and the Vestals who were supposed to have the last word. And yet, it never occurred in the minds of these Romans, that the mass gone wild on the Coliseum may become for that matter, anything else than what it appeared to be in the first place: an amorphous body of spectators or walk-on actors or ontologically passive entities.

Cacambo: How can you treat so lightly such a massive question? Had it not been claimed that the Masses and their various offshoots imprinted this time at the mass psychology are in reality the starting point for everything? Is not the crowd gone wild the ultimate reference of present day society, the ultimate justice, the ultimate natural law?

Pangloss: No, it is not.

Caliostro: Why?

Pangloss: Say Mass, Mass! Yes, just repeat the term for a time and tell me what do you imagine, what is before your eyes right now?

Caliostro: I see a crowd in place nearby. All see right now is a large black spot and it is only the sporadic wavering of its surface that reminds me of the ultimate nature of this spot, blackened by its constituent parts or individuals for that matter.

Pangloss: Great! This must be an image from the past of Ellis Island which is nearby. As for you Cacambo, what do you think of this same massive black spot on the horizon?

Cacambo: I think that the spot is the spot and it is a black, I mean a black spot.

Pangloss: I see. But is not what you say a little like the sky is blue because it is blue or money is money because it is money or Socrates is Socrates because it is Socrates?

CACAMBO: Listen I have been trained to see the basic thing, I mean, the ultimate staff in something solid, concrete and at this point I do not see anything more solid than precisely this same mass that you are talking about. So, when I stop there, my mind is just hammering all the time: the Mass is the Mass. The Mass is the Mass!

PANGLOSS: Yes. You are absolutely right my dear friend, your version of the mass as the ultimate staff is in reality a replica on a massive scale of the atomistic doctrine as we know it from Democritus with his Egyptian tutors or the atomists of Ancient India. The mass for you is the ultimate reference beyond which there is simply nothing at all, since otherwise your consciousness will naturally revert to the thing that is moving this same mass or the principle of the mass and this is something that, as we shall see later on, is contrary to the principle of fiat money. As a self-sufficient whole, the idea of the atom is turned toward the mass, whereas the Monad, being a reflection of the One in the Many is simultaneously separate and open to the Whole. However that may be, would you be so kind, as to put your glasses and to look closer at the black spot, the wavering of whose surface our friend Caliostro has just seen?

CACAMBO: Yes. Something is moving indeed within the spot or the mass before my eyes right now.

PANGLOSS: Is not the 'something' you see right now wavering, because it is a composite something where, its constituent parts are the number of individuals entering into the final countdown of the mass? Otherwise nothing would be wavering at all, since the black spot would have been a solid or an inert mass.

CACAMBO: I have been told that the individuals constituting the black spot somehow become a whole, a mass. Yes, a huge crowd displaying its congenital deformity from the inmost depths of the collective unconscious.

PANGLOSS: Did it ever occur to you to see a piece of concrete wall debating on the World Soccer cup in Swahili or a citrus tree playing chess on the tip of a needle or the stock market or just anything for that matter? My dear friend, this jump from something to nothing is in reality the latest Giorgio Armani suit in the Emperor's New Clothes wardrobe. C'est du n' importe quoi. (fr.).[5]

CALIOSTRO: Why?

PANGLOSS: A part of any whole as a replica of the Whole in itself or a Monad is always a part in the eternal present. Therefore, the idea of a fusion between the part and the whole is crude pantheism.

CALIOSTRO: What?

PANGLOSS: Yes. If the part becomes whole, the chain of causality or the endless series of the One should stop. Furthermore, this idea of fusion presupposes movement of the part toward the whole. So, should you play the role of a part, at some point you'll have nothing else to do than open a kind of Sesame like door and enter the Whole or the Absolute. There is no such door, since there can be no temporal or three dimensional path to the Whole. The Whole is always in the here and now. Otherwise the Whole would not be a Whole but a part. For this same reason, the Mass has always constituent parts or individuals or human beings.

CACAMBO: So should we eliminate the idea of the Mass altogether?

PANGLOSS: By no means. The Black Spot you have before your eyes right now is in reality a huge Black Hole.

CACAMBO: Is not this precisely du n'importe quoi?

PANGLOSS: If you do not have small change I can buy you, for example a ham and egg sandwich, since you may be hungry already and as I see you have trouble following the whole thing at this point.

CACAMBO: What does the Black Whole have in common with the Black Spot or the Mass?

PANGLOSS: The Essence of the Mass is a Black Hole, since nothing is coming from the Mass per see. The Mass is the receptacle absorbing the Energy from the entity or the center or whatever projecting this same energy toward the Black Spot. So, the more massive is the Mass, the less empowered is each of its constituents or individual members.

CACAMBO: So, you say nothing comes from the people or from the electors or from the citizens or the laborers or the peasants or the workers?

PANGLOSS: No, my friend. Each constituent part of the Black Spot is a vibrating spark of Cosmic Energy, black in potency and luminous in act. The combination of Light versus Darkness within each Spark or Soul is ingrained in the puzzle of the social domino. And this domino is constantly rearranged within the Cycle of Manifestation through the Triadic Principle. For millennia the constituents of the Black Spot came close to resembling a mass only in the rare occasions of natural calamities or when, following the taking over of a fortress for example, a panic ensued within the defendants and they just had been running like cattle to save their lives. Even then, however, some were less prone to mass kind of reactions than others, since the idea according to which everyone one is responding to something in the same way as everyone else is essentially possible only in the illusory realm of entropic universe of classical mechanics, where there is a place for everything except for the Soul.

CACAMBO: What is the Triadic Principle?[6]

PANGLOSS: The One in the Many or the Subject and its Object or the Whole and its parts rest on the interplay of extremes or opposite poles. Now, as there can be no meeting of opposites, the union is realized through a mean term and it is the distinction between the mean and the extremes that makes possible the Principle of Dynamics or the continuum of movement.

CACAMBO: Are you talking about real humans or about the point where the winds meet before dispersing on the four corners of the world?

PANGLOSS: Both, since there is no real human without a Soul. The cosmic interplay of extremes or opposite poles is taking place within the social, political, economic etc. scene at each infinitesimal point in time. And for the vital energy to flow there is one only way: from the one to the other.

CACAMBO: What?

PANGLOSS: Yes. Any form of contact is realized by the exchange of the cosmic vital flow or the Akasha or the Ether. And this flow is only made possible by the medium forms of the active and the passive expression of the Principle or the One.

CALIOSTRO: Are you referring to this master and slave kind of thing that inflames the imagination of the masses so much?

PANGLOSS: A real master has no slaves.

CALIOSTRO: Where does the idea of the Mass come from?

PANGLOSS: The starting point of the idea in question is a fallacy, since it assumes that the Mass is the Essence of the human condition whereas this is in reality only one of its possible expressions. Hence, the congenital vacuity of the mere abstraction by the name of Mass is effectively disguised.

CALIOSTRO: What is the Mass as a possible expression?

PANGLOSS: A temporary state of ontological, social and economic confusion brought by the conditions of Modernity. In the ancient traditional setting, the ritual character of social and economic activity, combined with the solid, although invisible pillars of the unwritten law or custom and the tripartite division, among Indo-Europeans in particular, rooted in the vision of Spiritual Rank or the ontological configuration of the Psyche or the Soul, which is by the way, a vision still present by the turn of the 19th century in its naturalistic version by the name of organic unity, prevented the irruption of depersonalization and consequently manipulation, as a key feature of present day reality.

CACAMBO: You left aside once again the subject of the Economy and the $20 bill.

PANGLOSS: The concept of the Mass has been used for political legitimacy as well as social, intellectual intimidation through the systematic propagation of cultural obscurantism, already going on for a fourth century in a row. It is precisely in the economic sphere however, that this view counts the most. Had it not been for the inherently leveling effect propagated by the concept of the Mass, the attempt to reduce quality to its representations or the expansion of quantity as a key feature of modern economic activity would not have been possible.

CACAMBO: Is it not time for dinner already?

PANGLOSS: Yes. I'll see in moment what I can buy on the counter of this coffee shop with a $20 bill and later on, I will retrace the value of these same $20 along the lines of mass production, mass consumption and their present day scriptural representation or fiat money.

NOTES

[1] Speech, *Bernanke -Deflation* - November 21, 2002. Federalreserve.gov. - http://www. federalreserve.gov/boardDocs/speeches/2002/20021121/default.htm. Retrieved 2010-01-3.

[2] Tamas (Sanskrit/tamas "darkness").

[3] See *The Revolt of the Masses*, Jose Ortega y Gasset, 1930; *Masse und Macht* 1960 (*Crowds and Power*, study, tr. 1962, published in Hamburg) Elias Canetti; *La psychologie des foules* (1895; English translation *The Crowd: A Study of the Popular Mind*, 1896), Gustave le Bon. By presenting themselves as the discoverers of a supposedly profound phenomenon of the highest importance such as the Mass, the above figures objectively aim at the following outcomes: First, since the Mass, according to their view is the ultimate reference, why should we object to any massive onslaught on the quality of Food, of clothing or the purity of Air or on human dignity or just anything that stands in the way of this ultimate expression of human nature? The message of Monsanto or KFC public relations specialists is no different, since thus the process of commercialization of any social activity will appear as being in conformity with the natural law or the essence of human condition. Second, by posing as sophisticated thinkers, the propagators

of this point of view aim at alienating those who aspire to intellectual activity from those who in the eyes of the former, appear as the Mass. Once you discover the natural law, embodied in the supposedly congenital mediocrity of the Mass, what else shall you do other than lamenting on the baseness of human nature in some obscure corner of your living room? Seen from this angle, the exploits of the heroes from the News of the World or the Sun or any other latest achievement of the Mass Media or the performance of the actors in the New York's or London's 'The Box Night Club' will appear as an initiation into the core of Human nature. Third, the leveling down of just anything will appear from this point of view as a confirmation of the ultimate Sovereignty of the masses, whereas precisely the opposite is true, since as an ontological black hole, the Mass is disempowered by the simple, fact of being a Mass or a crowd, since it is at the mercy of those who manipulate it by aspiring and directing its will power in a specific way. Fourth, since the Mass has the last word on everything it would be just a simple tour de magie to cast, for example a huge lot of collective guilt on millions of innocent people for something they just have nothing to do with. As for the idea of Socialism and the catch word 'Popular Masses', in the former Soviet Union and Eastern Europe, this notion had less effective meaning than in the present conditions of rapid commercialization of all spheres of social life, since once it became the core of the jargon providing formal legitimacy to the oppressive states of Soviet type, the congenital emptiness of this notion and the ensuing alienation of these same popular masses from the state apparatus, became manifest already at the earliest stages of these regimes. Hence, the present devastating effect of postmodern consumerism on the peoples from the former Soviet Union and Eastern Europe. As for the notion of the 'oppressed masses', this is the Jewel of the Crown of Socialism in the same way as India used to be the jewel of the British Crown. Here is the matrix, from which comes out in the open, the various modern and postmodern forms of methodical, systematic incitement to hatred against anything that on the level of ontology stands above the ground. Gustave le Bon has some credit on this point, since he stated that the idea of Socialism, at its core is nothing else than a display of outright puerility. However, things do not stop at this point, since there is much worse: here is a conspiracy of the envious and the blind against the human condition.

[4] Thomas E.J.Wiedemann, *Emperors or Gladiators*, Routledge, 1992.

[5] N'importe quoi (Fr.) Just anything.

[6] See Rosán, L. J. *The Philosophy of Proclus*. New York,1949. (Bibliography).

TALE XIV

The Adventures of Gulliver

CACAMBO: It is late afternoon already and you are still debating on your never ending points. We are in a coffee shop after all. So, why do not you just go to the counter and buy something with your valueless bill of $20?

PANGLOSS: That is precisely what I intent to do. So, if you are patient enough to wait for a while, I'll be back in a few minutes with what a $20 bill can buy on the 19th of May 2012.

CACAMBO: Fine. In the meantime we'll be conversing with Caliostro on the subject of ghosts and spirit invocation formulas.

Pangloss leaves the place and comes back at some point, one hour or so later.

CACAMBO: Where have you been? We were about to leave. But, wait a second! Where the food and the drinks you had to buy with your $20 bill is?

PANGLOSS: I had an argument with the cashier on the counter since he did not accept my cash.

CALIOSTRO: What? Is not this because you are dabbling in this fake kind of thing on which I knew so much in my own time?

PANGLOSS: No my friend, the ham and egg sandwich and the three bottles of Coke that I had just attempted to buy have a different price right now. So my $20 bill is not enough.

CACAMBO: If $20 is not enough, how much is enough then?

PANGLOSS: According to the employee on the cash register, prices suddenly changed this morning. He said there is a new price regulation.

CALIOSTRO: What is this all about?

PANGLOSS: A $20 bill is a $20 bill both in potency and in act. Its value is one hand an infinitesimal fraction of the Aggregate Money Supply or the Total Priced Value of all financial and tangible assets and on the other hand, the sum of all possible combinations that are to be made with this same fraction. When you buy what a $20 bill can buy, as in my case, I got three bottles of Coke, a ham and egg sandwich and a medium coffee, at the moment when the exchange takes place, that is when you hand your $20 bill to the cashier and you get a cash receipt with the purchased goods for it, the banknote of $20 ceases to be an infinitesimal fraction of the total money supply or a part of all priced assets either in circulation or in store and becomes an effective combination of this same total money supply or all printed or scriptural banknotes. However, when it comes out of your pocket and it is shelved in the cash register, the $20 bill retakes its previous condition by playing once again the role of an infinitesimal fraction of the Total Money Supply. A $20 bill in potency and in act is the same as the nominal and the effective value of fiat money or the virtual versus the real economy or money as a unit of account versus money as a medium of exchange.

CACAMBO: And so, what all this has to do with my ham and egg sandwich?

PANGLOSS: The nominal value of your sandwich may at any time, as we shall see later on, infringe upon its real value.

CACAMBO: Listen, it is half past three in the afternoon already and I still have nothing for dinner.

CALIOSTRO: You'd better wait a few minutes for the four o'clock tea.

CACAMBO: Are you kidding? Ever since the heyday of the British East India Company, the four o'clock tea is exclusively for those who are full already.

PANGLOSS: Do you know how much I was asked to pay for these cokes and the ham and egg sandwich?

CACAMBO: $40, $50 or more? Tell me the exact price and I'll give you the money.

PANGLOSS: I am afraid you do not have that much. The total monetary mass or the overall amount of fiat money in the United States as of 2009 includes $50.7 trillion of debt owed by US households, businesses, and governments, representing more than 3.5 times the annual gross domestic product of the United States.[1] As of the first quarter of 2010, domestic financial assets A totaled $131 trillion and domestic financial liabilities $106 trillion.[2] Tangible assets in 2008 (such as real estate and equipment) for selected sectors B totaled an additional $56.3 trillion.[3] The net worth of the United States at the end of 2008 was $75 trillion or 5.2 times GDP. As a fraction of the Total Monetary

Mass, our $20 bill is an infinitesimal part not merely of the net worth but of the total amount of financial assets plus liabilities, since the so called creation of money is in reality the creation of credit, which through the money multiplier[4] effect, increases the monetary mass more than anything else. Therefore, if $20 = three large cokes + ham and egg sandwich + one medium coffee, then, you should divide twenty by 131 trillion (financial assets) + 106 trillion (financial liabilities) to see how much is the worth of $20 as a fraction of the total monetary mass. You'll get something like 0.119 000 000 000 000 or:

$$\frac{1}{237\ 000\ 000\ 000\ 000}$$

CACAMBO: So where is the problem then? Who cares what the worth of a $20 bill relative to the total worth of the aggregate money supply is? The thing is to go to the counter and just buy this god damn ham and egg sandwich for which I have been waiting all day long!

CALIOSTRO: You do not seem to make a distinction between the real total amount of fiat money or the banknotes and coins plus the scriptural bank money and the virtual evaluation of assets? If I have a house priced at 0.2 million and I do not sell it, these 0.2 million exist only in my mind, until or if the actual transaction is executed.

PANGLOSS: Yes, here we start with the total nominal amount of fiat money as a representation in the minds of all who take part in the exchange of goods and services, since this virtual figure as we shall see later on, counts for the decision making process, which is going on in the real economy. Now, the figure at the cashier desk said, there is something wrong with his computers today and all bills are treated only in potency or as a representation of the total amount of the aggregate money supply, whereas had they to be treated as usual, my $20 bill would have been only an effective fractional combination of this same total amount. And as a result, this same bill of $20 bill is valued as much as the total money supply, where the price of the Cokes, the sandwich and the coffee is only an infinitesimal fraction of these $20.

CACAMBO: Are you not one of those who cling to the best in the best of all possible worlds staff? When you subtract all parts or relative valuations other than the valuations or monetary expressions of the three Cokes, the sandwich and the coffee from the total aggregate money supply, the price of these same Cokes and so forth, will be less than a one millionth of a cent. So, what are you waiting for? You'd better find a truck for these sandwiches since you can buy at least one tone with your $20 bill!

PANGLOSS: Yes, but the employee at the cashier desk has been asking for his $20 bill since this is the quoted price before his computers broke up and these $20 he said, are now equal to $237 trillion, as in the world of my good friend Jonathan Swift with his Gulliver, where the infinitely great is like the infinitely small in the same way as a drop of the ocean is equivalent to the whole ocean.

CALIOSTRO: How can a $20 bill, be infinitely great and yet infinitely small?

Pangloss: Once again, a $20 bill as a unit of account is an infinitesimal part of all the monetary mass or a fraction of all different prices, constituting the sum of the whole monetary mass in equal proportion to this mass, which in our case is $237 trillion: as such, the $20 bill is infinitely great since all different prices or valuations of the aggregate money supply or the monetary mass, take part in this banknote in a proportion equal to the difference between 237 trillion and twenty. Now, as a medium of exchange the $20 bill is infinitely small, since among all possible combinations between the infinitesimal fractions of the whole or the total monetary mass only a few are chosen during the transaction, where the part or the chosen combinations or valuations are to be equivalent to the fraction of the whole, represented by the $20 bill. The three bottles of Coke, the ham and egg sandwich and the medium coffee = $20 =

$$\frac{1}{237\ 000\ 000\ 000\ 000}$$

CACAMBO: I still do not see why you are adding the assets and the liabilities, instead of equating the aggregate money supply with the net worth or the assets minus the liabilities?

PANGLOSS: My dear friend, had it been as you say, there would be simply no such thing as banks and fiat money on this planet. As we said it already, money creation is at least 80% credit creation, where debts always should exceed payments, since there is no interest to be charged from a balanced budget, be it a state, a corporate or an individual budget. This is so self-evident that it is no use wasting the little time left, on the point for the absolute necessity for debts, so that profit out of thin air could be made. Now, in my view there is no better we could do right now, than just subtracting the liabilities from the assets, imprinted in the $20 bill, as an infinitesimal fraction of the total monetary supply. So, Financial assets minus financial liabilities or 131 trillion −106 = 25 trillion where:

$$\frac{25 \times 100}{131 + 106} = 10.4\%$$

$20

So ---------------------------- = 89.6% debt + 10.4% net financial assets.

237 000 000 000 000

CACAMBO: Why did you not a make a distinction between thin air and repaid debt. The built in prerequisite for debt in the printing of fiat money does not imply that all debts at any time will not be repaid, but only a fraction of these debts.

PANGLOSS: Yes. And that is why the periodical cancelling of debts or devaluation or default, is never in reality indeed a default on all debts but only of a certain amount of these debts, since this is the way of perpetuating the whole system, based on debts and the charge of interest. Now, for the time being this is beyond our point. What is at stake here is that a substantial amount of our $20 bill rests on vague promises for something which may or may not take place or the eventual creation of value, a little like thin air which the creditor is expecting to solidify at some point in the future. Therefore 89.6% of our $20 banknote is not real money but a receipt for a value which is inversely proportional to the rise of debts, since the more these debts go up, the more a default or devaluation is likely to take place at some point in the future, effectively cancelling the claims of the creditors.

CALIOSTRO: Are you suggesting that those who loose at last resort are the creditors?

PANGLOSS: I told you already that I'll discuss this later on. In a word, this is indeed so, but provided that the ultimate creditor assumes temporarily the role of insolvent debtor, so that at last resort he becomes a creditor again. Following this line, once aware that his debtors are no longer able to pay interest on their debts, this same ultimate creditor will intentionally cause a chain reaction of defaults of the intermediate creditors, his subordinates and/or allies of yesterday, whom this same ultimate creditor is now sacrificing, since the periodical cancelling of debts is the condition sine qua non, of a system whose ultimate reference or reason for being rests on the charge of interest. The last creditor along this chain of successive defaults will be the ultimate looser, so that, as we mentioned it already, the first creditor now posing as the last debtor, might remain first in the future or reassume his initial role of the first creditor, after the consequences of the default have been made clear to all the actors on the stage. By the way, the very existence of fiat money is a sign that the end of the ultimate, mega default is just around the corner, although the whole thing is still fixed around this same Meta historical corner already for forty years in a row, ever since the closing of the 'Gold Window' in 1971.[5]

CALIOSTRO: And what about the tangible assets, you mentioned earlier on?

PANGLOSS: It is highly unlikely that the amount of these tangible assets does not include a substantial amount of the above discussed financial assets. The crumbling of the US real estate pyramid by 2007 confirms the validity of such an assumption, since tangible assets are simultaneously mortgages and therefore financial assets also. I see no reason why, for example Freddie Mack should not agree with this statement. However, let's assume for the time being that the tangible assets do indeed correspond to the figure of 56.3 trillion, of which our $20 bill is an infinitesimal fraction. Each incremental increase of real estate prices is an occasion for money creation, whereas the bricks or the concrete or the prefabricated elements of the houses are usually the same or in a still worse condition than before.

CACAMBO: And is not the opposite also true, since a decrease of prices should cause a decrease of the money supply?

PANGLOSS: Once printed fiat money, either on paper or scriptural is still fiat money. People do not burn banknotes, since they think the banknotes are a store of value and therefore each banknote is a unit of account and as such belongs to someone, an individual, a corporation etc. As a result of this, an eventual decrease of the price of one asset, leads, as we will see later on in detail, to the increase or the inflated price of another asset, since fiat money comes indeed from thin air but will not vanish into thin air incrementally but only in its totality.

CALIOSTRO: So are you adding the tangible assets to the total monetary mass or you just include them in the figure of the financial assets?

PANGLOSS: It is a tentative guess. Since 2006, there are no longer figures on M3 monetary aggregate.[6] Now, the relative price of the tangible assets are on one hand illiquid and therefore not directly related to fiat money and on the other hand the rise of their prices is an occasion for an additional increase of the monetary mass and the expansion of credit. Yet, we'd better include, say a hypothetical 50% from their total amount in our fractional twenty dollar bill, since a substantial amount of these tangible assets are mortgages and therefore are counted as financial liabilities, whereas the other half as relative valuations participate in the total monetary mass, very likely, on a separate account from the financial assets, already mentioned above. So 56.3 divided by 2 = 28. 15. Our $20 is now 25 trillion + 28.15 trillion = 53.15 trillion =

$$\frac{1}{\text{-------------}}$$

53.15 trillion, where 53.15 out of 236 is = 22.4%.

CALIOSTRO: Is this the final value of $20?

PANGLOSS: No it is not. The GNP, measuring the earnings derived from goods and services should be added to the final countdown, since by definition the assets are the already produced value and the earnings derived from these assets, is the GNP. However, an unknown, but substantial amount of the GNP is not related to the valuations of real goods and services constituting the basis for physical sustenance and well-being.

CALIOSTRO: What is the link between the GNP and the total value of the assets tangible and intangible?

PANGLOSS: For the time being, it is to be noted that, the more the nominal value of the assets relative to the GNP goes up, the less real is the value of these assets. These are the prices of stocks and other financial instruments,[7] inflated real estate prices, monopolistic and oligopolistic prices of intermediate inputs, being at last resort useless for the delivery of the final outputs or worse still, in the case of industrial food additives, antibiotics, plastics in cars and toxic synthetic materials, for example in building or the introduction of new dangerous drugs etc. representing harmful activities and ultimately a debt to society, whose exact amount may be evaluated only by future generations,[8] since you cannot know what a theatre play is all about without seeing the fall of the curtain or the effective end of this same, in this case, Meta historical representation. Following all this, it would be reasonable to subtract at least two thirds of the fractional GNP value of the $20 bill, since modern accounting is making no distinction between useful and harmful activities by putting in the same basket the use of cocaine and the growing of organic food, as in the accounting books both of these have prices and therefore the difference in the quality of these commodities is not taken into account, but only the difference of their respective monetary value. So, as the gap between the GNP and financial assets is widening, you could subtract a substantial amount of the 53 trillion as a nominal value reflecting in an ever lesser proportion the real value of these assets. Furthermore, you can subtract another amount from the GNP, or its negative percentage or the part of useless and harmful activities. So in case you add the GNP of about 15 trillion by 2009 to the 53 trillion of tangible and intangible assets, you get something like 53+15=68 trillion. Now, as we said it earlier, if you subtract the tentative figure of 28 trillion which is very likely to overlap with the overall figure of 53 trillion, which accounts for the harmful and/or useless activities and also at least half from the GNP, accounting for the useless and harmful activities or 7.5 trillion form 15 trillion, the real value of the $20 bill would be:

$$\frac{1}{(53-28)+(15-7.5)}=20\$$$

And now the final countdown is: 25+7.5=32.5 or 14-15% out of 237 trillion of assets+15 trillion nominal GNP, where, the nominal value of each banknote of $20 is equal to = 14-15% of its real value or $2.4-5, since 84-5% of the $20 bill represents either non-existent value (debts+ inflated assets), a substantial amount of which, will never come into existence (defaults) or negative value due to the inclusion of harmful activities in the nominal value of the GNP denominated in fiat currency.

CACAMBO: Your figures are arbitrary. You can subtract any amount you wish. This is a wild guess. Furthermore, as I told you already before, let the market judge what is harmful and what it is not.

PANGLOSS: You seem to have forgotten that I outlined my point on this matter, when, we were conversing on the cars of the past and the present. Now, it goes without saying that this point is a key epistemological point, and I'll present it in more detail later on. As for my approach, at last resort, this approach rests on the idea of the ontological essence of quality and the presumption that men are no rats, neither piranhas and therefore are able to make a distinction between quality, and its representations or quantity or between the original and its shadow, that is the copy. These statistics are not the starting point, but only an illustration, in our case, of the gap between the real versus the virtual, the effective versus the nominal evaluation of economic activity. Furthermore, the question of perfect statistics is related to the epistemology of Economics. Statistics are like facts: they never speak for themselves, since they speak in the first place for their user.

CALIOSTRO: What will you do with the difference between 20 and 2.5 or $17.50?

CACAMBO: Look! Look at the sky! What..? What is going on?

NOTES

[1] *Components of US debt*, https: www. federalreserve.gov/datadownload/Download.

[2] *Flow of Funds Report*, p. L.5, L.125, http://www.federalreserve.gov/releases/z1/current/z1.pdf, retrieved 3 July 2010.

[3] *Net worth of the United States*, https://www.federalreserve.gov/datadownload/Download.

[4] (Mankiw 2008, *Part VI: Money and Prices in the Long Run: The Money Multiplier*, pp. 347–349). (Krugman & Wells 2009, p. 395) calls the observed multiplier the "actual money multiplier").

[5] See *Nixon Ends Bretton Woods International Monetary System* - YouTube. In 1971 the total US federal debt stood at $436 billion. Today, that number exceeds $8 trillion. The 2005 increase in the federal debt of $571 billion was more than the total debt in 1971. Worse still, when calculated in accordance with Generally Accepted Accounting Principles (GAAP), and taking unfunded Social Security and Medicare obligations into account, the total federal debt is actually

$49.4 trillion. This equates to more than $160,000 for every American. 11 May 2006, Nick Barisheff, Bullion Management Services Inc.

***The ratio of the federal debt on which is focused the attention of the media in reality, is only a relatively small fraction of the total debt. In 1946, the total US debt-to-GDP ratio was 150%, with two-thirds of that held by the federal government. Since 1946, the federal government's debt-to-GDP ratio has since fallen by nearly half, to 54.8% of GDP in 2009. The debt-to-GDP ratio of the financial sector, by contrast, has increased from 1.35% in 1946 to 109.5% of GDP in 2009. The ratio for households has risen nearly as much, from 15.84% of GDP to 95.4% of GDP. (*Components of US debt*, https://www.federalreserve.gov/datadownload/Download.

TALE XV

The Meteor Syndrome

CACAMBO: Do you see that luminous point over there?

CALIOSTRO: It is growing so fast. It is a ball already!

PANGLOSS: Here is a meteor or a fire ball.

CACAMBO: Look at your left side: there is another one, a huge one, very bright. And still another one! They are about to come down on us! Let's go out!

CALIOSTRO: Being a ghost, I can just fly away at any time. So, I wish you good luck my friends! I am leaving you and the surface of this planet as well, for a more hospitable spot somewhere in the galaxy.

PANGLOSS: You are overreacting. There is no danger, at least for the time being. The collision will certainly be avoided.

Caliostro lifts himself in the air and disappears from sight.

PANGLOSS: As a figure always looking for something to take without giving anything in return, now he reacted in a way contrary to his credo.

CACAMBO: Why?

PANGLOSS: Usually he takes for real, what appears to be outside of his own self only, since he has full consciousness of his ghost like, virtual, nature, being the same, as a copy is to its original or as fiat money is to itself.

CACAMBO: You are distracting me from watching what is going on in the sky right now. Are we really out of the reach of these meteors or this is just another statement in line with your dogma of preconceived optimism?

PANGLOSS: You have nothing to worry about!

CACAMBO: This is wishful thinking! They are growing in size by the second...by the fraction...of the fraction of the second! So what? What shall we do now?

PANGLOSS: My dear friend, just listen to my point, because this is really a key point on the unilateral nature of fiat money.

CACAMBO: You are incorrigible, like Andersen's Steadfast Tin Soldier. The sky is literally falling at this very moment and you still expect me to listen to your nonsense! Why the hell, did I agree , when someone of the like of you, persuaded me to take the elixir, which extends the span of physical life, but makes it so much more difficult than the ghost like existence of the guy, who just spared himself from the constraints of real life, only a few seconds ago!

PANGLOSS: The point is the following: the unilateral nature of fiat money is ultimately the very opposite of the notion of exchange. When an exchange takes place, you give something and you receive what you perceive to be the equivalent of the something you gave already. Fiat money and only fiat money works only one way. There is taking of real goods for getting thin air in return. There is credit which has no intrinsic cost to the creditor, but a real cost to the debtor only. The likely objection that when you buy something, you give the equivalent of something else, as we saw it with the infinitesimal fraction of the money supply, far from being a contradiction, shows on the opposite, the lack of real universal mediator between the two opposites i.e. the buyer versus the seller, taking part in the transaction. By the way, here is another illustration of the very effective nature of Ancient Philosophy, since the notion of a mediator between two opposites, as we saw it already earlier on, is a key tenet of Neo-Platonism. Now, this mediator, to be a real and not only nominal or a deceitful mediator, has to be of value in itself and this is possible only if this same mediator is not in unlimited supply as in the case of fiat money, but on the opposite, in limited supply as the precious metals are. Because it is thanks to, and only thanks to, the limited supply of the substance from which the mediator is composed, that it becomes possible to fix the real price. Without real mediator, there are no real prices. There are fluctuations, approximations and the later stages of the fiat money expansion all that is left of real price valuations, is a wild guess, subject to radical changes of the quotation at any time. A price tag based on fiat money is the Maya per se, since at its core, such a price mirrors nothing but the speed at which the flood of liquidity or pure sand is shifting from one asset to another. Now, look at the shiny traces left by the meteors.

CACAMBO: What?

PANGLOSS: You still have time to look. These meteors are about to vanish at any moment since they will bypass the Earth this time and will fall somewhere else, by making another huge crater, for example on the Moon or on Mars.

CACAMBO: I see letters in the sky.

PANGLOSS: What letters?
CACAMBO: On the trace left by the biggest meteor, I can see...FFo... Oh Yes! This is: Foreign Exchange. Here is another one: Personal Debt and Corporate Debt. And another one still: Internet Start Up.

PANGLOSS: The modern or rather the postmodern economy rests on the Meteor Syndrome.

CACAMBO: Come on! Why should you go that far to present something, as down to earth as the economy? The whole of your verbiage does not have a single iota of scientifically correct value. The thing is to look to details and to separate what is relevant from what it is not by making your point as specific as possible.

PANGLOSS: I agree with you but only in half. Details do count indeed, provided that these details are related to a whole and the latter respectively related to the consciousness of the whole in itself. Details in isolation, by being cut from their source, only create the optical illusion of taking the place of their principle. Should we compare modern finance to an elastic band, as we did it already earlier on, the details on the relative resistance of this band, when stretched may shed light on the precise point when the band will tear down. However, should we take the decision to wander in the dark on a permanent basis, we will evaluate the elasticity of this same band in isolation and in this way we'll ignore its effect on the economy. When the day comes where the notion of absurdity will be erased from the human mind altogether, which by the way, by no means will necessarily be so for other minds, since men have no monopoly on Consciousness, the idea of a detail metamorphosed in its opposite will cease to appear as irrelevant. So, once again, should we cut the detail from its source, there would be no way to evaluate and therefore to see the significance, the role of this detail in relation to, in our case, the economic puzzle, that is taking place at this very moment. So let's start with the Meteor. What is a Meteor if not the expression of a broken equilibrium that occurred somewhere in the Cosmos in the first place, since this Meteor at some point, has been detached from a remote substance, a planet, as a result of this same broken equilibrium affecting its natural setting?

CACAMBO: Listen, people want to know what is going on at this very moment and at this very place. What is above has been evacuated from what is below, a long time ago, already at the time where most of the philosophers that you seem to like, used to be still alive, during the late Roman Empire. Have not our credo ever since been that, what is above is impossible to be reached so that we would not be hindered in our blind impulse to sink deep down to what is below?

PANGLOSS: Yes, the credo on the absence of the Spirit and respectively the omnipresence of the body obscures Consciousness by weakening its innate, intuitive capacity for perceiving reality at its core and thus naturally attracts the erring, residual entities from the sidereal space, and as a result this credo is sustained by the propagation of an assortment of absurdities on a massive scale. Following this, once again, a detail may never be relevant outside of the Whole. So, our Meteor is a representation of the here and now. By the way, the case of M-r W. Delbert Gann[1] who earned millions from stock market speculation by the use of Astronomy, back in the 1920s illustrates the very concrete effect of this other attitude, on the way economic activity may be carried out. Naturally, it goes without saying, that should you compare this very personal achievement to what may be possible to be achieved on a larger scale, following the perception of economic activity we have outlined so far, the fortune of M-r Gann would appear only as an infinitesimal fraction of the whole.

CACAMBO: What I have just heard makes me think that you may be an advocate of the same kind of speculation that on other occasions you apparently deny. Also, since I was not really convinced that these Meteors would not come down on Earth, I had no time to tell you something: you seem to like Gold very much. Are you not one of these Gold Bugs[2] spending their time by waiting for the Big World Economic Crash to come out?

PANGLOSS: Stock Market and Foreign Exchange trading is essentially related to the role of Exchange per se. Here is a crossroad with only two possible directions. Either you deny the very idea of Exchange at its core, or the opposite you affirm its key role as one of the pillars of Civilization. From Ancient Phoenicia to the Vaishyas in India, trading activities had their specific role in society sanctified by traditions at least as old and as enigmatic as the origin of agriculture. Seen from the angle of Meta history, the denigration of trade in Classical Greece and later on in the Middle Ages and so forth is a relatively recent phenomenon, in line with the fear of the four Elements characterizing the Kali Yuga, or the fear in the face of the blind impulse of desire preventing Consciousness from mastering the Elements. It is no coincidence that the Spartans had forbidden the use of gold and had only iron coins in circulation.[3] By the way, could you just tell me what are we doing at this very moment?

CACAMBO: What do you mean?

PANGLOSS: Yes, what are we doing right now?

CACAMBO: Well, we are having a something like a dialogue.

PANGLOSS: We are having a dialogue indeed or said in another way, we are exchanging views on the Economy, since the Cosmic Manifestation itself is nothing else but a gigantic Mega Exchange, including Stock Exchange. Had not there not been, for this Cosmic Exchange taking place at each infinitesimal fraction of the second, on all levels and on all possible combinations of the Monads built-in, in the Four Elements, there would be simply nothing at all. Now, as there is no such thing as nothing at all, there is no way to get away from the Cosmos and therefore from the Exchange going on throughout the Cosmos. To suppress Trade is like suppressing the Four Elements altogether, ultimately an impossible task.

CACAMBO: We are talking about trade here, not the Cosmos. Also, by the way, is there a place in your Cosmos for Distribution?

PANGLOSS: Being a form of Exchange trade is an integral part of the Cosmos. As, for Distribution, there is no such thing as Distribution, since whatever you give, you always take something in return, although not necessarily what you might expect, implicitly or explicitly consciously or unconsciously, in the same way as there is no action without reaction, since at some point the Principle is going back to itself. Trade is like Love.

CACAMBO: What? Have we not been told from Late Antiquity all the way up to now that Love is to give without asking anything in return?

PANGLOSS: As there is an original, so there are copies of the original. In the same way, there is the propensity for Love or its representations, Love in Consciousness, and Love per se. The propensity for Love, as an image, a copy of the original, is unilateral, whereas Love per se, is bilateral. This is a magical exchange, since Love requires Love in return and therefore by no means nothing in return. In the same way, buying requires selling so that the exchange may take place.

CACAMBO: And therefore we are somehow living in the best of the best of all possible worlds, right?

PANGLOSS: Yes, although this is everything but obvious at the point where the Cosmic Wheel is turning right now. Yet, should we eliminate any ontological confusion and make it clear, that trading is separated from stealing by the abyss of cosmic polarity, trading appears to be no different from any other form of spiritual activity, such as Yoga for example and so forth. Here is the ancient dice game, mentioned in the Vedas to remind you that the Cosmos is actually like a child playing a never ending game with the Four Elements.[4]

CACAMBO: Listen, the Meteors are gone already and I suggest you to get back to Earth and to my question on Gold. They say there is nothing more material than Gold, on this planet.

PANGLOSS: Do you remember a guy from our own time by the name of Jean-Jacques from the city of Geneva?

CACAMBO: Is this M-r Volontaire?

PANGLOSS: No. Jean-Jacques is someone who knew as much about the ancient past as you do, on the number of devils dancing fox-trot on the tip of a needle. Just like, any little boy, looking for the hidden cookie jar in the kitchen by grandma, Jean-Jacques equated civilization with the pain he had to endure while looking for the jar and respectively associated freedom, with the moment when he'd find out the jar and open the cap of the pot, at last. In the case of Jean-Jacques however, the intensity of this urge was much higher, since, already at an advanced age, he still had urges of the kind, the great majority of little children do their best to avoid at any cost.[5] So, he associated savagery with freedom and civilization with pain, since he saw somehow to justify his ontological surrender before his blind unconditional reflexes. Yet, contrary to others, he used to be a good man at heart and naively took what is below for its opposite end or what is above. Now, later on, another figure, a self-proclaimed healer, who never cured anybody and whose followers equated blind desire with freedom and in the process piled up tones of fiat money, by becoming the undisputed leaders in the art of institutionalized, methodical self-indulgence, through their animosity toward Gold put off the last garment from the Emperor's New Clothes back, leaving our sovereign completely naked in the process.[6]

CACAMBO: Was not Gold compared at some point to the rather unpleasant form of processed matter by the name of excrement?[7]

PANGLOSS: If you think as these figures implicitly did, that craving is the only alternative to the human condition, Gold will appear to be the symbol of the subjection to this blind impulse. The attraction or the submission to Gold will be inversely proportional to the repulsion, the latter, coming from the feeling of powerlessness that the perceived impossibility to overcome this same attraction, thought to be one's essence, will provoke. Should you stick to the false certitude, caused by such an attitude, leading in the last resort, to the absurd impression according to which, space is somehow not three dimensional or that you can only fall without ever going up, Gold may indeed be associated with excrement as this is shown in Ancient Babylonian Religion. However, these associations present also elsewhere, including folk tales, are based on a radically different perspective, and this perspective is the Law of Polarity, where the difference between good and evil is not in kind but in degree, in the degree allowing you to find out the sufficient reason or the inner equilibrium within the eternal interplay of the Four Elements. As a result, the excrement of hell will in no time turn into pure Gold, provided you do not let yourself be blinded by its shine, in the same way as a horse may be your best friend, provided you know how to mount it. The thing is that Gold may turn into excrement just like food may become poison, if left to decay or if one is overeating all the time. Let's there be no confusion on that matter. Gold per se is Gold just like excrement per se is excrement, in all its possible versions, either human or non-human. By the way, should men turn to the practice of Coprophagia[8] they will not be able to remain in the human condition for long, since an instant process of transition will be set in motion, from the human condition to something else, as this is a perception characteristic of many insects as well as animals, among them, in the first place, may be flies and rats.

CACAMBO: Is not Gold attractive to some and repulsive to others?

PANGLOSS: The question of what is pleasant and what is not nowadays is associated with emotions and the emotions in their turn are opposed to reason. The thing is that you always have emotions, and these emotions are of two kinds, the emotions deriving from the mastery of the elements, for example serenity and the emotions deriving from the subjection to the elements, such as envy or melancholy. So, as far as Gold is concerned, the point is to know what Gold is all about, and not whether Gold is pleasant to some or unpleasant to others. By the way, provided you do not sink into obscurity, you'll never even conceive of the possibility that Gold may not be more pleasant to some than others.

CACAMBO: Gold is greed! Gold is evil entrenched deep down the Earth!

PANGLOSS: The hatred of Gold, in its various forms, as we outlined this so far, is the undisputed proof of outright impotence grafted on all layers of Consciousness. Here is a perception reflecting the ontological inability of the Psyche to confront the elements, the failure to win the cosmic game. Should we make one more comparison, the whole thing is like a toreador who at the sight of the bull is deserting the arena and is leaving his red cape and his sword on the ground and asking himself in the process why is he to confront the bull at all, as he is expecting somehow to win without fighting. And as at some point along the way, he'd realize the absurdity of such an occurrence, he bursts into rage against the bull, against the arena, against himself and not least of all, against the validity of his own realization.

CACAMBO: Is not gold the embodiment of earthly desire?

PANGLOSS: Yes, but only in case you lose the game, in the same way as when you fail to tame a wild horse, you'll fall down in no time on the ground. Otherwise Gold per see does not come from the Earth but from the Sky.

CACAMBO: What?

PANGLOSS: As a universal medium of exchange, seen as such, by Humanity for millennia Gold is independent from any government and any subjective encroachment on economic activity. As for gold coming from the sky, this is by no means a metaphor but the literal truth, since Gold appeared a long time ago from a bombardment of Meteors falling down on Earth.[9]

CACAMBO: But who cares for Gold these days other than the Gold Bugs?

PANGLOSS: The erasing of Gold from the memory of Humanity is an impossible task. The thing is that the pursuit of such an impossible task is only apparent, since there is a high probability that Gold may resurface on the horizon very soon, on conditions that we'll specify later on.

CACAMBO: What conditions?

PANGLOSS: As we said it already, the Meteors, as entities from other planets are the result of a broken equilibrium somewhere in the Cosmos. Once detached from the natural physical limits imposed by Gold, the printing of Fiat Money is an example of a process that simply is impossible to be controlled. The flood of what they call, liquidity, inevitably leads to Pyramids of various sorts or to irrational changes of the prices and ultimately to a crisis of confidence that will destroy the world of Fiat Money altogether. This is something that is perfectly known in the first place, by the very few real actors on the stage of the World Economy. Now, let's assume that the planet, from where the Meteors are coming from is made out of solidified piles of paper banknotes and that there is a kind of Cyclops over there, who is digging below the surface and taking huge piles from the substance of this planet, so huge that the whole planet cannot remain in orbit without the periodical thrust of some of its parts, from the sides where the necessary equilibrium is broken, playing the role of Meteors in outer space. The more the Cyclops is digging in one location of the planet, the bigger part is detached from another location, so that the planet might remain in orbit. In this way, the mass of the planet is diminishing over time, until the last detached Meteor, makes the whole planet go out of its orbit altogether and thus this planet becomes a detached mass of paper in a free fall, until it makes a last final crush somewhere in another galaxy leading to its complete annihilation. Fiat Money is like these Meteors. Once a bubble bursts, the flood of paper is turning to another kind of assets and another bubble is already swelling in no time, up to the point when, as we shall see later on in more detail, the last coin from the credit of confidence is thrown away in outer space.

CACAMBO: I do not want to stay on this island any longer. Bring me to the harbor for dinner.

PANGLOSS: We have to stay at this place for now and we'll examine the three Meteors that bypassed the Earth this time: the Meteor of corporate and personal debt, the Meteor of Foreign Exchange, especially in the light of the recent moves of the SNB or the Swiss National Bank as well as the crisis of the Euro, and, the Meteor of the 'irrational exuberance' brought by the bursting the Internet Bubble more than a decade ago and its connection with the US real estate crash starting in 2006, and at last we'll make a point on the recent sudden shifts of the world' s food prices.

NOTES

[1]According to Aerodynamic Investments Co, interested in the methods of WD Gann, Gann made $56 million in the 1920's... and then entirely avoided The Great Crash. www.aeroinvest.com; *On Gann's Law of Vibration*, See www.wdgannslawofvibration.com.

[2]See Gretchen Ritter, *Goldbugs and Greenbacks: The Anti-Monopoly Tradition and the Politics of Finance in America* (New York: Cambridge University Press, 1997).

[3]Lycurgus The Father of Sparta From *Plutarch's Lives, 15 Ancient Greek Heroes From Plutarch's Lives A Modern English Edition*, abridged and annotated by Wilmot H. McCutchen.

[4]Dice Game in Old India, Heinrich Luders, Berlin 1906; Each kalpa is made up of 1000 maha-yugas. A maha-yuga is comprised of four yugas or world ages: Krita (or Satya) Yuga (1,728,000 years), Treta Yuga (1,296,000 years), Dvapara Yuga (864,000 years) and Kali Yuga (432,000 years). These four yugas are named after the four throws in a dice game, progressing from the best to the worst. See, Heinrich Zimmer (Edited by Joseph Campbell) *Myths and Symbols in Indian Art and Civilization* (Princeton, New Jersey: Princeton University Press, 1946); Luis Gonzalez-Reimann : *The Mahābhārata and the Yugas, India's Great Epic Poem and the Hindu System of World Ages* .

[5]*6 Famous Geniuses You Didn't Know Were Perverts* By: Clive Jameson June 01, Cracked.com http://www.cracked.com/article_18559_6-famous-geniuses-you-didnt-know-were-perverts_p2.html#Ixzz1YERbtwjD.

[6]Michel Onfray, *Le Crépuscule d'une idole. L'Affabulation freudienne.* (2010) Grasset (ISBN 2-246-76931-0) (The Dusk of an Idol. Freudian Fabrication).

[7]*History of Shit* by Dominique Laporte MIT Press, *2000 Review* by Adrian Johnston, Ph.D. Apr 6th 2001 (Volume 5, Issue 14).

[8]Greek κόπρος copros ("feces"); Lewin, Ralph A. (2001). <u>More on Merde</u>, *Perspectives in Biology and Medicine* 44 (4): 594–607. doi:10.1353/pbm.2001.0067. PMID 11600805.

[9]September 2011, <u>Meteorites delivered Gold to Earth</u> By Leila Battison, *Science Reporter*, www.bbc.co.uk.

TALE XVI

The Spirit In The Bottle[1]

CACAMBO: No. I want to go out to the shore, unless you make another attempt of buying my ham and egg sandwich from the coffee shop.

Pangloss leaves his companion for the nearby restaurant and returns later on with a plate of French Fries, sandwiches and beverages.

PANGLOSS: I was lucky enough to buy all these things, since the computers are still broken but the restaurant personnel happen to be more flexible this time, and as a result they accept Gold instead of the never ending alignment of zeros corresponding to tones of paper banknotes.

CACAMBO: I did not know you had gold coins on you. Are not precious metals rather heavy to be carried in a pocket, however deep this pocket may be?

PANGLOSS: I have a Gold Certificate. This time, came out in our rescue, the prevailing propensity of the Modern Economy and society for that matter, to take the copy for its original or the preference for the representation at the expense of the thing or the content, represented in the first place. Yet the cashier on the counter acted like one of these speculators who established all the Ponzi schemes in the last three centuries: he asked for ten times as much gold as he would have asked, if I had real Gold instead of a mere representation of Gold, since the Gold Certificate I have just found out in my wallet is nothing else.

CACAMBO: My dinner is here at last!

*****

Our heroes are now having a walk along the sea.

CACAMBO: Do you see one large bottle floating over there?

PANGLOSS: What bottle?

CACAMBO: There is a bottle on the crest of that wave approaching our island and something moving inside. It is very close to the shore right now. I'll go there and get it.

A minute or so later, Cacambo is back with the bottle in question. A little humanlike creature is springing up and down in the bottle, making, what appears to be, another vain attempt of pushing the cork of the bottle and getting on the loose.

CACAMBO: Who are you?

THE SPIRIT: Will you release me if I tell you who I am?

PANGLOSS: As I see in my Crystal Ball, I was farsighted enough to take with me from the other side, since these postmodern gadgets of the Blue Berry kind are nothing but a poor copy of the real thing, it is no coincidence that you happen to be at this very place by the name of Liberty Island precisely at this very moment, highly charged with a dense Meta historical current.

THE SPIRIT: Would you be just kind enough to open the cork of this god damn bottle? If you do, I will give you all the magic powers that Faust got from Mephistopheles with the notable difference that you will not have to make any bargain in exchange, in the sense that you will keep you Soul for yourself. So, can you imagine anything better than getting everything for nothing or more specifically, getting everything for the little effort of just pushing, this cork above my head out? My dear friend, open this bottle and all the Planet will be yours for free!

CACAMBO: He might be right after all. By the way, is not his present condition the perfect negative replica of the definition of freedom that has been specified back in our own time, as the absence of outward constraint?

PANGLOSS: Okay I'll let him on the loose although I know who he is and why he is here right now.

*****

At this very moment, a voice is coming out of the Crystal Ball that Pangloss is holding in his hand:

CRYSTAL BALL: You may know what this is all about but the point is to see, how the whole thing has been going on ever since it came out in the open. So, I suggest you to keep him locked for a while and to let him on the loose only after you see the two sides of his modes of perception, a little like the dark versus the bright side of the Moon.

The Spirit: What are you waiting for, my friend? Just push that cork out and you'll get anything in this world for free!

Pangloss: As far as I can see, you appear to be a Spirit. However, there are countless Spirits erring throughout the Universe and yet all of them have a name, because the state of confusion is only a temporary state, in the same way as any theatrical representation has several stages, since the whole process of acting is basically going on, by starting at the very first stage and is ending at the setting of the curtain, when the last or the ultimate stage has been over. Having said that, what is your name?

The Spirit: Will you release me if I tell you my name?

Cacambo: Yes, for sure. He will open the bottle, provided we know who you are.

The Spirit: I am the Specter from the *Communist Manifesto*.

Cacambo: How come you are the Specter of the *Communist Manifesto*?! What are you doing here?! You are supposed to haunt Europe, not wasting your time locked in a bottle![2]

The Spirit: The thing is that I had to make a transatlantic crossing in a way that, as you can see, I do not really appreciate. So, I am in no mood to go into details right now. Let me out first!

Pangloss: I am about to make a point on the Meteoric rise of present day finance and I would be very pleased if you take part in the debate.

The Spirit: Any meteor is rising at the beginning only to fall in the end.

Cacambo: (*To Pangloss*): He seems to agree with you on this point, doesn't he?

Pangloss: Do you know where the beginning of present day Finance is?

The Spirit: In Venice, Amsterdam, Geneva, in the City of London and then right here, in New York.

Pangloss: No. The whole thing starts with the Sphinx in Egypt.

CACAMBO: You like talking about sufficient reason for this and that. So, where is the sufficient reason for such a statement? Is not the beginning of your whole thing, the Dismal Science founded back in our own time by such figures as A. Smith, Giammaria Ortez, Malthus and so forth?

PANGLOSS: Sphinx's erosion was due to water rather than wind or sand.[3] The reason for this is that there used to be a time when the desert around the Sphinx was no desert. It was a green valley.[4] Modern Finance is like sand. Fiat money is as valuable and as abundant as the sand of Sahara. The green valley that once surrounded the Sphinx and later on became a desert is a perfect replica of the ultimate effect of Fiat Money on the Modern World.

CACAMBO: There are many places that have been transformed over time. Why do you place the Sphinx at the center of the stage?

PANGLOSS: The Sphinx is much older than the present day science of Egyptology is willing to admit.[5]

CACAMBO: What all this has to do with Economics?

PANGLOSS: It has to do with 'la raison d'être'[6] of Modern Culture and indirectly with the question of the ontological, Meta political legitimacy of Fiat Money as an embodiment of blindness or blind desire, on the subtle level of consciousness, where the perception of reality is taking place. If the traditional view of the Sphinx is to be acknowledged, the whole planet of Fiat Money will crumble 'comme un château de cartes"(fr.).[7]

CACAMBO: How did you get there?

PANGLOSS: The professing of Materialism leads out of itself to the unwillingness of looking beyond the surface of reality, since once you deny the existence of the Soul simultaneously you also deny the very possibility of reaching the Essence of just anything under the Sun. As a result, the distinction between the way things appear to be and the way they are, is realized either in act, more or less unconsciously or as a transgression of one's convictions. Now, since reality is no more sunflower than materialists are the Sun, so that it could turn itself in the direction of their expectations, just to please them, the latter attempt to resolve the contradiction between what they do in practice and what they profess in theory by playing with words, just as once the Sophists did. Hence, there are essentially two outcomes: First, these views are at last resort always dogmas since once you deny the Spirit you have nothing else left other than finding a substitute to the Spirit, inevitably appearing as its opposite double. In such views the starting point of reality may be just anything: atoms, genes, neurons, electrons, photons or whatever provided you stick to the ultimate, at its core, anthropomorphic dogma of taking the copy for its original. The words expressing these views are to be taken literally since looking beyond words is an anathema to a doctrine professing the primacy of the form over its content. Second, the propagation of Materialism on a large scale, by denying the very possibility of meditation on the First Causes, leads to an atrophy of those centers of Consciousness where the subtle reality is perceived. As the reality of the witches flying through the chimney on their way to the Sabbath was taken for granted almost up to our own time, in the 18th century, so the dense fog veiling today's reality appears in the clothing of the GNP growth statistics, the obsession for counting or the blind submission to the categorical imperative of Quantity. Now, however massive and tall this Giant may be, he has his own kind of Achilles' heel since sooner or later, any dream is melting into thin air.

CACAMBO: I do not see where this Achilles' heel might be. Is there a single portion of today's perception of reality however small that is not literally stuffed with figures?

PANGLOSS: All economic theories, either in the form of Distribution or Socialism or in the form of Appropriation or Liberalism are based implicitly on the false premise that Humans are in the first place a self-regulating or a rational, or a walking and talking digestive tube. The eruption of the present day volcano of greed with its endless ghostlike images, invading modern Consciousness from all sides, is a self-evident refutation of the basic premise of the essentially mechanistic perception, standing behind the formal tenets of Economics. Objects do not experience greed. Piranhas and Sharks do not experience greed either, since they are made that way by Nature.

CACAMBO: Are not men also made in the same way, being at last resort no different from animals?

PANGLOSS: The modern perception of reality is no revolt at all but a massive denial of free will. As we said it already, the very greed that is pouring from everywhere right now is the best refutation of present day Materialism and Primitivism.

CACAMBO: Why?

PANGLOSS: Because greed would not have been greed if it had limits. The very fall into the trap of blind greed indirectly reaffirms that the core of human Consciousness is based on the perception of the Absolute or Non-Duality, in the same way as the experience of humiliation reaffirms indirectly the existence of honor. Now, should the free fall into the abyss of greed to be going down still further and further, there has to be a veil on the spiritual nature of Consciousness. Greed has to be justified both inwardly in the form of a false perception of the self, sustained by the modern assembly line type culture of self-delusion and outwardly in the form of political and social legitimacy.

CACAMBO: And where is the Sphinx in all that?

PANGLOSS: The traditional view of the Sphinx rests on the doctrine of the Cosmic Ages, Cyclical Time and Eternal Recurrence. There is no place for the straight line of Progress in such a view, neither for the idea of endless approximation, where you can observe a process of transition going on before your eyes as much as you wish, but you are not allowed to raise the question of the nature of this same transition, since this question would reveal the ever present Forms or Monades behind the Maya of the Elements and therefore would curve the straight line in such a way as to make it a circle. Furthermore, the very foundation of this ancient view rests on the idea of Equilibrium, since otherwise the Principle of Unity or Non-Duality is unconceivable. Now, at this point, is revealed the abyss between these two views, standing on opposite directions. The cult of progress by its very nature is a legitimation and a sanctification of intellectual nihilism and blind greed, although most of the time this is an unconscious process. The real meaning of the Economics Cult is to put a veil on Consciousness and thus to disguise the ultimate outcome of the obsession for quantity. Also, Progressivism and the whole assortment of 'Ideologies' has no other purpose at last resort than creating an intellectual confusion on a global scale and achieving the impossible dream of usurping the throne of the Original or the arcane doctrine of Non-Duality at the expense of the copy. Here is the doomed attempt of the shadow to free itself from its essence of a second best. Inversion in all of its expressions is as much part of the whole cosmic design as his opposite.

CACAMBO: And where is Fiat Money in all this?

PANGLOSS: The very idea of Fiat Money was barely conceivable only a few decades ago. What made it happen, from the inside, is the conditioning of the modern Psyche, pushing the frontiers of obscurity and greed to their utmost limits. From the outside Fiat Money is related to the specific conditions created after the end of WWII. Had Germany, Japan or South Korea been, fully sovereign states, their unreserved acceptance of the USD as medium of exchange would not have taken place. By the way, the Gold Reserve of Germany is kept right here, in the city of New York.[8]

CACAMBO: And where is the Achilles' heel of the world of Fiat Money?

PANGLOSS: It is in the idea of Equilibrium. Progressivism and Materialism can digest just anything except the perception of Cosmic Equilibrium as the ultimate law of the Universe. Fiat money is fiat money, precisely because it is based on excess. And this excess is not an economic excess, in the first place. It is a metaphysical failure of the Psyche, and only later on, an economic failure as well.

THE SPIRIT: Great! Congratulations! I see that we agree on all that really counts!

Capitalism is doomed! I knew it, ever since my friend now still in a mausoleum, wrote on the role of Finance and Monopolies.[9] So, let me out now!

Pangloss: Wait a minute. Are you not seeing this very thing that I just presented from its opposite end or from the angle of mechanistic determinism?

The Spirit: Listen, I am somewhat confused since I am turning so often upside down in this stupid bottle! If you let me out I am sure we'll agree on just everything!

Cacambo: Will you still claim the same thing once on the loose?

The Spirit: Yes! For sure!

Pangloss: And another thing. As we said it, earlier on, Fiat Money is as abundant and as valuable as the sand of Sahara.

Cacambo: Great! Yet, I do not see why you do not raise up to the fact that you can buy nothing with sand, but you can buy what you can buy with a $1 USD, just anywhere including in any store of the $1 Dollar Store variety, now in operation on a global scale.

Pangloss: Have we not referred already to the question of the Metaphysical, including Meta historical, tension around the literal versus the figurative meaning of words? When we say that fiat money is sand, we refer to the following: All traded goods and services have a literal, i.e. physical form and a figurative, non-physical form, a representation where one good is exchanged for another according to its relative value in comparison with the total value of all tradable goods in circulation, so that the sum of all physical goods is to be equal to their total represented value. It goes without saying that the valuation of all traded goods is impossible without a medium of exchange, and when this medium of exchange is in unlimited supply i.e. has no intrinsic cost, there is no real valuation, only a virtual valuation, subject to changes at any time, since you can print as much paper banknotes as you wish and affect the price of any good without any reference to its intrinsic i.e. fair value. As traded goods, whatever their volume, are in limited supply at any given point in time, so their valuations should also be in limited supply. There is nothing further from the truth than the term 'liquidity', used today to designate the circulation of fiat money, since had not the water in the desert been in short supply there would be no desert at all.

Cacambo: Is not the real valuation possible through the relative exchange rate of one currency versus another?

Pangloss: Here it is! This is the first of the Meteors that bypassed us a short while ago: the Meteor of Foreign Exchange. They say there is a virtual versus a real Economy, where what is going on in the one side does not affect the other side and vice versa.[10] So, there should be two different types of exchange, one real and the other virtual or unreal. So, if you have bought, for example, 100,000 World.com stocks[11] in the late 1990s, for, say $60 a share, we can retrace these two parts in the following way: $6 000 000 = Real fiat money taken from a Bank Account, the selling of a Real Estate property, of a Business or whatever = 100,000x60 virtual stock market valuation. When, the World.com stock price, reached, shortly before being delisted, $0.20 per share, the 6 000 000 (real fiat money) = 0.20x100,000 (virtual stock markets shares) = 20,000 real fiat money. According to this theory, the missing $5,800,000 are somehow transmuted into a virtual loss or the very real initial amount of 6,000,000 became unreal after the transaction has been completed. The question is: How did this amount came to make the transition from the virtual to the real economy? So, following all this: if you keep 6,000,000 in your pocket, this is real, and then, if later on, all that it remains from these 6,000,000 is 20,000, this is still real but the missing 5,800,000 is not real!

CACAMBO: This is because all that really counts is the present. You had 6,000,000, before and now 20,000 and that's it!

PANGLOSS: Yes. When you climb stairs all that is in front of you at each point in time is the next step, although you are still on the present step, right? So, would you be able to climb any step of the stairs, if you do not see the next step?

THE SPIRIT: Definitely not.

PANGLOSS: So, is the cause and effect of any act, including, the passage from the virtual to the real Economy. Here, the pile of fiat money, growing by the second, is creating a huge gap between the monetary mass on one hand and the part from this same mass, for the accounting of the real Economy, on the other hand. The apparent separation between the two is only a matter of time and appropriate circumstances before the imminent financial reunion takes place in the form of gigantic Ponzi schemes and various Tulip mania type bubbles with all their devastating effects, at last resort beyond the limits, set within the present system of exchange. The containment of the natural propensity for inflation on the retail level by Central Banks in the name of political stability is no different from a sea wall, where the flood is stopped from pouring from one crack, but it is only a matter of time before it pours from another, inevitably appearing under the pressure of the ever growing mass of water. By the way, at last resort there is no other reason for the on-going real estate crisis, in practically all places, starting from Japan in the 1980s, the US in 2007, now Spain, later on China etc. ever since 1971.

NOTES

[1] The Spirit in the Bottle (German: *Der Geist im Glas*) is a German fairy tale collected by the Brothers Grimm, tale number 99. D. L. Ashliman, "*The Grimm Brothers' Children's and Household Tales*".

[2] *The Communist Manifesto*, originally titled *Manifesto of the Communist Party* (German: *Manifest der Kommunistischen Partei*) (1848) K. Marx and F. Engels.

[3] *Scholars Dispute Claim That Sphinx Is Much Older*, Published: February 09, 1992, *The New York Times*, Archive.

[4] *Sahara Desert Was Once Lush and Populated*, Bjorn Carey Date: 20 July 2006 www.livescience. com.

[5] *The Mystery of the Sphinx*, Dr. Lee E. Warren B.A., D.D.(C) 1998 *Plim Report* Vol. 7, www. plim.org.

[6] (Fr.) Reason for Being.

[7] (Fr.) House of cards.

[8] *Germany should end the secrecy and bring its gold home, By: Lars Schall*, www.goldseek.com.

[9] *Imperialism, the Highest Stage of Capitalism* (1920) V. Lenin.

[10] *World of Unreal Finance Hitting the Real Economy Politics / Credit Crisis Bailouts*, Sep 28, 2008 - 03:48 PM By: David Chu www.marketoracle.co.uk.

[11] See www.worldcomfraudinfocenter.com.

TALE XVII

International Trade

Cacambo: Do you remember what International Trade used to look like back in our own time?

Pangloss: Up to the end of the 18th century, the way International Trade was carried out ever since the Phoenicians had hardly changed, if at all.

Cacambo: What is this all about?

Pangloss: The origin of Long Distance Trade has nothing to do with what is referred to nowadays by the term 'Economics', neither with the logic of physical survival.

The Spirit: I may well be locked in that god damn bottle but I still cannot refrain from replying to the sheer nonsense that I have just heard. Trade, dear comrade is nothing but the dialectical interplay between the relations of production and the productive forces taking place in a historically specific mode of production.

Pangloss: Would you be kind enough not to interrupt me? I'll reply to this later on.

Cacambo: If Trade is to be detached from Economics, then why not starting the whole subject with an introduction to the underworld of the Hades type, where misty ghosts are greeting themselves by exchanging fire whirls of thin air to each other?

Pangloss: Because, first, in Hades there is practically nothing that is not already right here, in one way or another and second, our notion of truth rests on the point of intersection between the Soul and the Body. What we just said above, is not idealism but realism, since the reality represented by idealism is as reduced to absurdity as its opposite double or materialism. So, once again: Trade and long distance Trade in particular is totally unrelated to physical necessity. The origin of Trade is a function of the Psyche and nothing else.

Cacambo: And from here to the claim that Trade is ultimately useless there is no more than an inch, right?

PANGLOSS: No, my friend. What is useless is a Body from which the Soul has departed and what is even more useless is the illusion that a Body can be animated on its own, without the mediation of a Soul.

CACAMBO: Why do not you just get to the point of Trade?

PANGLOSS: International or Long Distance Trade in recorded history came from the craving for rare and consequently, luxury goods. These goods, as we shall see later on, are designed to bring excitement to the senses or to enhance the imagination. Their reason for being is the ultimately extra-physical quest for the thing in itself or for value in itself.

CACAMBO: What are these goods?

PANGLOSS: We can start with the Minoans[1] and the Phoenicians, who had a monopoly on the production of Purple.[2] Here is a color fast (non-fading dye) and it was believed that the intensity of the purple hue improved rather than faded as the dyed cloth aged.[3] The technology of producing purple has been lost today, ever since the fall of Constantinople in 1453 because the Byzantines never let the secret of making the purple dye pass to others.[4] It is purple which provided the impetus for the development of Trade in High Antiquity.

CACAMBO: What the hell has all this to do with the present? Have we not been told from all sides that what really counts is the future? If Progress is to be taken for the compass of economic activity, the past is nothing but a way to evaluate the distance we have covered by bettering ourselves in a given period of time.

THE SPIRIT: Yes. Here is the law of Progress. So, infallible is this law that not only me, but also all that stands on the left of the scene, and even almost all of those believing to be on the right, take the idea of Progress for granted.

PANGLOSS: Trade is a Monad. The Monads are on one hand without windows i.e. in themselves and on the other hand, infinite. Had a Monad been finite, it would be not a Monad but an atom and since any atom, is indivisible all economic activity would repeat itself just like the white rabbit from Alice in Wonderland who, is having tea all the time. Now, Progress had been made possible to come out as an idea or a dogma, only because its ultimate, organic link to atomism has been either shelved through the matrix of various modern 'ideologies' or disregarded in full consciousness.

CACAMBO: Are you not contradicting yourself at this very moment, since on one hand, you do not miss any occasion to suggest that the economic activity is a reflection of the supposedly immutable laws of Consciousness and the Human Psyche in particular, and on the other hand, you refer to the inconsistency of the ideology of Progress on this same matter, as an implicit expression of the Atomistic, Mechanical world view, where the Economy just as anything else is to be subjected at last resort to the repetition of one and the same combination, which by necessity is to reappear indefinitely in a mechanical Universe composed of indivisible material particles?

PANGLOSS: No, for sure. Have I not told you already that the Monad is the very opposite of the Atom, since the former is a simple expression of the immaterial or Substance, whereas the latter appears to the imagination as an inert hard mass, a tiny billiard ball. Now, should we apply the Monad to the sphere of economic activity, the Universal Law or the Forms of Consciousness are indeed one and the same, and it would be sheer absurdity to claim otherwise, but the action of these laws, their imprint on the manifested reality is never identical, since the Monad by being simple is simultaneously infinite. During a sea storm, the shape of the waves is always different, however slightly, but the sea is still the sea.

CACAMBO: Okay, fine, but is it not time to go back to Trade? You said earlier on that Long Distance Trade comes from the Psyche and has nothing to do with material necessity? Following this, would you be so kind as to enlighten me on the difference between those on the quest for the Grail and any ambulant salesman of spices, shouting to the passers-by, from some the dark, tiny alley of an Oriental Souk?

PANGLOSS: Already centuries before our own time, there appeared an inverted mirror, reflecting the Whole as divided in two antithetical halves. This is the here and now or the sensual perception of the body on one hand and the ever escaping horizon of the future where is erring a light and an essentially useless, harmless soul, on the other hand. The more the one is certain and solid, the less so is the other. As we said it already on several occasions, this optical illusion is related to the cyclic law of Manifestation. In the present Iron Age, the Maya appears as Essence and the Essence as Maya. Now, should we narrow the scope to the conditions of what is referred to as recorded history in the mainstream sources, this same optical illusion has been unfolding in basically three stages. The first stage, at least in the West, may be characterized as the Orphic stage, where the Soul together with the belief in Metempsychosis among both the Etruscans and the Thracians,[5] being depositors of the fragments of Scientific Knowledge, inherited from previous meta historical cycles, is already entrapped in matter, although the awareness of his true nature is still not extinct. During the second stage, the Gnostics and the Manicheans saw the Soul not as a mere stranger looking for his way in a hostile environment but as a harmless, although beautiful bird, locked in a cage and lamenting itself on his condition. The third and last stage comes out with the likes of Cesare Cremonini,[6] where the Soul is denied altogether. Later on however, this initially very conscious attempt to erase once and for all, one's awareness of being other than the body, has been gradually dissolved in the blind impulse for gratification, in the unconditional reflexes of livestock grazing the pasture of present day crass materialism within the confines, of what appears on the way to become, a global enclosure. Today, anyone is selling just anything to anyone else, except for one's Soul to the Devil, since there is no Soul nor a Devil any longer or is there after all?

CACAMBO: Have you not spoke on this already at the hotel?

PANGLOSS: The dichotomy between Spirit and Matter is a Pandora's Box, from where spring present day illusions, including the false perception of economic activity. Any occasion to mention this once more in a different setting and with different words is not to be passed by, since these illusions are dissolved in all spheres of modern life.

CACAMBO: The kind of continuity you are referring to is a textual, paper continuity, what is called these days history of ideas. Could you just specify how the dust on the pages of a forgotten manuscript somewhere on the shelves of a remote Monastery's library may be in a position to affect so to speak, the mainstream consciousness? Who cares about your Gnostics, Manicheans and so on, other than a theology or philosophy student, impatiently awaiting the grade for his latest term paper or an erudite of the like in Erasmus' 'Praise of Folly'?

PANGLOSS: What has been stated so far is based on the premise that the content precedes the form. The meaning of these writings is not tight to the ink that had been imprinted on the letters of the text, since it can fly away at any time from the pages of the manuscript.

CACAMBO: Okay, but how should you know where this same meaning once on the loose, ends its journey? What if it does nothing more than affecting in an unknown way, only a few isolated Monads scattered in some remote corner of the Universe, whereas at the same time you deceive yourself by taking the effect of this textual reality, on the world as a whole, for granted?

PANGLOSS: What is at stake here is the perception of reality as it is manifested in …

CACAMBO: Collective Consciousness?

PANGLOSS: By no means. Have we not insisted a short while ago on the essentially illusory, deceptive nature of such an absurd concept? The unfolding of Consciousness is going on through the Monads i.e. under no conditions these Monads so long as, there is a Manifested Consciousness, do dissolve in such an abstraction, devoid of inner consistency. The only reason for which this notion of Collective Consciousness or rather the Collective Unconscious is put forward, is to divert the attention from the center to the periphery and delegate the responsibility from its real place of origin i.e.

the center to its projected place of origin or the greatest number or the masses or most of the humans subjected to the supposedly and apparently free will of this same center.

Cacambo: So what then?

Pangloss: Look at our friend in the bottle!

Cacambo: I have seen him already.

The Spirit: What are you waiting for? Sadly, I am still here. So let me out for God's sake! I heard your speech where you just mentioned the Devil. Yes, I definitely agree with you! There is no Devil these days indeed and that is why if you release me, as I promised you already, you'll get everything you can imagine for free! I will not bother you with this soul kind of thing any longer! So, you'll have nothing to worry about!

Pangloss: I'll let you out! Just, be patient for now! (*To Cacambo*) Look at the Statue of Liberty this time!

Cacambo: Why?

Pangloss: I'll tell you later on. Now, just look in front of you right now!

*****

Cacambo: And so what?

Pangloss: Look again and keep your eyes in that direction.

Cacambo: You did not tell me why.

Pangloss: Watch at the Statue for a while without taking your eyes off and then tell me, what you see.

Cacambo: I see…wait a second. I see fire in a crowded place. An old man is burning on a pyre..And now the sea, a ship in the sea, a drummer is beating in a galley and the rowers act accordingly…A letter… more letters still, figures, triangles, squares in what appears to be a sheet of paper or a scroll…

Pangloss: What you see is the projection of the term Liberty in your mind corresponding to the Statue in front of you.

CACAMBO: Are you attempting to say that the concept of Liberty is coming out of these incoherent images and figures? They are already gone. I see nothing right now.

PANGLOSS: Yes. When you reflect on Liberty or anything else for that matter you see a succession of entities and then you forget about the whole thing. For a time, your consciousness appears to be a Tabula Rasa. And then, all of a sudden the concept comes out in the open. You say to yourself: 'This is so because it is not otherwise' or in other words, here is the limit of the object of Consciousness on which you have been reflecting, by the name of sufficient reason. And another thing: there is not a single iota of doubt on this point: I see, therefore I am. The puzzle of reality is rearranged in a way as to project an endless alignment of arguments in favor of the sudden appearance of the meaning or the genuinely rational limits, providing the substance of your concept. Once this synthetic, magic operation, involving countless entities has been completed in your Consciousness, you are certain that you saw what had to be seen. The non-physical nature of the whole process, and the outcome, deriving for this same process, so to speak, on the psychological level, has been made clear, for example, by Iamblichus, in his *Theurgia*, or *On the Mysteries of Egypt*.

CACAMBO: My dear friend, you seem to suggest that ghosts have priority in the assessment of objective reality over real creatures, be they humans, mosquitos, or whatever.

PANGLOSS: The apparent abyss separating, the senses from the invisible point of sufficient reason cannot be retraced empirically on a microscope, in the same way as the nature of electricity is not in its conductors such as copper or aluminum, or the meaning of the words you hear over the phone is not in the waves or in the wire that are conveying it, but in the Consciousness uttering these words. As a part is by necessity is conceivable only in relation to a whole, so the senses have no existence outside of the entity or Consciousness that is projecting them. Therefore, the sufficient reason is no other than the invisible to the naked eye, point of equilibrium between the Principle and its expressions taking place throughout the Cosmos.

CACAMBO: If it is invisible to the naked eye, so what is it visible to, then?

PANGLOSS: The visible is visible precisely because it plays the role of representation in relation to the invisible. Have I not told you before about the difference between a point in Consciousness and a point on blank paper? Whenever you attempt to arise, awareness on this same point as well as on the uncertainty of its precise location, the term intuition comes out of itself.

CACAMBO: Any animal has intuition, but does not have reason. So, is not following from your statement that the reflection on your point of equilibrium is hindering the intuition where the ultimate wisdom has taken shape?

PANGLOSS: Intuition is within Reason, not above, nor below. Emptied from the awareness of one's nature, Consciousness is like a broken clock spring, when for a time before coming to a halt, the clock's hands are still moving by inertia. The glorification of animal's intuition is a way to veil human's intuition. As a result, here is in reality an implicit glorification of blindness. It is also a false representation of animal's intuition as well, since the unconscious, built-in reflex is not the best appraisal of reality in given specific setting but the only possible appraisal for a creature that is essentially unable to make a free choice. So once again: intuition is the point of equilibrium between the visible and the invisible, where all layers of Consciousness intersect to produce awareness or the sufficient reason. The real origin of Knowledge is beyond the senses i.e. within itself.[8]

CACAMBO: What is standing in the way of Intuition in the present, so to speak, postmodern context?

PANGLOSS: At last resort, nothing, since the Monad having no windows, does not affect anything and it is not affected by anything either. However, these Monads are not really visible at this point, because the Sun is about to complete its daily cycle and therefore is about to set, and as a result of all this, it is getting dark. So, the whole thing at this stage appears not as a pack of cards, but as an intricate, synthetic, web of causes and effects affecting one another along the chain of being.

CACAMBO: As I see, there is no better than just take a rest and wait for the Sun to rise, right?

PANGLOSS: No, since the Cosmic Play or the dance of Shiva never stops. Otherwise I would not have been in a position, to bring you to this island, by the name of Liberty Island. By the way, do you have any matches?

CACAMBO: I did not know you are a smoker. Wait a second. Yes, I found one small matchbox I happen to keep in my pocket.

PANGLOSS: No, do not hand it to me. All I want you is just to strike one match, so that a flame appears in sight.

CACAMBO: Here is apparently another of you Night Club type illusionist tricks. Let me know, at least when the white rabbits will start coming out of your hat!

PANGLOSS: Would be so kind as to strike one match?

CACAMBO: Okay, and so what now?

PANGLOSS: Have you seen the flame?

CACAMBO: Yes I did.

PANGLOSS: The act of striking a match is an act of free will since you may have acted otherwise, after all.

CACAMBO: Definitely.

PANGLOSS: And yet, had it not been for the propensity of you own self for freedom, as an expression of the Human Self, you may not have struck the match and as a result there would be no fire, right?

CACAMBO: Why do not you just get straight to your point?

PANGLOSS: The flame we saw appeared only because phosphorus has something in itself that is making it catch fire.

CACAMBO: Fine.

PANGLOSS: Now, is it you who created fire or simply you set in motion something that was already there beforehand or the very existence of Fire in the first place and then, the possibility or the propensity of Fire to burn when a phosphorus match is stricken against the coarse striking surface on its edges?

CACAMBO: Yes, it is me.

PANGLOSS: It is you indeed, but has not all this been possible to take place, only in so far as you have the built-in propensity for Freedom, just like the Fire or the Phosphorus have also qualities in themselves, although these are different qualities from you own human like quality of Freedom?

CACAMBO: Are you not flatly contradicting yourself?

PANGLOSS: Only an infinitesimal amount of the intuition, we have been discussing so far is enough to make the absurdity of what you say self-evident. The Monad is pre-existent and free at the same time.

CACAMBO: Is not your intuition a quality in the first place?

PANGLOSS: Yes. I said 'amount' in the sense that any effort, apart from being an emanation from its ultimate source, in the same way as the rays of the Sun originate from the Sun, (and hence the frequent use of this symbolic representation in Antiquity.) does not take place in a separate compartment, but simultaneously, in the eternal here and now, and the immediate three dimensional here and now, where the intensity of this same effort may indeed, be measured. Now, free will is the quality per se, the sign of Life, where the cosmic game takes place. The contradiction is only apparent, since what initially appears as a pre-set mechanism, at a closer scrutiny turns out into the awareness of the Self, represented in ancient records, always negatively. Now, the expression, the manifestation of this awareness is conditioned within the ever shifting combinations of the four elements, in the same way as any game has its rules, so that even if you do not play by the rules, these same rules still apply but negatively. Now, what is therefore referred to, by the term 'conditioned' here, is the very opposite end of 'determined', let alone pre-determined. Determinism may appear as relevant only if you stick to the surface of reality. Now, the instilment of confusion between these, in reality opposite poles, is may be the most efficient way of making your natural propensity for reflection dysfunctional.

CACAMBO: As it is always the case with you, your initial point on the… International Trade, I guess, has been lost already a longtime ago.

PANGLOSS: No. Later on, you'll see why we had to take this turn, away from the subject per se. So, let's stay for the time being on this sub-subject of the subject of International Trade, in the same way as you may well open a window on a computer screen, then open another one, a link, and revert back to your first window in the end.

THE SPIRIT: What is this computer for? When I started wandering out there, Progress was measured by the speed of Steam boats and locomotives.

CACAMBO: You have missed the whole action, my friend. (*To Pangloss*) Why do you not let him out? He seems to be so far away of everything, which is also to say, he is harmless.

THE SPIRIT: Yes. I am definitely harmless! What I am really, is an innocent ghost waiting for some good rest on the loose!

PANGLOSS: I kindly ask you for some patience. Now, our sub-subject again: let's go back to the matches of a short a while ago. What if you are still in a position to execute this same operation that is, striking a match and thus, making Fire coming out of the dark, but without being aware of what you are doing?

CACAMBO: So where is the problem if you are still able to perform the task of striking the match?

PANGLOSS: At first, there should not be any problem, unless you repeat the whole operation and something goes wrong along the way. So, if your matchbox happens to be wet, after a rainfall, for example, you will not be able to produce Fire and since you are acting out of an automatic, blind impulse, you will not be aware why, this time there is no Fire and as a result, the whole operation will be aborted. Otherwise, you would have known that the match is to be dry and you would act accordingly, either by drying up your matchbox or by going to the nearby convenience store for another matchbox. In such a dreamlike, sleepwalker type condition, any change of the execution of the operation may turn out to be a puzzle that you are simple not able to resolve.

CACAMBO: What does your matchbox have to do with Economics?

PANGLOSS: The act of striking a match, as we have seen it already, is an expression of the intuition or the right effort for the appraisal of reality, and in our case economic reality in particular. Have you noticed that we insisted on the pre-established propensity for equilibrium of the Monad and on the essentially illusory nature of the very idea of cause and effect, since at last resort, reality is a pack of cards, in the sense that nothing affects anything, since ultimately everything is in itself or everything or every entity has its own sufficient reason. That is why the Monad has no windows. Things being what they are, you cannot alter reality in any way. What you can do however is to project your will either to what is above or to what is below, since you have will and this will is free. When you project it to what is below, your intuition becomes atrophied, and as a result you no longer have the awareness that is making you fully alive. You go down the road of conditional reflexes, where false images and systematic self-delusion will follow.

CACAMBO: So, there must be on one hand reality, that is economic reality, and on the other hand a projected reality. Yet I do not see why you had to take this turn toward abstract theory, whereas it would have been enough here, simply to state that basically you have the free will to say the truth or not to say the truth.

PANGLOSS: Once caught in the trap of self-delusion, Consciousness is divided between itself and its inverted or false representations. The whole world is projected in a gigantic reverse mirror. A new fantastic perception of Reality comes out, where the unreal by substituting itself temporarily to the real, becomes a reality in its own right. And this reality is the fantastic reality of present day representation of economic activity. Now, what has been of concern to us, up to this point was not to present our view on the consistency of modern economic theories, but presenting a perception of reality based on the Monad. Later on, we'll go to the question of the antithetical opposition between this same perception, based on the Monad and the false perception that made these theories or doctrines or ideologies possible in the first place.

THE SPIRIT: So what follows from this, is that one is not aware of one's actions.

PANGLOSS: Yes, and also that, one is not aware that one is denying in his thoughts what one is doing in his actions.

CACAMBO: Who is this 'one'?

PANGLOSS: All those who appear to be under the spell of what we have characterized as false perception of reality and the process of economic activity, imprinted in this reality, whoever they are and whatever they do, since this 'one' is confined not to the social, political or other limits but to the invisible limits of the perception itself.

CACAMBO: You refer to a kind of normative Antiquity all the time and when I asked you to stick for once to the present day post-modern context, you apparently eluded my question.

PANGLOSS: Before getting there, I had to present, however briefly a perception, which far from being a mere normative rhetoric has a living continuity, simultaneously with the ancient past as well as with the eternal present and all this has no other intent than retracing what the immediate present is all about.

CACAMBO: Listen, I am fed up with your propensity for sweeping generalizations and your basically incorrect insistence on, say, the completeness of the whole versus the incompleteness of its parts.

PANGLOSS: Do you see this forgotten newspaper on the next table. Could you just bring it here?

CACAMBO: Don't you see it is covered with mud, in all likelihood brought about by the latest rain in combination with the last summer wind.

PANGLOSS: Bring it here and when we go back to the shore, I'll offer you the best dinner fiat money can buy.

THE SPIRIT: And me? What about me? I am also hungry.

CACAMBO: How come you are hungry? You are not supposed to be hungry under no circumstances. I wonder what kind of ghost you are, after all. (*To Pangloss*): Okay. Your God damn paper is right here on the table now.

Pangloss tears down the paper in several parts.

CACAMBO: What are you doing?

PANGLOSS: I am tearing down the remnants of this newspaper. Could you just tell me what do you see on this cut in front of you right now?

CACAMBO: I see what it remains of something that appears to have been a picture at one time.

Pangloss tears down the rests of the paper in ever smaller parts.

PANGLOSS: And now?

CACAMBO: There is apparently a text like spot on the left corner, just above the number of the page, one or may be eleven or fifteen or whatever, since the other part is missing.

PANGLOSS: Great! What you just saw is the so called 'objective' reality, the reality provided by your senses, by empirical observation, by, so to speak, several centuries of cultural development.

CACAMBO: I agree on your last point. Have not newspaper cuts of the same variety been wrapped in the label Art and sold for tones of fiat paper throughout the world?

PANGLOSS: Would you let me finish? I was just about to make it clear that these same newspaper cuts would indeed have been all that is left from reality, save for the Intuition we talked about already. It is this Intuition and this Intuition only that makes it possible to find out the One in the Many or to distinguish gold form sand. It is this Intuition that unveils the abyss separating the Human condition from the surrounding flora and fauna on this planet.

CACAMBO: So your Intuition is the essence of Humanity and therefore the most human feature within anything that seems to be human.

PANGLOSS: Definitely not. Intuition is the Spirit or the Essence or the ultimate Monad or the Universe. Man is a circle within a circle.

CACAMBO: Fine words, yet you can relate your conclusion about the nature of so to speak, the whole thing, on just anything under the Sun, where our subject of International Trade is only one among so many other subjects.

PANGLOSS: Once you leave the intuitive point of awareness of the One among the Many, where the principle of uncertainty prevails, you confuse the innate, a priori perception of unity with the Elements, by ascribing absolute existence or perfect simplicity to what is in reality a composite entity.

CACAMBO: And what about the Monad? Are you not proceeding in the same way with the Monad? How is it, that such a simple entity may be simultaneously entrapped in the composite nature of the Elements?

PANGLOSS: The Consciousness of the Monad is precisely this same intuitive point, since the ultimate Essence or Unity is manifested within the sufficient reason or the right effort or the right perception, where nothing is entrapped in nothing, but it is only projected as the rays of the Sun are projected in the composite reality of the Earth. The division of Consciousness with itself leads to the falsest of all false representations: the apparently insurmountable abyss between the One and the Many, the Body and the Soul, Spirit and Matter.

CACAMBO: Where is fiat money in all that?

PANGLOSS: Let's assume for the sake of courtesy that Fiat Money or Gold or Silver, are essentially the representations of the attraction of the Psyche to what is below or to Matter, since there is no better term for describing the nature of this same attraction as greed, which comes somehow out of itself or is simply self-evident.

CACAMBO: This time you definitely contradict yourself. Have you not already forgotten that you insisted a short while ago on the spiritual essence of Gold?

PANGLOSS: Any medium of exchange is by definition oriented toward the visible with naked eye since it is not possible to buy an Essence or a Quality per se. It is only possible to buy its expressions and what is more, its physical expressions that may be counted and moved. You can collect and sell solar rays but you cannot sell the Sun, no more than you can sell hot Air or Sympathy or the entire Galaxy, since for the time being there is still no way of transferring any constellation from one corner of the Universe to another or deposit a Star in someone's bank account. Therefore, it is in this sense and in this sense only that we said that Gold and any other medium of exchange are the expressions of the attraction to what is below. However, since in the last resort, what is below as well as what is above are the two sides of the same coin, where the ultimate Unity stands in all eternity, there is a point of equilibrium or a point of intuitive awareness of the ever present possibility of counteracting the attraction to Matter with the attraction to Spirit, and thus having a free reign on the Elements. The ultimately Spiritual nature of any form of Maya becomes manifest in the meditation on the Principle of greed. The assumption according to which, it is somehow impossible to master greed in general and in respect to Fiat Money or Gold in particular is an absurdity, since implicitly such an assumption means that greed has no principle of manifestation and in practice leads to a form of Consciousness characterized by the abject surrender to blindness or blind greed.

CACAMBO: If someone is really blind, this is definitely you! You are disserting on something that is so omnipresent, so self-evident!

PANGLOSS: It is omnipresent, indeed in the same way as darkness is no more real that light simply because you have just woke up in the middle of the night. Now, let's stay for a while on what we referred to above as the Principle of Greed. So, would you not agree that if greed is everything that really counts, since greed is the body, the impulse of the body, then there would be no such entity as Soul? It is this same perception, based on the dichotomy between body and soul that is making appear injustice, disloyalty, greed and outright cruelty as natural as the rising of the Sun on a permanent basis, since the daily volume of the transactions on the various world markets is in the tenths of trillions.

CACAMBO: How is your dichotomy related to the syndromes you described earlier?

PANGLOSS: What we saw as the Digestive Tube Syndrome, the Liverpool Syndrome and the Woodstock Syndrome are the modern and postmodern versions of blindness or the veil of Maya. Being essentially empty i.e. without any positive content all of these by their very nature are impermanent states of mind, whose crystallization naturally leads to their own negation and to a tide of socio economic destruction. The waning of ancient structures, be it Egypt or Pre Colombian America or China etc. based on Metaphysics required thousands of years, whereas modern forms follow one after the other in a frenzy that started only a few centuries and may end from one meta historical moment to the next. As the likes of Sardanapalus knew it very well in their time, the power exercised by slaves, at last resort turns to be as shaky as the ground sustaining a forest of skyscrapers built out of low quality concrete during an earthquake. Now, you as you can say 'No' so you can also say the opposite or 'Yes', since there is no Yes without No, right?

CACAMBO: And so what?

PANGLOSS: If you think or rather believe that greed is omnipresent but in spite of this, there is still a Soul, would not this Soul appear to you as being somehow detached form the Body?

CACAMBO: Yes, such a Soul would be, by necessity, separate from the Body.

PANGLOSS: Separate and at the same time alien and weak, since let's not forget that what is real and therefore omnipresent and all powerful from this point of view is the Body, right?

CACAMBO: Maybe.

PANGLOSS: Now, what if you submit to the impulses of the body and yet you still love the Soul? Would not your version of the Soul appear as beautiful and the more beautiful it would be, the more you'll attempt to alienate it from the harsh, and yet real form of the Body?

CACAMBO: Where are you getting at?

PANGLOSS: Would you not get in this way, the best of all possible worlds, since on one hand, you submit to the impulses of the body or blind greed and nothing is hindering you from doing so, because this is the only possible reality in the immediate present and on the other hand you take your ideal, beautiful self to be your real self by convincing yourself of the impossibility to reach it anywhere else than in the ever escaping horizon of the future?

CACAMBO: Yes, the ideal would become real only in the future whereas the real would remain real only in the present.

PANGLOSS: Is not this abyss between the Soul and the Body justifying your submission to blind greed in the here and now at the expense of the eventual freedom of the Soul in the future?

THE SPIRIT: Yes. Let me out and I'll tell you a lot on that, since I am an expert on the future, after all.

CACAMBO: Hello, I did not know, you happen to be an expert at all! I always thought that you are essentially evolving within the limits of a term, invented back in our own time, that is: 'ideology'.

PANGLOSS: Do you realize that what is at stake here is not the future per se, but a perception of the future, following the ontological separation between Body and Soul in the Psyche?

CACAMBO: If the future is already unfolded in your perception, then why should you bother looking beyond the present at all?

PANGLOSS: When you see an egg, be it a serpent egg, a chicken egg or the Cosmic Egg itself, provided you are in the human condition and beyond, you may well know when the chicken will come out in the open and how it will come out. Furthermore, if you happen to distinguish a serpent egg from a chicken egg, you'll make no mistake about the form of the being that will hatch the egg at some point in the future. What you cannot know, however, at least most of the time, is what will happen to the chicken when it will already be out of the egg since an earthquake may take place, at this very moment and the existence of the new born chicken may take an unexpected turn as a result. Now, you my friend in the bottle, you and the kinds of you, as we shall see more closely later on, when I let you out, you had the absurd pretention of knowing all moments of the above chicken' s life in their entirety. And if this had been so, it is because you implicitly refused to make a distinction between what is alive and what is dead. You simply transposed the grotesque mechanics of the free fall kind of thing to society and as a result, under the label of Historical Materialism you draw the most extravagant conclusions, and you wrapped the whole package under the name of 'Scientific…' whatever!

CACAMBO: You perception seems so opaque! If it is to become more transparent, there must be some obstacles along the way.

PANGLOSS: At last resort, there are no obstacles whatsoever since electricity is forever present in the atmosphere whether you like it or not.

CACAMBO: Okay, fine. You already presented all these generalities. Do not you have something more specific to say at this point?

PANGLOSS: The perception in question is veiled at least to some extent, by the meaning ascribed to the term Freedom by the modern and now postmodern cultural assembly line. The shadows operating the whole thing, find it, on one hand, rather correct to diffuse in one way or another, the most absurd, outright grotesque type of determinism and on the other hand, in the name of their version of Freedom as well as in the name of what they call, 'objective truth' these same figures, pretend to free themselves from pre-conceived notions, where nothing appears as more pre-conceived, so to speak, in their eyes than precisely the perception we spoke so far. Should we retrace the source of their concern for the Freedom of thought, we have to look at the concept of the Tabula Rasa, invented back in our own time. Freedom, they say is simply nothing.

CACAMBO: How come nothing? Is not there a Statue here, devoted to Liberty?

PANGLOSS: Yes, had there been possible for 'something', including the chicken from above, to come out in the open as 'nothing', there would be no way to erect a Statue or a monument of any kind to Freedom, since the latter would have been emptied of any positive content.

CACAMBO: Except I guess the content of…well…the thing you just said…

PANGLOSS: Yes, Tabula Rasa.

CACAMBO: Is not this Tabula Rasa by its mere existence as a concept a flat contraction of its own content?

PANGLOSS: Yes, and at the same time it is an attempt, for instant annihilation of any positive assertion or representation of the sufficient reason for any entity. Should we assume that the perception or the intuition of the One in various degrees of self-awareness is immediately present to Consciousness or is Consciousness per se, the idea of Tabula Rasa would appear not as a mere veil, but as a thick curtain obscuring the nature of Consciousness and leading to an atrophy of the Psyche now having no access to the subtle reality or the intelligible essences, which, as in a true reverse mirror are reflected in the mind as details and the details as substance. How many times have you heard the allegedly profound truth of the so called 'harsh reality' of life or whatever, where the supposedly self-evident 'objective validity' of the crudest sensitive impressions is taken for granted without a blink of an eye?

CACAMBO: Yes, but being hidden your perception does not seem to be of any value, since it is not operative.

PANGLOSS: Any tyrant, including the Monarch in this… short story by the name of 'The Little Prince',[8] who if you do not remember or you do not know, is living on a small planet, where his only subject happens to be a mouse, and is spending his time by giving orders to the Sun to rise and set, so… any tyrant basically, likes the idea of, so to speak, modeling, of molding reality, including the way of thinking of his subjects, at will. As a result, the tailors came out and made a new garment for our Sovereign with incrusted 'narratives' on his sleeves and his collar. Having said that, our perception is equally valid either veiled or unveiled.

CACAMBO: So, why then bother of presenting it at all since your perception happens to be so indifferent to the plight of living creatures, including humans?

PANGLOSS: There is hardly anything more human than the awareness of the Self or the perception of Non-duality. If there is to be Human nature, the free will in the way to or respectively out of this awareness would be its key feature.

CACAMBO: How your perception is affecting International Trade and the Economy?

PANGLOSS: The perception of the One in the Many in itself, as we said it already on many occasions, does not affect anything. What does affect reality, however, is the free will or the awareness of this perception. You always act on what is possible to happen or you never act on what is impossible to happen. Yet, when you act consciously the outcome is one and when you act unconsciously the outcome is another. Reality has two layers, the relative and the absolute.[9] Now, should you take the awareness of this perception as a starting point in the appraisal of today's economic activity, there are two ways of expressing this awareness: a descriptive way, where reality ceases to appear as it seemed to be within the framework of the various economic concepts, as these were established starting from our own time in the 18th century. And an active way, where a specific freely established cause gives a concrete and a predictable result.

CACAMBO: How does the Modern Economy look like from the angle of your perception in its descriptive dimension?

PANGLOSS: The Modern Economy, starting from a little further than our own time, at the beginning of the 19th century, at its core, is a crystallization or the outward expression of a false perception of reality, where the positive representations of Consciousness remain dormant or latent or in potency and the negative representations take an outward expression or appear in act.

CACAMBO: This is an empty abstraction, a fantasy.

PANGLOSS: Words are like fiat money, since you can borrow words in the same way as you can borrow paper, and now plastic banknotes, with the only difference that when you take credit from any Bank you know at least its initial amount, that is the principal without the interest, whereas when you borrow words under no circumstances you are to know that these words are taken from the Invisible Hand or the Invisible Bank of the Psyche. Now, the more your individual Consciousness is alienated from itself, the less access you have to the Thing in itself and respectively the greater is the propensity of your mind to fill the resulting vacuum with staff from this same Invisible Bank or from the outside or from the inner space of the Psyche or in a more restrained sense, from a given state of mind. Further on, it goes without saying that all concepts or images that tend to put your Reason on a sleep mode have the notable contribution of raising the stock price of the Invisible Bank, so to speak, on a bubble type level. Also, the already mentioned estrangement of the Mind from its Essence naturally leads to intellectual immaturity and an enhanced herd like reflex, where a given term or combination of terms sets in motion the pre-established effects of those propagating them, including the suppression of a free reflection on the difference between things as they are and things as they seem to be.

CACAMBO: So, according to your perception, there are two Economies, the one perceived, in a reverse mirror and another one, a real one most of the time unperceived in full consciousness.

PANGLOSS: Yes, in the same way as a sleepwalker is not aware that at this very moment he may well be on the roof of the Empire State Building or may be passing by Socrates, at the moment when the latter is still debating on the Thing in itself with his opponents, the Sophists. The starting point of the real economy is not in the solid matter or what appears to be so. It is in the specific atmosphere or invisible form of the Psyche, where lies its modern and now postmodern substance. In the same way, when you plant seeds deep down the Earth, these seeds do not arise spontaneously from the soil, although they are to be in an appropriate environment, since it is you who planted them from the outside or so to speak, from above the ground, and their subsequent evolution has been already built-in themselves and therefore by no means created from nothing by the soil that is surrounding them. Once this atmosphere or invisible form becomes accessible to full consciousness, what appears in the first place, is the abyss between Body and Soul or the built-in unawareness of the existence of a mediator between the one and the other, where the point of Primeval Unity is coming out of obscurity. Now, it is here, within the atmosphere permeated by this division of reality in two halves or separation or dichotomy that is hidden the ultimate source of Modernity and the matrix producing on the visible surface or the cultural, economic, social etc. sphere one absurdity after another. Presenting a Modern History of Ideas, including Economic Ideas, without any reference to this atmosphere or from the Tabula Rasa of pseudo objectivity is in reality the same as simply refusing to acknowledge that the newspaper cuts, that I just dispersed on the ground a short while ago, have been at one time a whole, that is an integral part of a newspaper, and that this same newspaper initially was not covered with mud, since it came out of the printing press clean and undamaged.

CACAMBO: How this separation is affecting the economy, including International Trade, on which up to this point you said not more than a few sentences?

PANGLOSS: Do you see that stone over there, behind the next table?

CACAMBO: What stone?

THE SPIRIT: Yes I saw it, right there. This is at least a five pounds granite stone.

CACAMBO: And so what?

PANGLOSS: Could you just bring it here? You have it? Great! Now, would you tell me what will happen if you just throw this stone into the sea?

CACAMBO: It will sink to the bottom, I guess.

PANGLOSS: This stone is a Body with no Soul. The free fall of this stone is like the coming free fall of the Modern Economy, based on the sanctification of greed or the blind impulse of desire. Some of the participants in this process are aware of what is going on, others are aware only from time to time or for briefs periods of time and still others are not aware of anything. Yet all of them take blind desire to be the only possible ultimate expression of the human condition. Anything that stands against greed, from this angle appears as a mere convention, a temporary departure from the state of nature or from the very essence of life. It goes without saying that we can give credit for this notable achievement to the various developments in the sphere of the history of ideas, taking place in Europe, more than a century before our own time, including the core precepts of the then dismal science, since the latter had already made its appearance in Venice. Beyond the changes that took place during the various stages of the modern economy, since our own time, beyond the real meaning of the many apparently different economic theories, beyond the spider web like legal framework of the Basel III[10] variety, beyond the convulsions of the Great October Crash type, there is a specific perception of reality, imprinted in the most subtle layers of the Psyche. This blind subjection to what is below in the human nature is the result of several centuries of methodical nihilism denying the very idea of equilibrium, on which rests the awareness of the Spirit or anything of real value in this world and in the best of the best of all possible worlds.

THE SPIRIT: Why do you put all your eggs in the same basket? If it had been as you say, why then should I have come out in the open to haunt Europe back in the 19th century?

PANGLOSS: If fiat money is to be equated with something other than paper, it is the blind impulse of desire or greed, as they say.

CACAMBO: Great! You just seem to have discovered a new key Natural Law!

PANGLOSS: No my friend, if there is to be a Natural Law, here is the Law of all Laws or the Law of Polarity, where the whole Universe gravitates around the cosmic point of equilibrium emanating from this same Law. Further in this vein, there is nothing to discover at this point and at any point, since this Law has been all around form the beginning of time. Had it not been for this Law, there would not be a single stock market in operation throughout the world or else there would simply not have been possible for any financial Bubble to burst, ever since the very idea of exchange came so to speak, into existence.

THE SPIRIT: Do you remember that I stood against…well…against capital and money… and therefore against greed?

PANGLOSS: Yes, you denied money or blind desire in the name of this same blind desire.
THE SPIRIT: What?

PANGLOSS: If Money = Blind Desire = Body # Soul = Modern Economy or as you say: 'Capitalism', then you denied Money and therefore, Money = 0 = Blind Desire = Body

= 0 = Modern Economy = 0, since for you there should be no longer Blind Desire, no more than a Body a Soul or anything for that matter. Now, this, say, integral denial is in reality no other than the universal leveling down, labeled as Equality.

Cacambo: If all this is thin air or pure vacuum how is it that our friend is still alive and what is more, how was he able to make such a perilous transatlantic crossing? And there is even more: how is he alive at all, since something does not come from nothing in the sense that it is always coming from something else?

Pangloss: What else may be the propelling force of the bulldozer that had been leveling down any vertical arrangement of the Elements in the inner layers of the Psyche other than, this same greed in its negative expression of envy that led to the denigration of the very idea of exchange and therefore Money as well?

Cacambo: You did not answer my question.

Pangloss: The world of fiat money being essentially a huge soap like bubble has been unfolding within a particular time sequence, which as you very well know started somewhere at the end of the 17th century. So, as any pre-set mechanism of the time-bomb type, fiat money has its specific way of manifesting itself, it has its own forms with a very precise meaning, whereas you my friend in the bottle, you wanted to destroy this world, before the latter had been destroyed out of itself, and you had nothing other than mere envy and resentment to fill the empty space that you would have caused, were your plan to succeed, following the end of WWI. Now, as the very idea of empty space is never the ultimate expression of reality, but only an appearance, since at last resort there is no such thing as emptiness, you filled this apparent vacuum in the places where your experiment was carried out with the display of the most absurd decisions, such as for example the home made steel furnaces in China, including your uncontested expertise in Production Fetishism in general, bureaucratic chaos, senseless brutality etc. These are the most absurd decisions that had ever been taken, at least in the last few thousands of years of recorded history. So, you unleashed the same current of blindness and greed in the name of the denial of fiat money.

Cacambo: And the cause for all this, say, fascination with fiat money, as an expression of greed is I guess, according to you, in the distorted perception of the Self, where the last cause lies in the absolute separation between Body and Soul or the visible versus the invisible?

Pangloss: Yes, Materialism at last resort is either a denial of the Spirit, including the Soul or the evacuation of the Soul in an inaccessible beyond, so that the outbreak of blind desire may not be hindered to reach its utmost limits, somewhere on the bottom of the sea.

Cacambo: Is your exposé over?

Pangloss: Only the part dealing with the Principle is over. Now, from this same ontological separation or Manichean optical illusion springs, so to speak, in the open the institutionalized, sanctification of greed or blind desire or quantity for its own sake or fiat money or the worship of the Golden Calf, resulting at last resort in spiritual mutilation and material self-destruction.

Cacambo: Have you finished already?

Pangloss: No. This same cult of Quantity or fiat money, as we know it on both sides of the Atlantic has another side, in the same way as any coin has two sides.

The Spirit: Yes, That is why I have been haunting Europe, and now the whole world ever since your own time, the 18th century.

Pangloss: The other side of the coin is the denial of fiat money or any form of money and ultimately any form of exchange. This is a wave of pure, unrefined, condensed hatred of oneself as well the Thing in Itself. So, on one hand there is the worship of fiat money and on the other hand the opposite, the denial of money. However, as we said it already, this denial is not in the name of the opposite end of greed or the spiritual end, but in the name of the very reason that made possible the emergence of fiat money, that is in the name of greed, although in an indirect, implicit way. It goes without saying that at a closer scrutiny this implicit way, becomes explicit in no time, since the pseudo ideal of equality or what is a leveling down from below in reality is driven by envy and greed or the blind impulse to what is below.

Cacambo: Is not this denial a legitimate reaction to the whole process of monetization and now, say, 'fiatisation' of social and private life as well?

Pangloss: Let me finish what I am presenting at this point, at least for the time being without an escape in the realm of 'what ought to be… or what has to be' since right now, what counts is to see what is really going on, not what should be going on.

Cacambo: What is going on is that greed is just everything.

Pangloss: It is everything to a form of Consciousness where the world appears in a reverse mirror. When they say that greed is driving the economy, including profit, most of the time this is another expression of the massive, monumental self-delusion that is at the very core of Modernity and yet in some, rather rare occasions it may be simply a blatant lie, since among the tailors, there are those who are aware that the Emperor is basically naked. Greed is a passive state, a blind impulse and as such cannot drive anything. Hence the constant confusion between greed and profit, where greed is taken for what it is not, an active force, whereas the opposite is true: greed is an effect and not a cause. It is a passive state of being or a subjection to the blind impulse to what is below. This is in all likelihood, the most effective way of making parasitism appear as the opposite, since, on the ontological level, greed is a reverse effort.

CACAMBO: Do you see from your Ivory Tower, the on-going fight between Bears and Bulls, on the still functioning floor of the Stock Market right now and the wavering of the crowd gathered around the very places where these daily combats are taking place?

PANGLOSS: There is hardly anything more intimate to any living creature on this planet that the rays of the Sun and yet, these same rays are coming from millions and millions of miles, where their source is to be found. Further on, if you happen to be lost somewhere in a dark tunnel of the Underground during a power cut, would your eventual knowledge on electricity and conductors of electricity be of any help?

THE SPIRIT: My dear friends, would you just pay attention to the fact that, only me and me only, I am able to direct the movements of the wave of agitation that is going on right now?

PANGLOSS: That is why for the time being you'd better stay where you are.

CACAMBO: What will happen if fiat money is suppressed in the name of Equality and the exchange of goods replaced by Distribution?

PANGLOSS: The root of such an occurrence is precisely in the false perception of Body and Soul, where the Soul seems either inexistent or separate from the Body. Hence, the Psyche makes the fruitless attempt to free itself from the subjection to the representations of blind greed standing behind the orgy of the printing press, propagating countless banknotes in the air, by burning these same banknotes in a huge furnace built for that purpose. Yet, once the banknotes are no longer on the loose, there is nothing left other than the very impulse that had made the whole operation of burning possible. So, you are back at blind greed, with the only difference that there is a kind of vacuum now, in the sense that this impulse of greed is waiting to be filled with something. As we said it already earlier on, at last resort there is no such thing as distribution, since nothing is free, although this may appear to be so for a time. Now, both the expansion and the suppression of fiat money are essentially directed to the same goal: the deconstruction of Civilization or the dissolution of the human condition in something else, but in different time frames. Compared to the 'expansion', the 'suppression' is unfolding within an accelerated time frame, since a general repetition of this same scenario already took place following WWI.

CACAMBO: How is it that you put in the same basket two seemingly antithetic entities? Are not those who stand against fiat money opposed to those who stand against distribution?

PANGLOSS: These are different branches of the same tree. In the very likely event of a storm in the forest, these branches due to the strong wind may indeed oppose each other or even break at some point. Yet, below the surface of Politics, are the immutable laws of Consciousness, including Meta Politics.

CACAMBO: How do these apparently antithetic entities come to express their Metaphysical essence in the sphere of Meta Politics and lastly Politics?

PANGLOSS: The wind shaking the branches of the tree is this same blind desire we spoke of in so many occasions up to now. Once Distribution takes the place of Exchange, in the sphere of Economics comes out the problem of Economic calculation. Now, at this point, whatever the rhetoric or the immediate social or historical surroundings the only possible way of allocating resources is through subordination and the corresponding irresponsibility, leading to the destruction of the whole system, since, economic voluntarism or irrationality becomes the only norm of exercising economic activity. Now, this same process as we said it already, may be started all at once, from above or as the result of a radical political change or gradually through the 'fiatization' of the Economy and the corresponding 'communization' of Society.

CACAMBO: Is not something like a radical change to take place also along what you refer to as the gradual path of creeping 'communization'?

PANGLOSS: Yes, but in this case, it is not the radical political change that comes first, but the very opposite, it is the economic change, in the sense that the political change has to be preceded by an economic crisis, as the last step before the establishment of the new economic system based on Distribution.

CACAMBO: Have you not said already that such a system is doomed, since there will be no rational way of economic calculation?

PANGLOSS: This is so only on the last resort. So, the question at this point is how long such a 'last resort' may last? It may be a whole historical epoch. History does not repeat itself in the way similar to the rabbit from Alice in Wonderland, who, if you do not mind, is in hurry for an appointment and is having tea all the time. The last experiment with Distribution, starting in 1917, and ending with a fiasco a few decades later, may be only an accidental repetition on a smaller scale of the world to come, since everything is global these days.

CACAMBO: I guess by 'economic' calculation you mean market prices, which cannot exist in a context of Distribution?

PANGLOSS: Yes, but now it is my turn to remind you that, our initial subject was on the origin of International Trade and that is why we'll pass to this key point later on, for example after you have taken the dinner you have been expecting so far.

CACAMBO: You used to speak on Purple and the origin of International Trade and I asked you, if you still remember, to specify the difference between the quest for the Grail and the selling of spices in any oriental souk, since according to you Purple, and I guess Spices too, have a non-economic origin and are essentially also a way to look for the Thing in Itself?

PANGLOSS: Yes. The difference in question is only a difference in degree and by no means a difference in kind, since if International Trade in its very source appears as antithetic to the quest for the Grail, this is so because of this same optical illusion in the Psyche, we spoke so far, where the ultimate Unity between Body and Soul is obscured and the resulting, dichotomy is paving the way for a social deconstruction on a large scale. By the way, this dichotomy was not as pronounced as it is today, since, something like three centuries before our own time, the quest for the Grail may not have been that different for the then Psyche, than, for example, the quest for the Kingdom of The Prester John.[11]

CACAMBO: What is the difference in degree?

PANGLOSS: A difference in degree is not a difference in quantity: it is a difference in direction.

CACAMBO: So, these are opposite ways, I guess.

PANGLOSS: These ways are like the journey of Columbus to the western hemisphere, since you can go to India both ways, either heading west or east, where the only difference is the time frame. International Trade has its source, as we said it earlier, in substances related to the condition of the Psyche, and hence, is different from the basic agricultural produce, dealing with physical survival. Purple as a representation of beauty is related to contemplation, sugar and spices to pleasure for the senses, coffee and tea are pleasant to the mind and opium to the idea of happiness, where a certain price is to be paid for a representation of happiness, since this is not the result of one's own effort, but the effect of an intervention grafted from the outside and therefore, a simulation or a copy of happiness.

CACAMBO: Is International Trade the shortest way to the Grail?

Pangloss: According to one of the eighty four Mahasiddhas, a guru by the name of Kankanapa: Once upon a time, there lived a king in India who was very proud of his wealth. He was approached by an ascetic monk who told him: Do not let yourself be blinded by your Gold, since in this world suffering and the cycle of rebirth turn in circle as a wheel' The King said: 'In my position, I cannot serve the Dharma in the cloth of an ascetic. But if you can give me an advice that I could accomplish in conformity with my own nature and abilities without changing outwardly my way of life, then I am ready to accept it.' The Yogi knew that the King used to like precious stones in particular very much and that is why he chose, this very inclination of the King as a starting point for meditation. In this way he transformed his own weakness in a source of inner strength. He told the King: 'Contemplate the diamonds of your necklace, direct you spirit on them in the following way; they shine with all the colors of the rainbow; and yet all these colors that make me feel happy, do not possess their own nature. The spirit itself is the shining precious stone, the incomparable, priceless stone, from where all things get their passing reality.'[12]

Cacambo: My dear friend, had your tale been known by the onetime Conquistadors, sailors of the Pirate or East India Company variety and other fortune - hunters of the Gold Rush type, the world as we know it today, would certainly have been a very different place. By the way, once we get back to the shore, why do not you just make this suggestion to the horde of money changers operating at this very moment on the island of Manhattan?

Pangloss: At this point, my tale may indeed seem irrelevant, because gold and precious stones do not count any more, since banknotes have taken their place. Furthermore, the Soul in any of its versions does not seem to possess enough imagination so that it might reincarnate itself in a piece of used, low quality paper. However, I still insist on the validity of my tale, since the nature of International Trade is not a figure neither an accounting nor a statistical unit.

Cacambo: So what is it then?

Pangloss: Have we not pointed out already on several occasions that the prevailing assumption, either explicit or implicit, according to which Trade came out in the open somehow from an amorphous, anonymous, unconscious process of quantitative accumulation, which our friend in the bottle used to call 'surplus' or 'division of labor' is a fiction or so to speak, pure sand or thin air? Should we admit the traditional separation of the human self, where the Physical body envelops a little like a Russian doll, an Astral and a Causal body, the items which made possible the emergence of International Trade correspond to the second body and the third body, since Purple, Sugar, Coffee, Tea or Opium affect in an ascending degree, the centers of consciousness where the human and only human state of the Psyche is present, based on the perception of the Thing in itself or Non-Duality. Now, from a Meta historical point of view, it is no coincidence that International Trade appeared precisely in the Iron Age or the Kali Yuga or after the Deluge, since the veil of consciousness, at this stage causes, a constant confusion between appearance and substance, where the relative is taken for its opposite. Therefore, the mere realization that the body is not cut from the soul, in the same way as a shadow has no existence by itself leads to a different appraisal of reality, including economic reality.

Cacambo: So, being illusion, International Trade in your vision should be pure evil, I guess?

Pangloss: By no means. In the post-deluge conditions, the wanderings of the Psyche along the lines of International Trade is not only inevitable, but also very positive, since although an illusion as far as the ultimate essence is concerned, it is still an effort and therefore, a free opportunity to restore the lost mastery over the elements during the previous Ages and at the same time it is a representation of the cosmic game taking place throughout the Universe.

Cacambo: What is the problem, then?

Pangloss: It is the proportion, the relative importance accorded to such an activity. After a certain level the further expansion of International Trade is a time-bomb, disrupting the last remnants of economic and social equilibrium.

Cacambo: How did International Trade disrupted this equilibrium, which I guess you'll take for granted, still existed in our own time?

Pangloss: The point of equilibrium as far as trade is concerned was indeed still in place, up to the end of the 18th century. You should not forget however, that the larger point, or rather circle or Globus, was already much too heavy for Atlas' shoulders with the beginning of the Iron Age or Kali Yuga, where all sources on the use of cosmic energy and practical metaphysical knowledge were a mere souvenir, represented in the ever more fragmentary, cryptic records dating back form the distant antediluvian past, that, by the way, may have been presented, for example in the lost books of Manetho or Berosus.[13] As you'll see later on, the ancient galleys which used to be more or less the same from the time of Odysseus up to the battle of Lepanto are no match to a present day Liner of the Queen Elizabeth variety. The thing is, that once the tremendous progress that has been accomplished since our own time, reaches a certain point of development, the unwillingness , so to speak, for an ontological reversal, turns the use of technology into the most efficient destructive force or time bomb on record.

Cacambo: Would you be more specific on what you really mean by 'reversal'?

PANGLOSS: In the first place, a reversal of perception. Once the veil of materialistic obscurantism is lifted from the inner layers of Consciousness, the ghostlike nature of present day economic reality will simply vanish. The economic activity will no more be separated into what one is really doing on one hand and what one perceives to be doing on the other hand, since, once applied to the exchange and the production of goods, the Principle of Polarity or Equilibrium will arrange the puzzle of all variables into a harmonious whole. Present day Economy, will be put on a balanced diet, and thus will no longer be looking like the swelling giant from the logo of the Michelin tires, stuffing himself with one ham burgher after another.

CACAMBO: Why do not you just give a concrete example how your perception is operating on the micro economic level?

PANGLOSS: Every stock trader up there on the shore as well as on our own continent Europe, where most of the Foreign Exchange is still carried out through the City of London, does not have to go to the zoo for observing the behavior of Bulls and Bears, since both are constantly displayed in his view, either on the floor or lately, on a computer screen.

CACAMBO: Are you a veterinarian doctor?

PANGLOSS: No. The Bull is a representation of the blind impulse of desire or greed, whereas the Bear epitomizes fear. Now, it is the right effort or the balance between greed and fear that is the key for financial survival or better still successful trading. This same right effort, the trader has to make is no other than an expression of the perception or the intuition we have described so far by using terms, borrowed from philosophy and metaphysics. What is in action here is the cosmic polarity or the law of equilibrium, since the right effort is identical with the point where these two opposing trends intersect. However, once out of his screen, our trader who makes this same effort, most of the time, unconsciously, will profess consciously exactly the opposite view, since he has been indoctrinated to pay homage to materialism or blind greed, and hence, he will take for granted views that are not really his own, but borrowed from the writings of individuals who in reality never exercised this activity. Had not the worship of blind desire been established, in one way or another as the credo of Modernity, there would simply no such thing as fiat money on this planet. Fiat money is not exchange either, since it is essentially based on the illusion that you can take something without giving anything in return.

CACAMBO: And where is International Trade in all that?

PANGLOSS: Modern International Trade is like the scattered torn cuts of the newspaper of a short while ago with the notable difference that these same newspaper cuts, in this case, somehow miraculously reappear as a reassembled, packed whole with a price tag, on the shelf of the nearby supermarket.

CACAMBO: I am really fed up with your never ending metaphors. Where are the proofs for your credo? Where are the statistics, the sources, the citations, the quotations? Any serious inquiry on the subject, should whiten with chalk at least one blackboard of the kind displaying the evolution of the National Debt on Time Square.

PANGLOSS: The problem with statistics is just like the problem with the figures from any piece of theatre, where the number of actors, the replicas they address to each other, the whole plot, so to speak, is pre-set right from the beginning, since otherwise there would be no theatre at all. Statistics are another form of wishful thinking where the desired end leads to the appropriate rearrangement of the figures. Furthermore, as we said it before, there is no such thing as quantity per see, because any quantity is the expression of a given quality. Hence measuring economic activity by taking quantity for an implicit starting point is an exercise of a permanent self-delusion, and the validity of this self-delusion or self-deception is no less than 100%.

CACAMBO: Give me at least one example.

PANGLOSS: There is a magazine, which started appearing in Europe shortly after our own time, 'The Economist' from where, I guess, came out in the open, among other things, new series of statistics under the licensed label of Big Mac Index. So, they say, the exchange rate of fiat money around which International Trade is gravitating counts for much less than the comparative price of a French fry, a Coke and a Burger of the kind I just bought you a short while ago.

CACAMBO: What is that?

PANGLOSS: According to the Big Mac Index, if you buy the item in question say in Geneva compared to a place, such as Bucharest or Shanghai, the value of fiat money is apparently melting like Ice on the Sunshine. Following this assumption the GNP per capita calculated in accordance with the actual or current exchange rate simply ceases to be a tangible criterion of accounting for the fluctuation of assets, goods and services from one place or one country to another and as a result, what they call, the PPA or GNP according to purchasing power parity swells the GNP of low income countries, to the point of obscuring the very nature of fiat money and, as we shall see later on, the key role of Foreign Exchange in International Trade, including the possibility of its manipulation by those who take discreet decisions at each point in time, when and how much fiat money to print.

CACAMBO: Is not a Burger cheaper in Bucharest than in Geneva, after all?

PANGLOSS: Have you heard of the Monaco Grand Prix formula one race?

CACAMBO: You did not answer my question.

PANGLOSS: So according to the Purchasing Power Parity kind of thing, the relative price for a drive on a Bugatti along the tiny streets of Monte Carlo is to be the same as a ride on a bus, stuck in a Cairo or a Dacca traffic jam, or the few cents for the Cairo bus ticket in terms of PPP should be equal to the at least hundred times more expensive price, in nominal terms or according to the current exchange rate, for the drive on a Bugatti, if the amortization costs, the insurance etc. are taken into account. Therefore, we can safely assume, following the lines of the PPP view that a $100 USD bill in Monaco is worth less than $1 USD in Cairo or Dacca and indeed the opposite, 1 buck in Dacca or Cairo has a purchasing power equal to a banknote of $100 USD in Monaco. Now, it goes without saying that there are some basic prices such as rent or transportation, as in the above case, which are essentially inelastic and this is so, once again for extra economic reasons, since as a resident of Monaco, if you have a hundred times higher income than a resident of Dacca, you will not take hundred more rides on a bus, even in the unlikely event that a bus, in a similar condition and with the same charge for one ticket, as the average bus on the streets of Dacca, was indeed available in Monte Carlo. Other than that, the more the International Trade grows in importance, the more the difference in relative prices throughout the world tends to be erasing itself and correspondingly the more the urge to obscure the phenomenon in question, assumes a higher priority on the global agenda. After all, this is one among countless other illustrations of the indeed Meta historical dichotomy between the Thing in itself and its representations in Modern Consciousness.

CACAMBO: And how about the Burger?

PANGLOSS: $1 USD is $1 USD everywhere. On the aggregate level, higher incomes lead not to different prices, but only to different relative price allocations of the assets and goods in circulation, where at last resort, the sum of all prices in the place A, are to be equal to the sum of all prices in the place B. The price of a Burger in Geneva is indeed higher than the price of Burger in Bucharest due to higher salaries in Geneva. Yet, you only have to go to any Geneva supermarket, of the Migros or the Coop variety, where under the green label 'Budget' you can find items on discount prices with a corresponding lower quality, similar to that in Bucharest, where the leveling impact of International Trade on local prices is manifest.

CACAMBO: You started your point on International Trade with its supposed origin in High Antiquity and Purple. Yet you did not retrace the evolution of Trade up to the present.

PANGLOSS: How come I did not? I presented a certain view on the nature of Trade in its Meta historical and Metaphysical dimension. As for the quantitative trajectory of International Trade during the formally recorded history, there are two things: first, as we said it already, the utmost caution is required when a consideration is given to the flood of statistics or the supposedly accurate economic data and their exponential growth due to the expansion of modern Universities and now the advent of the Internet etc. since as we said it already, the sources of these data, are objects only in relation to a subject, where the nature of the subject may give different replicas to the same object, in the same way as one can change at will one theatrical representation with another. Second, there is a point of natural equilibrium and once the threshold of this equilibrium has been broken, the further expansion of International Trade becomes more and more negative for the economy as a whole, where each incremental increase in Trade leads to an incremental decrease of the efficiency in the global allocation of resources.

CACAMBO: How did you get to such a notion of efficiency?

PANGLOSS: Can you measure something which is nothing in itself, a non-entity, a pure vacuity? If it happens that there is no way of measuring nothingness, after all, then you will have to provide a given substance to any notion of efficiency and it is coming just out of itself or in the same way as rabbits do come out of the magician's hat, that your substance has to have a quality or some kind of filling. Here is a problem or the famous problem of finality, which has been either eluded by modern culture as a whole, including philosophy, political economy and present day economics or described in vague terms to say the least, as for example our friend in the bottle was essentially preoccupied by the world In the 19th century and by the way of bringing radical changes to this world, and that is why his description of the future or communism is as consistent as thin air. I wonder how many times a day the world GNP or the GNP of this and that country is mentioned, analyzed, dissected with the outmost statistical accuracy and printed in millions, indeed already may be billions of copies, without hinting even for a second, why bigger is better, why anything that is moving under the Sun and therefore accounted as a good or a service and consequently included in the GNP without taking into consideration its quality or its intrinsic value is seen as a positive phenomenon or economic progress or an increase of the real wealth.

CACAMBO: Would you be, so kind as make it clear how efficient is International Trade today?

PANGLOSS: Do you remember the fable of the Tortoise and the Hare?

CACAMBO: Yes.

PANGLOSS: And what if we just change somewhat the setting of the story and instead in the open, the race between the two competitors takes place around the shelves of the nearby supermarket? So, the run will start from the entry, where usually are located the cashiers and will end, say, in the pastry section, where a prize consisting in a cup of coffee and a basket with groceries will be awarded to the winner. And another thing: the Hare will not take a nap this time,[14] since the winner is the one who gets first to the shelf with the groceries and the coffee by a particular time frame, when the coffee is still hot, but not too hot nor too cold. Let's assume that this time frame is twenty minutes after the start of the race. So the Hare, as might be expected, will reach the basket first in a minute or two by making a complete U turn around the hall of the supermarket, whereas at the same time the Tortoise has been advancing only a few meters from the start. So our friend the Hare, impatient as he may be, will be taking the basket and leave it again on the shelf, each time he is reaching his target before the scheduled time frame of twenty minutes. Now, what it turns out at this point is that the Hare makes a complete U turn of the supermarket in two minutes and the Tortoise, judging from its own pace, in nineteen minutes. So, one time, two times, three, four… the Hare is running and running and each two minutes he is lifting the basket, only to leave it again on the shelf with resentment and growing impatience. In the meantime, the Tortoise has been slowly advancing. Eighteen minutes has passed already. Now, soon comes the point, where the Hare is about to complete its ninth consecutive U turn of the supermarket. One minute is left, fifty seconds, forty, thirty, twenty…The Tortoise is also close to the final. So, our race is in its last seconds right now…five…three….. two…and one. The Tortoise has just completed its first U turn and…won the race, since the Hare was left behind by a whole minute.

CACAMBO: You know what? I was just wondering what, is inside this basket after all, since I am still expecting the dinner you promised me once we get back to the shore, whereas the Tortoise, in all probability may be full already.

PANGLOSS: The Tortoise may be full indeed at this point, but this is definitely not the case of the Hare, since as the one time' Maître à penser' of The Peripatetic School put it in his 'Metaphysics', you cannot say Yes and No at the same time. The Hare is like Modern International Trade, save the statistics in which our friend had been wrapped, so that his rabbit like nature may not become explicit.

CACAMBO: And what about the Tortoise?

PANGLOSS: We will get there later on. Now, let's see for the time being why the Hare completes his first U turn around the shelves of the supermarket.

CACAMBO: He is basically running fast and at the sight of the basket full with groceries, he runs still faster.

PANGLOSS: Your statement is definitely true, but it is too general. We would say the Hare makes the first U turn so that the red pork chop in the basket may be dyed in red.

CACAMBO: And so what?

PANGLOSS: Commonly used food dyes, such as yellow 5, Red 40 are made from petroleum and pose a rainbow of risks.[15]

CACAMBO: Do you know that these food colorings have been banned in Europe?

PANGLOSS: No, my friend. They banned six food colorings,[16] and by no means of all of them. So, it goes without saying that these colorings are to reappear later on, with a new name and a new price tag, since the Emperor is constantly preoccupied by the periodical filling out of his wardrobe.

CACAMBO: Okay, but your Hare made, I guess, nine or ten U turns, right?

PANGLOSS: Yes, although these nine U turns are not enough to fill all the components included in the price tag of the goods in the basket. So here is the second one, for the sake of: Synthetic Pesticides, the third one: Chemical Fertilizers, the fourth: Genetically Modified Organisms, the fifth: Irradiation, the sixth: Food Additives, the seventh: Antibiotics, the eighth: Growth hormones.

CACAMBO: I wonder how many million times, all of these are mentioned or talked about in every single day.

PANGLOSS: The ninth U turn of The Hare is for the transportation costs.

CACAMBO: And where are the others?

PANGLOSS: Once the race is over, our Hare will have to make at least as many U turns as he has made already, since all of the above components included in the final price tag of the goods in the basket have to be transported separately, before being shipped to the place where their final assembly will be taking place. Wait a second. I think I forgot the expenses for publicity, telemarketing calls or consumer surveys or whatever and well... also, the cost of the telecommunication equipment, allowing a telemarketing employee from India to make phone solicitation in New York or Toronto for the various inputs along the production line, leading to the final output, contained in the basket.

CACAMBO: They say only 19% of every dollar spent on food in the US covers raw materials costs.[17]

Pangloss: Yes. These reportedly 19% however, include the cost of all of the above, pesticides, additives, the cost of oil etc. It is highly likely that the price tags of the goods in the basket are to be decreased by may be more than 90% and even 95% if they are delivered unprocessed to the shelves. Furthermore, the prices are to fall still further if the on-going global oligopolistic retail trade arrangements are suppressed and real competition reintroduced on the market place.[18]

Cacambo: This is not so. You cannot separate the chemical, synthetic inputs from the basic stuff, since otherwise the price will go up, as it is the case with organic food, right now.

Pangloss: If present day agriculture switches to organic farming[19] at this very moment, the final price may indeed rise somewhat but not as much as you think. Furthermore, should we take into account the long term effects of all the consecutive U turns of The Hare on human health and the environment, including soils and the water supply, the prices of the goods in the basket may increase by the thousands, but not now, only later on. So, clearly, at this point, you have a potential for an annual double or triple digit rate of negative growth of world GNP for at least a century.

Cacambo: Listen, this debate has been going on for decades now.[20] Was not what you say at this point, already classified as a holistic approach? Seriously, you promised to bring me to the harbor for a dinner and if I can choose between organic food in two hours-time and conventional food right now, I will prefer the latter without any hesitation.

Pangloss: Have you heard of the New York black out of 1977?[21]

Cacambo: What is that?

Pangloss: The whole city had no electricity, I guess for more than twenty four hours. Now, could you just tell me, what would you do if it happened that you were stuck in the elevator of one of those towers up there?

Cacambo: I would stay until electricity comes back.

Pangloss: I see. You would wait for something that was already there before and that may be still there in the future, right?

Cacambo: Yes.

Pangloss: So, will electricity come back if you just say: I believe in you! I believe in you!?

CACAMBO: What this has to do with food and International Trade?

PANGLOSS: And how about that? Listen to me Electricity: I prefer you to Fire! I prefer you to Water! I prefer you to Air! I prefer you to just anything! So, you know what? Do not be nasty and do come back, please!

CACAMBO: What is your point?

PANGLOSS: My point is on International Trade and Organic Food. For the guy in the elevator there is in reality one only option left: it is the hope that someone out there will make a sufficient display of knowledge on electricity per see or so to speak, in itself, including the conductors of electricity and thus, being able of making a consistent effort to save him from staying indefinitely in the dark. It is the only knowledge that can make the elevator function again and nothing else. And this is not a Holistic view. This is not one view among other views. This is the only real view.

CACAMBO: What is making you think that the artificial ingredients in the food supply are harmful?

PANGLOSS: Synthetic products stand against natural ingredients in the same way as a copy is related to its original or a shadow to its substance. They stand against Quality and since Quality is an emanation of the First Principle or the Monad of all Monads, they stand at the same time, against Nature. And this is a sufficient reason to end all debates on the number of pesticides or GMO dancing on the tip of a needle or on the cutting edge of any microscope. Agriculture from its very abrupt beginning, as this is attested in countless myths and traditions, including the Mysteries of Fleusis used to be a gift from above or from the point of view of the present state of knowledge, from the unknown. Given that the integral cognitive process following the perception of an ever present Natural Order, on which ancient Agriculture was based, is no longer available, this path is to be followed along with the effort, one of whose expressions is Ecology, to recover in part or one day, in whole, this same lost or forgotten knowledge.

CACAMBO: Okay, Okay. Why do not you just stop there? Where is International Trade in all that?

PANGLOSS: Modern or rather Postmodern International Trade is represented in our case by The Hare and Pre-Modern Trade by the Tortoise, where the relative efficiency of the one versus the other may be measured through the application of Zeno's Paradox. Do you still remember the coffee that had to be awarded to the winner in the supermarket?

CACAMBO: Coffee?! What coffee?

PANGLOSS: Together with the basket, there was also a coffee for the winner, and it is because of this same coffee that the race had to be completed within twenty minutes, since this had been considered as the best time frame, so that the coffee should not be too cold neither too hot. On a larger scale or on the level of Macro Economic Theory, this time frame has been referred to as the Economic Cacambo Calculation Problem,[22] which by the way, used to be the Achilles Heel of the now defunct Soviet System of Central Planning.

CACAMBO: Why are you also referring to the Zeno's paradox?[23]

PANGLOSS: Because Pre-Modern International Trade is more efficient than, its Post Modern version.

CACAMBO: Why?

PANGLOSS: How many U turns of the supermarket did the Hare make?

CACAMBO: I do not know. I guess, at least ten or more.

PANGLOSS: Should we admit that one U turn of the supermarket, the U turn that the Tortoise made is enough, since this is the U turn is in line with the Universal Law of Equilibrium or the Dharma or the Cosmos, all other U turns, those made by The Hare are an exercise in futility, a massive waste of resources and later on a toxic time-bomb, leading at last resort to the systematic destruction of society and in the end to the deconstruction of Humanity itself. Each U turn of The Hare corresponds to an incremental rise of the synthetic and other essentially toxic inputs, standing behind the absurd expansion of Modern International Trade, which today's accounting standards, together with the GNP kind of fetishism, present as a source of power and wealth. Here is the most massive deception in recorded history, something like the famous ghost ship by the name of *The Flying Dutchman*, yet on a scale of 1 to the thousands, may be millions.

NOTES

[1] Cooksey C. J. (2001). "*Tyrian purple: 6,6 Dibromoindigo and Related Compounds*" (PDF). *Molecules* 6 (9): 736–769. doi:10.3390/60900736. http://www.mdpi.org/moleculespapers/60900736. pdf. John Edmonds, *Tyrian or Imperial Purple: The Mystery of Imperial Purple Dyes*, Historic Dye Series, no. 7 (Little Chalfont, Buckinghamshire, England: John Edwards, 2000).

[2] Reese, David S. (1987). "Palaikastro Shells and Bronze Age Purple-Dye Production in the Mediterranean Basin," *Annual of the British School of Archaeology at Athens*, 82, 201-6); Stieglitz,

Robert R. (1994), "The Minoan Origin of Tyrian Purple," *Biblical Archaeologist*, 57, 46-54.

[3]Vitruvius, *De Architectura*, Book VII, Chapter 13.

[4]*Silk and religion: an exploration of material life and ...Parties* 600 à 1200, p 78.

[5]See *Derveni Papyrus*, Gábor Betegh, 2004. *The Derveni Papyrus: Cosmology, Theology and Interpretation* (Cambridge University Press). A preliminary reading, critical edition and translation. ISBN 0-521-80108-7. Janko, Richard, "The Derveni Papyrus (Diagoras of Melos, Apopyrgizontes Logoi?): a New Translation," *Classical Philology* 96, 2001, pp. 1–32 .Laks, André, "Between Religion and Philosophy: The Function of Allegory in the Derveni Papyrus", *Phronesis* 42, 1997, pp. 121–142.

[6]See David Wootton: *"Unbelief in Early Modern Europe"*, *History Workshop Journal*, No. 20, 1985, pages 83–101 : Averroes, Pomponazzi, Cremonini.

[7]*The Origin of Ayurveda in the Cognitions of the Vedic Rishis*, by Nancy Lonsdorf M.D. www. virtuelscience.com 'What is Ayurveda?' www.neelkanthdhaam.org.

[8]St Exupery, '*The Little Prince*'.

[9]See Nagarjuna and Madyamika School.

[10]Basel III rules published January 2011 www.whitecase.com.

[11]See *Catholic Encyclopedia*, Prester John.

[12]Cited by A. Govinda, '*Foundation of Tibetan Mysticism*', p 73.

[13]See *"Berossos and Manetho"* by Gerald P. Verbrugghe and John M. Wickersham (Michigan 1997); Harold T. Wilkins '*Mysteries of Ancient South America*' P77, Lost Books, Manetho The London quarterly review, For April 1859 Volumes 105 à 106, p221 Bunsen's Egypt and the chronology of the Bible.

[14]The Tortoise and the Hare is a fable attributed to Aesop and is number 226 in the Perry Index.

[15]Center of Science in the public interest '*Food Dyes: a rainbow of risks.*' www.cspinet.org.

[16]Europe wide food color ban call BBC News, 10 of April 2008.

[17]*Record Food Prices Causing Africa Riots Stoking U.S.* (Update1) By Alan Bjerga and Tony Dreibus - Jan 18, 2011 2:55 AM PTTue Jan 18 10:55:02 GMT 2011www.bloomberg.com.

[18]NEW YORK (Reuters)- For the small club of companies who trade the food, fuels and metals that keep the world running, the last decade has been sensational. Driven by the rise of Brazil, China, India and other fast-growing economies, the global commodities boom has turbocharged

profits at the world's biggest trading houses. They form an exclusive group, whose loosely regulated members are often based in such tax havens as Switzerland. Together, they are worth over a trillion dollars in annual revenue and control more than half the world's freely traded commodities. The top five piled up $629 billion in revenues last year, just below the global top five financial companies and more than the combined sales of leading players in tech or telecoms. Many amass speculative positions worth billions in raw goods, or hoard commodities in warehouses and super-tankers during periods of tight supply Commodity traders: The trillion dollar club By Joshua Schneyer NEW YORK (Reuters)-21 oct. 2011.

[19]See '*Look to the land 1940.*' Walter James, 4th Baron Nortbourne.

[20]Paul, John (2011). "*Attending the First Organic Agriculture Course: Rudolf Steiner's Agriculture Course at Koberwitz, 1924*". *European Journal of Social Sciences*' 21 (1): 64-70. http://orgprints. org/18809/1/Paull2011KoberwitzEJSS.pdf).

[21]Frum, David (2000). *How We Got Here: The '70s*. New York, New York: Basic Books. pp. 14–15. ISBN 0-465-04195-7.

[22]Hayek F.A. 1937 Economics and Knowledge *Economica* V4 N13 33-54.

[23]*Zeno's Paradoxes*. First published, Tue Apr 30, 2002; substantive revision Fri Oct 15, 2010 Stanford Encyclopedia of Philosophy.

TALE XVIII

The Political Economy of Foreign Exchange

CACAMBO: Look at our friend The Spirit in the Bottle! He must be sleeping right now, since his eyes are closed. Strangely enough, his head is not in the empty portion of the bottle where there must be air, after all, but in the other half filled with water or a kind of liquid, as the latter is appearing to be of a pale red color. He may be snoring! Do you see the bubbles all around his petrified face, making their appearance, each time he is taking and then releasing his breath?

PANGLOSS: Yes. These are small bubbles indeed. He may be dreaming of the world to come after all, where the small bubbles of the fiat money type, will be growing by the day, or better still by the hour, by the minute, by the second and eventually by the fraction of the second. The present day issuers of banknotes seem to dislike the physical world their own bills are supposed to represent. Any payment in cash nowadays, appears to be the most economically incorrect way of settling a transaction, since the overall expansion of quantity has been accompanied by the multiplication of the copies of any given original. Yet the replacement of cash by credit and debit cards on the retail consumer level is only the tip of the iceberg, since the emergence of, say, the junk bonds in the 1980s, appear in today's financial flora and fauna as the fossilized remains of a monster from a by-gone era.[1] By the way, where is the wrapping paper of the Burgher and the fry I bought you a short while ago?

CACAMBO: I do not know... I do not want to know... I threw it somewhere. You would better bring me to the harbor for dinner instead of asking me such a futile question. You did not specify that the transmutation of metals is not included in the potion with the Elixir of long life you gave me back in our own time. So, if I become at some point a wandering pauper this will be your fault.

PANGLOSS: No, my friend. You have apparently forgotten on how many occasions I gave you donations already in the 19th century. Now, if you do not mind, I'll go to the trash can over there to look for the remains of the wrapping paper.

CACAMBO: Okay.

PANGLOSS: I found it. Do you see this small stone next to your chair?

CACAMBO: And so what?

PANGLOSS: I will wrap it up. Here it is. It is whole package right now.

CACAMBO: Great! Why do not you also just wrap this cigarette butt below the table? Here is another one…and another one still! Do you see that empty can right there?

PANGLOSS: I prefer to stop at this point, since basically there is no object on this planet that cannot be wrapped in one way or another. Now, for the on-going process of massive 'Fiatization' of economic activity, one wrapping is as good as another wrapping of just anything, including thin air, since debts are an essential part of any financial package, whose, so to speak, inner essence consists of being a derivative of another derivative. The expansion of the Modern Economy is in reality, a ghostlike labyrinth, where huge mirrors project a hidden original into an endless alignment of copies, simultaneously within the inner layers of the Psyche and the outer configuration of the Body.

CACAMBO: If you are about to repeat what you said already on the printing of fiat money, I am to remind you that your subject right now is on Foreign Exchange.

PANGLOSS: The allocation of resources taking place, on today's Post Modern economic stage rests on the stroke of a pen. Foreign Exchange is Foreign Exchange in name only. Being epistemologically inaccessible to the lexicon of present day self-proclaimed science of Economics, the realm of essence refers to the very notion of exchange, whenever the conditions of free will are present. Are these conditions to be lacking, there is no such thing as Foreign Exchange. There is distribution and respectively appropriation. Present day, Global Financial System, is a coin, and once tossed this coin falls either on the side of Distribution or on the side of Appropriation and nothing else.

CACAMBO: You spoke on the question of Gold and the Gold Standard already. So, I guess you will say at this point that what you refer to as Distribution is due to the suppression of the Gold Standard. Following from this, the Gold Standard as it used to function, a century after our own time, from the City of London is to be considered in your view, as the very best in the best of all possible financial worlds, right?

PANGLOSS: The real meaning of the Gold Standard and the precious metals as a whole, here, is not derived from History, be it Financial History or any other History. It is derived from the eternal present within the Human Monad or the immutable Laws of Consciousness. Furthermore, although the precious metals backing the issue of any bills is indeed a prerequisite for any real form of exchange, this is by no means the only prerequisite, since the very first prerequisite for the possibility of an exchange is no other than Freedom.

CACAMBO: Listen, you promised to take me for dinner to the harbor, already more than an hour ago. Could you at least be more, so to speak, specific about the whole thing? Why Foreign Exchange is to be something else than it what it appears to be? What happens when you take the decision to show up at the desk of any Foreign Exchange Office? There are various currency pairs, displayed in front of the entry, where the rate of one pair is to match the rate of another pair, according to the amount that has been exchanged either way or according to supply and demand.

PANGLOSS: There is no part of any whole that is not implicitly taking for granted the existence of this same whole, in the first place. In the same way there is no house without foundations. Foreign Exchange has to have an ultimate reference. Up to September 1931, this was Gold and up to 1971 it was still Gold but in a different way. Now, in 2012, as we said it already, it is sand, provided that the supply of sand is no less abundant than the supply of paper and now plastics, used for the printing of fiat money.

CACAMBO: Fine. Yet, it is still not clear to me why do you apparently exclude a priori, the theoretical possibility that the sum of all currencies in circulation be they fiat currencies, may serve as the reference in the last resort for a new system of International Trade?

PANGLOSS: Such a system would be based on the presumption that it might be somehow possible to conceive a composite entity as being composite by itself, that is without being a part of a whole, which is a manifest absurdity, since only a whole may be composite. So is the case of the SDR of the IMF, being in circulation since 1969.[2] These SDR's may well coexist or function in parallel with the ultimate reference, Gold or now the USD, but they cannot replace it.

CACAMBO: Why?

PANGLOSS: Look, shall I buy you another burger until we get to the harbor for dinner at the Waldorf Astoria Hotel later on? You stubbornly cling to something which may not be self-evident only to a mind, under the spell of the most abject form of dogmatic empiricism or statistical fetishism, which by the way may exist only in an ivory type environment of the semantic variety, since in real life no human can function in such a condition of methodical obscurantism for more than a fraction of a second.

CACAMBO: First of all, I do not want another of these sandwiches or whatever, since the taste definitely has nothing to do with the food in our own time. Furthermore, you did not specify why this cannot be done, after all.

PANGLOSS: Okay. Imagine that the currencies of all countries, currently members of the

United Nations are a kind of a universal SDR, whose components are freely floating on the surface of a global Mare Nostrum.

CACAMBO: Great!

PANGLOSS: So what would happen if one of the states listed in the U.N. for any reason, political, geopolitical or whatever simply stops accepting these SDR's?

CACAMBO: A crisis of confidence will follow and in all likelihood there will be a flight from the SDR's since these, will be reduced to ashes or to their components in no time.

PANGLOSS: Yes. So how would it be possible to react to this situation?

CACAMBO: There would be two ways, I guess. State or rather Global Intervention in favor of the SDR, resulting in compulsory measures for the enforcement of the SDR system or the creation of a Global Currency.

PANGLOSS: So what now? Would not this global currency be one complete whole, assembled from its parts or the SDR's?

CACAMBO: There is no such currency at this point.

PANGLOSS: The currency playing this role is the USD.

CACAMBO: If the USD is the whole, and other currencies its parts, then it follows that in today's world, there is in reality one only currency and this currency is the USD. Does it not appear from all this somehow out of itself that the position of the USD in today's world has somehow evolved, as a result of deep meditation on the nature of the Universe and the relative place of fiat money in this same Universe?

PANGLOSS: No. What it does appear is that the USD ever since 1944 and later on, 1971, came to play the unique role of a global currency and this is due to an intense reflection on the subject of Foreign Exchange, starting already in 1913, since there is no History per se, in the same way as there are no parts without a whole and better still, there is no escape from the whole.

CACAMBO: Since history per see including Historicism, is only an optical illusion, there certainly must be a Universal Law, where the USD is to play a key role.

PANGLOSS: Yes. The USD is the negation of Universality, but since as we said it already in reality there is no escape from the Intelligible Essence, in the last resort this same negation is still an expression of the Universal Law, so to speak, a reversed triangle.

This is the same triangle, standing behind the Principle of Dynamics, where the Meta historical forms follow one after the other as the waves of the sea.

CACAMBO: So, everything is definitely the best in the best of all worlds, right? I knew it!

PANGLOSS: Seriously, why do not you just accept a new sandwich? We presented already our view on what the best of all the possible worlds is all about. Now, had you been full and therefore rather more relaxed right now, you would have asked, why the role played by the USD ever since Bretton Woods, and more so since 1971, is contrary to the positive expression of the Universal Law, I guess.

CACAMBO: Yes. You said it yourself: Why is this so?

PANGLOSS: We mentioned this on many occasions, but not in the specific context yet. So, by the mere fact of being a currency backed by nothing but itself, the USD is the very embodiment of subjectivity or 100% pure, unsweetened, pasteurized economic voluntarism.[3] Should we expand further, what we said, already on the ontological nature of exchange, the USD plays the role of a universal medium of appropriation for the issuers and distribution for the holders of assets denominated in the most arbitrary form of resource allocation in recorded history.

CACAMBO: Wait a minute. Has not something of this kind been around already for decades, I mean a similar view on the subject, save for your best in the best of all possible worlds metaphysical staff?

PANGLOSS: You refer to some observations made on the course of modern financial history, when the post war arrangement of Bretton Woods had been put into question, I guess?[4]

CACAMBO: Had not been what you refer to as a flood of paper and now computer clicking or scriptural money, been contained by the Basel Accords, including the reserve requirements for Banks?

PANGLOSS: The easiest answer would be to take the events of 2008 as a proof precisely of the opposite. This is indeed the case. However, our intent here is to go beyond what appears to be the immediate reason, by surfing along the series of conditions, where the different layers of reality unfold as a pack of cards thrown on various points of the Earth.

CACAMBO: Your way of approaching things is mistier than the thickest London fog. Is not clarity and consistency an exercise of complex equations, as present day economic science seems to suggest?

Pangloss: The introduction of mathematics on a large scale on the Stock market and the FOREX by the heirs of an entity as misty as the ghostlike modern corporation, invented a century after our own time, is one of the most pervasive examples of massive waste of economic and human resources. The sheer magnitude the phenomenon in question may be surpassing in absurdity even the systematic mutilation of scientific research by the use of statistical methods at the expense of the genuine effort for insight into reality. Here is also, a perfect example of what is referred to in Macro Economic theory as a Demand driven by Supply or a Demand creating its own Supply. Had it not been for the ontological vacuity of Modernity, leading to the constant preoccupation with figures, starting already at the time of Descartes and consequently leading to the expansion of computation techniques in the Curriculum of present day Universities, the on-going replacement of simple common sense together with the intuitive search for the sufficient reason in the sphere of investing and trading by these equations, that might have made the delight of Pinocchio, most of the bubbles, taking place in recent years would have been at least half smaller and respectively half less devastating for the overall economic activity as they happened to be.

Cacambo: Great! Would you just stick to the Foreign Exchange at this point?

Pangloss: Before going any further, we stay for a while on the question of epistemology.

Cacambo: Have you not talked already on the different ways of perceiving economic reality?

Pangloss: Yes. However, these different perceptions are no more of equal value than the broad daylight is identical to its own absence during the night. There are entities, invisible to the naked eye, operating simultaneously within and beyond the protocols of a Davos or a Club of Rome conference for example, including numerous other meetings and decisions on the way of regulating the flood of liquidity that is pouring into all segments of economic activity. And another thing: the question of the transparency of these meetings, ever since the hay day of Venice and the gathering on Jekyll Island is a key epistemological question with several possible answers ranging from the imprint of the Akashic records on the points of gravity of our blue planet, the Earth to the monotonous utterings of a parrot of the Arara variety. On the surface, there is no reason why all the good intentions for the containment of the fiat money supply should not work and yet in practice things turn out to be different.

Cacambo: Is not the question on the intentions, in reality the most relevant? You can say, you aim at one thing and doing just the opposite. Is not the expansion of liquidity with its corresponding debts and so forth, the condition sine qua non for the expansion of power per se, including economic power?

PANGLOSS: We will get at this point later on. For now, we will only say here that, at last resort there is no such thing as an arbitrary decision, since there is no escape from the natural law. Following this, the notion of equilibrium is to be taken into account along the way of any finality, whatever this finality might be.

CACAMBO: And what about the rest? You dislike equations, but would you at least provide the sources on which your view on the Forex is based?

PANGLOSS: No. I will not.

CACAMBO: How come you will not? Do you realize that a presentation of a subject like that does not appear to be credible in the slightest degree, unless each paragraph you write is stuffed with references and quotations?

PANGLOSS: There is no better quotation than free reflection.

CACAMBO: Are you simply attempting to ignore the sources?

PANGLOSS: By no means, since the Monad of Foreign Exchange is essentially the right effort for interpretation of these same sources.

CACAMBO: Okay. What is the source to begin with?

PANGLOSS: The source of all sources is the USD.

CACAMBO: You just said that the USD is backed by nothing but itself? Is this really so?

PANGLOSS: Yes. When the last link between the USD and Gold had been cut off, by the closing of the Golden Window in 1971, the currency emitted by the FED came to play the role that the Monarchs, or Emperors of by gone ages, such as Rudolph II for example and countless alchemists, including Newton, had been attempting to do but were unsuccessful of achieving so far: this is the establishment of a monopoly on the Gold supply through the know-how of the transmutation of metals.

CACAMBO: How come? Had not the basic know-how on the printing press already been, patented back in the 15th century by Guttenberg?

PANGLOSS: No my friend. The free printing press, as the hyperinflation of the Weimer Republic shows, tends in no time to make of the issued banknotes, a pile of worthless pieces of paper. So, the patent of the printing press is not enough. A different variety of patents is to come out on the stage and these patents are no other, than the so called Cold War from 1945 up to 1989 and Oil, respectively. By the way, should we adopt this synthetic view on the whole thing, the division of data and events in different separate compartments such as History, Economics, Political-Economy, Politics etc. is no more relevant than the famous devils dancing on the tip of a needle of the Medieval Scholastics. I wonder in which dusty library depot the whole junk of the one-time science of Kremlinology, has been piled up at this point, since this, so to speak, science had been keen on any subject concerning the now defunct Soviet Union, except on the date when the Berlin Wall was to fall.

CACAMBO: Oil? Is not this the Gold of the present age?

PANGLOSS: No. You can store Gold, but you cannot store Oil since you have to burn it at some point. Gold is primarily a medium of exchange, whereas Oil is a commodity and as such has to be denominated in something other than itself, that is, either in Gold or fiat money.

CACAMBO: Have you not just said that the USD is backed by Oil?

PANGLOSS: Yes, but in this case, the opposite is equally true, in the sense that Oil is also backed by the USD.

CACAMBO: How come? Is not Oil imported by each of the 190 states currently, members of the United Nations? So, there must be other currencies as well, right?

PANGLOSS: No. The price of Oil is quoted in USD and better still: Oil is traded only in USD. So, a country without Oil reserves and without US Dollars would revert back to our own time, when, as you very well know, there was no such thing as Oil.

CACAMBO: I see. Therefore, the demand for USD is assured, I guess?

PANGLOSS: Yes it is. But there is more: the issuers of USD have also decided that the USA would pay for all the goods and services that are imported from the rest of the world only in USD and consequently never in a foreign currency. In addition to that, there are 15 other dollar market commodities.[5] And at last, there is the market for US treasuries, owned, contrary, for example to that of Japan, primarily by foreigners.

CACAMBO: Sounds great! So, the demand for the USD must be…who knows how many times higher than the US terms of trade would suggest?

PANGLOSS: Yes. For all other countries, except to some extent for the U.K. and Switzerland, the value of the currency is essentially a function of the terms of trade. This is not so only for the USA.

Cacambo: How come? Are not the terms of trade also relevant for the USA?

Pangloss: These are relevant, but no to the same extent as for practically all other countries and in a different way.

Cacambo: What different way?

Pangloss: The relevance of US terms of trade is in inversely proportional or negatively correlated to the relevance of the USD. The higher the US trade deficit is, the more the position of the USD as a reserve currency is strengthened, since, as we said it already, this is one of the ways to flood the world with US Dollars and therefore to assure the position of the USD in the future. Once in possession of US Dollars, the foreigners in reality are taken hostages, and well in line with the Stock Holm Syndrome, they have no better to do than making consistent efforts for preserving the apparent value of their Dollar denominated assets and as a result, the USD itself.

Cacambo: You speak very often of equilibrium. So following this, are not there constraints also for the USD, although these, may be constraints of a different nature that is, not the same as those of other currencies?

Pangloss: Yes. Nothing is without limits, even the free printing press. The question on the constraints of the USD is related to the world demand for Oil and the other Dollar denominated commodities and therefore to the statistical expansion of quantity leading to higher money supply or the growth of the global GNP. Up to this point, the macroeconomic balance from a statistical or financial point of view may be achieved without any difficulty by the issuers of last resort of the USD. Before going any further let me remind you that had it not been for the long term devastating economic effect of this quantitative and statistical expansion, our friend the Hare, from above would hardly even bother to move, let alone run and complete all the U turns around the shelves of the Supermarket. Now, the right balance may be difficult, if not impossible to be achieved in the end, when it comes to credit, debt and the ever growing list of financial assets denominated in USD. Once the world is flooded with something in unlimited supply as the USD, the tendency for the debt, state, corporate or private, is to rise on a level that otherwise, as in the old days of gold and silver was simply unthinkable.

Cacambo: Why in your view, debts cannot be controlled even from above or from the issuers of last resort whoever and wherever they are?

Pangloss: This is the key question of postmodern political economy. The very foundation of fiat money rests on the inherent dichotomy of debts, denominated in pure sand on one hand for the issuers and in real goods and services, on the other hand, for the debtors. Now, even the most tightly attached knot of oligopolistic strings is still a knot. The ultimately composite nature of the whole process, so to speak, of issuing of debts denominated in fiat money makes that the restraint or the containment of the unleashed blind forces operating behind the printing press at first glance seems rather unlikely.

CACAMBO: Are you suggesting that the constituent parts or the various strings of the knot are necessarily doomed to disagree? These strings are no more than the first few prime numbers, after all.

PANGLOSS: Not necessarily. Should we compare the world of fiat money to a house, the disagreements are most likely to happen, not on the roof, where is located the heliport of each New York building worthy of self- respect, but on the first floors, as there, everything is done under the compulsion of competition.

CACAMBO: So, the competition in your view is for the individuals not for the corporations, I guess?

PANGLOSS: Listen, I am about to finish my point in a minute and we will be heading straight to the harbor for dinner, since as I see your patience is definitely running out and as a result you appear to be much more distracted than usual. Because, my friend, it is precisely the opposite. Do you still remember by any chance my previous point on the 'Revolt of the Masses' kind of thing, where it has been made clear that the sufficient reason for any social phenomenon is never on the level of a mere abstraction, such as the essentially empty concept of collectivism, but on the concrete representation of separate Monads or individual entities? Although, it goes without saying, that the latter in their turn, are the embodiment of metaphysical forces with all their highly charged Qualitas Occulta erring throughout the Universe and so forth. By the way, that is why, any little child is trying to make a distinction between the good and the bad all the time, since in this way, his Consciousness is making the effort of transcending the world of appearances or complexity for the world of simplicity, where the sufficient of all sufficient reasons or the Essence itself is anchored from the beginning of time. It is worth repeating here, that from our point of view, nothing is further from the truth than all these theories, such as' totalitarianism' and the like, based on the optical illusion of an all-powerful mechanical state apparatus, which is nothing but a mere replica of the dead soul dogma of classical mechanics. Big Brother does not rule for its own sake, because there is no such thing as an entity for its own sake, other than sake of human nature and the sake of the eternal final truth or the ultimate sufficient reason or the last Monad. A Big Brother, not inhabited by the urges of blind desire for power and the constant fear of losing the grip on this same power, would be a little like a stock trader, in a state of indifference to the fluctuation of the price of his own assets on the Forex or the Dow Jones.

CACAMBO: Okay, fine. So, you said all of the above just because, the competition is between the corporations and not individuals, I guess?

PANGLOSS: There is on one hand a competition in name only and on the other hand, the ever present threat of a breach of even of the most entangled spider web of oligopolistic deals, which is in itself a source of tension and therefore, a degree of real competition. However, should you take the elevator from the roof to the downstairs floor, the more you go down, the less the competition appears to be a fake, since the shareholders of banks or any other corporate entity, including, for example, pharmaceutical companies, do indeed expect higher returns and therefore, the unlimited supply of fiat money gives a powerful and arguably uncontrollable impetus for a fast escalade of the mountain of credit, debt and hence the inevitable abrupt fall from the top to the bottom. So, there is competition between the corporate ghosts, although their ultimate substance is provided by the very concrete individuals owning and operating in one way or another these entities. Now, as we said it already, the point of equilibrium between the oligopolistic Entente from above and the competition for credits and clients from below, is resolved by periodic economic crises, in the following ascending order: recessions, depressions and at last, say, major collisions.

CACAMBO: So, your view is at last resort no different from precisely the economist perception based on the idea that production exchange and gratification are all that counts on this planet, I guess?

PANGLOSS: Economics, in itself is nothing but a link for the extra-economic reasons that at last resort, condition the whole process of production and exchange. The collisions we just mentioned, after a certain threshold are beyond the logic of greed, even in its metaphysical representation. This is a power struggle.

CACAMBO: Would you be more specific?

PANGLOSS: The present system of exchange based on fiat money and the categorical imperative of International Trade lacks any true consistency in itself, since it is, in the first place a mean to an end. You can spend eons on complex derivative schemes, econometric formulas or elaborate strategies for the detoxification of the financial system from its various toxic components, without even being aware that all this is simply a joke.

CACAMBO: What?

PANGLOSS: Yes. Can you comprehend a message addressed to you, say, over the phone if at this very moment, you have no better to do than disassembling the various components of the phone box with a screwdriver instead of listening to the content of this same message? The technical side of Foreign Exchange may be useful as a way to loose one's assets if you happen to follow the precepts of some sophisticated trading strategy, based on complex equations or to give a forecast on the likely price of the USD or any other currency for the next few trading sessions, but it is irrelevant as far as the nature and therefore also, the long term effect of fiat money on the economy, are concerned. When you give something, for example, your old shirts to the Salvation Army, you are well aware that you get nothing in return. In the case of Foreign Exchange based on fiat money, you give, for example, an amount of your time in the form of labor and you think you get money in return, whereas the very opposite is true, but you are aware of that only later on, when in time of economic cataclysm, the sand like nature of fiat money becomes obvious and at last you realize that you have been deceived about the whole thing right from the beginning to the very end.

CACAMBO: How is all this related, say, to the present crisis of the Euro?

PANGLOSS: Before the emergence of the present day Foreign Exchange system, based on the USD, you got something which by the mere fact of being in limited supply, provided substance to your assets: this was Gold. So, the cancelling of debts and the issue of new currency used to be a much more serious matter, since the risk of losing your Gold was a constant preoccupation for the various players on the scene. As for the Euro, we will get there later on.

CACAMBO: Have you forgotten that cheating and Ponzi schemes were almost as common in our own time, than they are at this very moment?

PANGLOSS: Yes, Gold in those days used to me somewhat like the Flying Dutchman.[6] Yet, the magnitude of these bubbles is by its very nature destined to be infinitely smaller than the coming economic Deluge caused by fiat money.

CACAMBO: Why?

PANGLOSS: It is the limited supply that provides the intrinsic value of the precious metals on one hand, and the independence of the very idea of the value of Gold from any central authority. Empires and States come and go but that does not affect the shine of Gold in any way, since once fallen on Earth gold is here with us, on this planet till the end of time.

CACAMBO: So, present day finance is to be taken very lightly, I guess? Since fiat money has no real value, then the whole system is a joke, right?

PANGLOSS: Yes, a joke but a very bad one. From the point of view of the lender, especially the lender of last resort, all debts...Yes!...All debts can be cancelled tomorrow and the funds required for a new cycle of economic expansion can be issued in no more than forty eight hours.

CACAMBO: Why then is not this happening? Why is the world economic crisis still there?

PANGLOSS: Had you been aware from the beginning that what does appear before eyes right now is not the horizon of the sea, but its representation, just like a seaside image imprinted on a wall paper and consequently, that instead of walking in the open, you are in reality enclosed within the tiny space of a soap bubble, fiat money would lose its entire self-proclaimed worth right on the spot. As we mentioned it already, for the issuers of last resort or for the designers of the whole thing, all financial assets, loans, treasuries and the like may be created or put into circulation right away, or literally thrown out of helicopters at any time. The problem here is not the creation of assets. It is how to sustain the illusion of the intrinsic worth of sand or fiat money. The figures on the basement and the first few floors of the social fabric have to be deceived on a permanent basis, so that a crisis of confidence may be prevented. As for those on the top floors and on the roof itself, the periodically resurfacing question of the enforcement of their loyalty to the system of fiat money would have to be resolved, so to speak, in a constructive way. It is also, the question of accountancy and therefore ultimately responsibility. If you hand piles of cash to someone on the street, simply to stimulate the Aggregate Demand and you do not ask anything in return, you bypass the present system of exchange and production and as a result you make it dysfunctional.

CACAMBO: Are you not on the Moon right now? Will not any Bank go bankrupt if liabilities exceed assets?

PANGLOSS: In a major crisis, only the issuers of last resort remain on the scene. The periodical cancelling of debts is an expression of the power of the lender of last resort and a sine qua non condition for his position or survival on the political, and therefore also economic scene. Now, for the sake of this same ultimate survival of the whole system of fiat money, the smaller players, such as Banks, Corporations may be sacrificed in time of crisis by the lenders of last resort without any hesitation, since new entities may be created out of nothing at any time. Now, up to WWI, even these lenders of last resort used to be subject to the theoretical threat of bankruptcy, since everything turned around the most tangible of assets, Gold and/or Silver. They had to run after gold, since it is the possession of gold that assured their position on the top of the mountain. The suspension of gold convertibility in 1931 is only a prelude for the world to come.

CACAMBO: Why do not you just stay where we are right now, in 2012?

Pangloss: A brief comparison between 1931 and the likely termination of the post 1971 world may shed light on the way things happen to be at this very moment.

Cacambo: If you promise to bring me to the harbor after that, I will be l paying as much attention to your point as possible.

Pangloss: On Sunday, September 20, 1931, the British government went off gold by suspending the clause of the Gold Standard Act of 1925 requiring the Bank of England to sell gold at the fixed price. This event is a key Meta historical event. The course of the world economy accelerated simultaneously in three directions:

1)Quantitative expansion.
2)Virtualization. It is the methodical infusion of blind greed within all tissues of the social organism that initiated, the on-going process of virtualization of consciousness, including all spheres of economic activity.
3)Communization. The access to ever greater amounts of sand like liquidity, naturally led to the institutionalization, either in its state or corporate variety and the bureaucratization of economic activity, followed in turn, by a corresponding flight from real economic responsibility.

Cacambo: Are you not going too far? Did not the default on gold lead precisely to the opposite of what you say? There was a contraction not expansion of the overall activity, since this is the true cause of the Great Depression. As for the sand of Sahara, the abundance of liquidity did really take place, but much later, after 1971, not in 1931.

Pangloss: What we referred to as a Meta historical point is in no way contradictory to the immediate effects of the event, which indeed caused initially a contraction of activity and credit, including the corresponding political climate favorable to an outbreak of war or the Second World War. As for the flood of liquidity, had there not been for the suppression of the Gold Standard, there would be simply no such move as the closing of the Golden Window by Nixon in 1971.

Cacambo: Okay fine. Yet had not Gold already been suppressed after WWI?

Pangloss: Yes, but it was only for a time, since this is more than anything a matter of consciousness. In the then, way of perceiving economic reality, a suspension of Gold may have been only a temporary measure, since the permanent use of fiat money, would have appeared to the players on the world stage, as no less than an outright robbery or a grotesque joke. The flight from reality had still not reached this high point of virtualization, when, for example, some otherwise apparently rational individuals, proclaimed in the height of the Internet Bubble, that the rules of finance had somehow changed and therefore, no pyramids would be erected in such a new environment any longer, however much the P/E ratio of the then NASDAQ stocks had been raising.

CACAMBO: I still do not see why happen to regret the suppression of gold so much. If you think that there is no better than the 19th century Gold Standard, I suggest to you to read Dickens and even the *Capital*.

PANGLOSS: As I see your impatience is growing by the minute. Have we not talked on Gold in length on several occasions already? So once again: Gold is the most rational way ever devised way for solving the problem of economic calculation, based on the idea of equilibrium as a representation of the Natural Law. Now, we are in the Iron Age or the Kali Yuga, where blindness and unrestrained greed are the rule for millennia. Gold in such an environment, although a reflection of the cosmic equilibrium on a deeper level, has been evolving simultaneously along the lines of hoarding and appropriation. At no time, have we claimed that Gold alone, by itself, is a formula for harmony and prosperity. The key is in the effort for the mastery of oneself first and then of the four elements. What we have insisted upon, is that however much greed there might be for the possession of Gold or under the system of exchange based on Gold, it is still incomparably less than under the categorical imperative of pure Sahara type sand or fiat money. On the ontological level or the reality of the eternal present or the intelligible essences, fiat money is at the very opposite end of Gold, where the one stands as blind desire and the other as the containment of desire. Now once more: this is the instilled inner meaning of Gold and fiat money by the ultimate Monad or the form of consciousness, within the causal body, which by no means excludes the possibility of Gold, being itself an object of greed. Had it been so, there would be no Gold default in 1931.

CACAMBO: What are the immediate reasons for the Gold default of 1931?

PANGLOSS: Wealth in our own time, you know it very well, used to be measured by the amount of Gold in one's possession and therefore the hoarding of Gold, as innumerable buried treasures of the Ali Baba type attest was a constant preoccupation of the Kings, the Landowners, the Merchants, including the Merchant of Venice and so forth. In the 19th century, the Gold Standard suited the interests of the British Oligarchs, since manufacturing based on Cotton, Opium, Diamonds and Gold from South Africa and Australia, provided a trade surplus and therefore an influx of Gold to their coffers. After WWI, however, the debt ridden British Economy had no longer the industrial base for maintaining a trade surplus and therefore was not in position to preserve the Gold Standard and the role of the City as the world's financial center.

CACAMBO: So, the British economy was initially competitive and therefore up to the Great War, the influx of Gold was a natural reward for its success on the world's stage, I guess?

PANGLOSS: The export of British Textiles in the 18th and the 19th century has nothing to do with competition, since the main market, absorbing at least one quarter of the whole production, used to be in India, Bengal in particular, where British manufactured goods based on cotton had a monopoly at the expense of the local high quality industry, which had been utterly destroyed by the East India Company[7]

CACAMBO: Are you not once again beyond the subject of the Gold default of 1931?

PANGLOSS: The thing is that, when the Gold Standard had been reintroduced in 1925, The British were no longer in a position to retain the Gold, backing the Sterling by themselves, since British manufacturing was no match to the German or the US industry. So they embarked on their way for the building of an elaborate Pyramid or Ponzi scheme. The ultimate goal was to raise the value of the Sterling artificially, by the manipulation of the interest rate and embark on a massive shopping spree for the acquisition of tangible and intangible assets throughout the world. The bubble that burst in 1931 had been initiated and engineered right from 1925. The coordination of the interest rates between the FED and The Bank of England was such, that the US interest rate had to be low, so that the value of Sterling might be high, creating the US Stock Market bubble and consequently the 1929 Crash in the process.[8]

CACAMBO: Have you not said already that the scale of the Gold Bubble of 1931, by the very fact that it is formed on a medium of exchange of a limited supply such as Gold, however far reaching for its own time, is still nothing in comparison with the Bubbles to come, based on fiat money?

PANGLOSS: Yes.

CACAMBO: Look left! Someone out there seems to be waving at us.

PANGLOSS: It is a girl dressed in what appears to be a bright silk dress.

CACAMBO: She is walking toward us. Odd as it may seem, this girl does not have the look of one of these..? How do you call them?

PANGLOSS: May be, you mean, tourists? She does not look like a Lady from our own time either, since as far as I can see there is no trace of a corset on her, at this point.
CACAMBO: Is she not of the kind of this ghost Caliostro who left us when we were still on the harbor?

PANGLOSS: She is going to be right here in a second. So I expect you to be courteous and reserved, since, I guess, you still remember the good manners of our own time!

Cacambo: What is your name?

The Girl in white gives a smile, before replying: Dorothy.

Panlgoss: You are not really looking like the little girl caught up in a tornado with her farmhouse.

Dorothy: Have you not noticed that I still keep my Silver Shoes?[9]

Pangloss: I am glad to be in your company.

Dorothy: You said so much on Gold. So, what about Silver?

Cacambo: We were debating on the 1931 Gold default. Is not your question somewhat beyond our point?

Dorothy: I heard, although from a distance you friend by the name of..?

Pangloss: Pangloss.

Dorothy: Nice to meet you Pangloss! I paid special attention to your last point on the link between manufacturing, exports and the Gold backed Sterling in the 19th century. This may have been indeed so, but if you do not provide another more substantial reason for the 1931 Gold Default than the mere reversal of the terms of trade, after the Great War, you miss not only this point in particular, but you miss nothing else than simply the whole thing.

Cacambo: What do you mean?

Dorothy: The medium of exchange from the ancient to the very recent past was not based on Gold only, but on Bimetallism or Gold and Silver. The Gold Standard is in reality a modern phenomenon, dating only since 1822, and it used to be as unprecedented in its own time as fiat money is today.

Cacambo: When did Bimetallism collapse?

Dorothy: The Gold Standard formally introduced in Britain in the first place, in 1820 I guess, was adopted later on, in the 1860s by Germany and France, in 1873 by the US, and in Austria, Russia, India and Latin America by the 1890s. Now, it goes without saying that had it not been for the key role of the City of London, the Gold Standard would not have spread to the rest of the world. The opposition to Gold came for a time from France,[10] from the US, even after 'The Crime of 1873'[11] and China, the latter remaining on Silver up to 1913. Bimetallism had been around since the beginning of recorded History, including in the Middle-Ages, when various objects were used as money: various disks made of gold, silver and copper. These disks had the design on them by which one could determine where they came from and how much metal they contained.[12]

CACAMBO: It is still not clear to me, why such a system from time immemorial suddenly came to a halt?

DOROTHY: The most cited explanation that has been put forward is based on the mechanistic view, where humans, react just like stones to the pressure of pure entropy: they say it is the discovery of more gold that put an end to Bimetallism.[13] But had not Gold, Silver and Copper been discovered and in the case of hidden treasures, rediscovered, ever since the Deluge or the beginning of the present cycle?

CACAMBO: What is it then? By the way, had it not been claimed from all sides, after the Gold default took place in 1931, that the event in question counted for no less than 'The end of the world'?

DOROTHY: Yes. The argument of those advocating Bimetallism in the US, more than a half a century before 1931, was that the Gold Standard would restrain credit and therefore would create unfavorable conditions for the great majority. Now, both the End of the World mood on both sides of the Atlantic following 1931 and the supposed tight credit policy of the Gold Standard reveal implicitly an attitude of trust in the then central financial authority.

CACAMBO: Where are you getting at?

DOROTHY: What is interesting here is that in the eyes of the public the Gold Standard was not taken for what it really used to be, but for what its proponents, made it appearing to be. The Gold Standard was taken at face value. The general public seems to have forgotten in the process that any coin has two sides. The tight credit, kind of thing, would indeed have taken place, if the Sterling had been backed by Gold not in a figurative, metaphoric way, so to speak, but literally. Had this been indeed so, there would be simply no such thing as Gold Standard.

CACAMBO: What?

DOROTHY: The Gold Standard was nothing less than an elaborate, long term Ponzi scheme and what it did happen is that the bubble simply had to burst in 1931. Throughout the whole period, the proponents of Gold had the following message to the outside world: Do you want to be paid in Gold on demand? If you really insist, basically you have nothing to worry about: we will find ways to restrict your access to your own Gold and to persuade you that this is good for you after all, and more than anything we will see that you have no idea of the ratio at which one ounce is exchanged for its paper equivalent. It goes without saying that this can be done on the condition that all that is happening, takes place behind closed doors, out of the reach of any real public scrutiny, the kind of thing that only a central bank in private hands such as the Bank of England could have provided. By the way, after 1925, and up to 1931 the Gold Standard was nominal or as they say, only a partial Gold Standard. Now, when we say, that the whole thing was a Ponzi scheme from the very beginning, we mean that the world of fiat money in reality starts with the Gold Standard itself.

CACAMBO (*to Pangloss*): Have you heard what she said, my friend? And you spent an hour praising your precious Gold with all your metaphors and misty philosophical abstractions!

PANGLOSS: I was speaking of Gold as a natural limit to the sand like nature of fiat money, as a universally acknowledged medium of exchange, and a shield against tyranny, from the point of view of Non-duality. What she said far from contradicting with my point of view, is in reality only reaffirming it. The specific role of Gold up to 1931 is like a disguised masked, actor, playing the very opposite role of his real nature.

DOROTHY: The very opposite role you just mentioned had been made possible by the suppression of Bimetallism.

CACAMBO: Is not one precious metal enough?

DOROTHY: Gold is in limited supply just as Silver is also in limited supply. Should Silver coins in circulation be backed by Gold, providing their ultimate reference, the very possibility of Ponzi schemes and speculative bubbles of any kind is eliminated altogether, since the one will be mirrored by the other. That is why ever since the Phoenicians, the exchange of goods was carried out not only by Gold alone, but by all the precious metals simultaneously, that is Gold, Silver and Copper. Ever since 1833, when the Bank of England began issuing paper money that was legal tender, Gold Standard is in reality a Fiat Money Standard in disguise, since Gold was no longer priced in an entity with its own intrinsic value such as Silver.[14]

CACAMBO: Where did the idea of the Gold Standard come from?

DOROTHY: The immediate circumstances from which, various larger entities take their origin, are obscured most of the time and numerous different reasons are often invoked in parallel, not only as far as Gold is concerned but also many other things, for example scientific discoveries, patents, cultural or political events. The idea of the Gold Standard apparently came from Newton but also the impetus may have been provided by the British Silver deficit with China before the Opium Trade and the fact that China was on a Silver Standard up to the beginning of the 20th century.[15]

CACAMBO: If Gold is fiat money in disguise, so what are the Lincoln's Green Backs, then?

DOROTHY: Lincoln was for transparency, public supervision and accountability, since contrary to the present 2012 Greek government he was unwilling to pay a double digit interest to private loan sharks for financing the war against the British backed south. Fiat money, in such a context may play, at least for a time a positive role, since once in the open, paper banknotes have a limited bubble like potential.

CACAMBO (*To Pangloss*): Is not this exactly the opposite of your praise of Gold and Silver?

PANGLOSS: No, it is not. Under public scrutiny fiat money may indeed function rationally for the benefit of society and the economy as whole. However, this may be so only in the short run, and in an exceptional context. As I told you already on many occasions, Gold and Silver, by their very intrinsic limits provide a natural protection against the outpouring of blind greed, irrationality, voluntarism and the ever present threat of tyranny in any form of government, and therefore a permanent fiat money system, however transparent at its beginning, when confronted with corruption may become more and more opaque by the day and thus assume the role of a weapon of mass economic destruction.

CACAMBO: You still did not make it clear what is the immediate reason for the Gold default in 1931?

DOROTHY: This is the termination of the post war process of buying up assets throughout the world with inflated pseudo Gold backed Pounds Sterling. This process of investing throughout the world with fake Gold or Pounds Sterling and getting tangible assets in return was further facilitated by the provisions of the Gold Exchange Standard, according to whom countries could hold gold or dollars or pounds as reserves, except for the United States and the United Kingdom. There is also, the less immediate reason, dealing with the structural inability of the then British economy to keep Gold at home.

CACAMBO: How do you compare the 1931 Gold default with the recent 2008 crisis?

DOROTHY: There is a difference and this difference is not in kind but in degree. The default of 1931 counts more than the Crash of 1929. Now, despite the fact that the Crash is predating the Gold default chronologically, it is the forces set in motion behind the default that caused the stock market bubble on Wall Street, through the policy of low interest rates of the FED and respectively high interest rates of the Bank of England. Here is a bubble within a bubble, where the smaller bubble, that of 1929 is bursting first and the larger one, last. As for the 2008 crisis, this is still another bubble, but of a much larger size than the default of 1931.

CACAMBO: Is not the Depression of the 1930s much more significant in its impact on the then society and economy than the crisis of 2008?

DOROTHY: Yes. The Gold default, including the Depression of the 1930s, is like an individual who had fallen ill and recovered by his own efforts, whereas the Crisis of 2008 appears as a temporary cure for this same individual, extending his lifespan for a while with artificial respiration and toxic drugs, but at the same time reducing his chances for ultimate survival to zero, because of the side effects of the whole treatment. A Ponzi scheme of the like of the Gold default and earlier on the Mississippi Bubble, by their very nature, and whatever the ways of hiding and restraining the access to Gold are no match to the free printing press, either of Papiermarks, Zimbabwe Dollars or USD. When they say, that the devastating, far reaching effects of the Great Depression, will no longer reappear, essentially nothing of substance is meant other than a disguised hinting on a spree of paper banknotes thrown out of a helicopter.[16] The post-modern sand like economy in reality simply collapsed in 2008. And if the illusion that this is not exactly so, has been sustained ever since, it is at the price of a flat denial of everything on which the very idea of money as a medium of exchange, of private property and responsibility stand for, at least from the time of late antiquity. The rescue of the patient put on artificial respiration was accomplished by the free printing press and hence the role of the State, have been how to legitimize the essentially obscure origin of the so called funds with all their never ending alignment of zeros, coming apparently out of nowhere. This is in reality only a repetition for the next mega move, when the patient will be relieved of his pain on a permanent basis, by the removal of the apparatus for artificial respiration altogether.

CACAMBO: Was not the nationalization of the Bank of England in 1946 flatly contradicting the categorical imperative of privacy in these matters?

DOROTHY: Ever since the default of 1931, the real action was no longer there, but in its former subsidiary, the FED of New York and even more so after 1971, when a full-scale offensive for Global Dollarization or so to speak, Fiatazation was undertaken. Following these lines, after the Bretton-Woods agreement, the City of London turned to money changing on a scale never seen before, since there is no better exchange these days than Foreign Exchange.[17]

I have to leave now my friends, since it is the subject of Silver that made me come and

I have basically, nothing else to say on that. Here are these two white flowers for each one of you!

CACAMBO: Wait a minute! Where are you going? Will you not come with us to the harbor for dinner? You are such a charming Lady!

*****

PANGLOSS: The Gold default of 1931 is no less relevant for the present and for the future than it is for the past.

CACAMBO: I see. So, where your fortune telling is leading you now?

PANGLOSS: If we paid so much attention to the Gold default, it has been in the intent of outlining the intrinsic difference between a bubble based on a limited ultimate reference and a bubble on an unlimited reference. In the last resort, the volume and the likely impact of the former on the economy and society as a whole, by necessity, is to be much smaller than that of the latter. The Gold default of 1931 is not the end, but only the beginning of the end.

CACAMBO: How do you see the next Mega fiat bubble coming out of the sands of Sahara?

PANGLOSS: When in 1971, the last reference to Gold was scrapped, the USD as we mentioned it a short while ago, made a fast escalade to the roof of the world. It goes without saying that the more Dollars are in circulation outside of their country of origin, the higher is the importance of the USD in the world economy. Seen from this angle, the US twin deficits that had caused such a stir in the mainstream media, in the years before the Crisis of 2008 are in reality, a sine qua non condition for the continuing role of the USD as a the world's ultimate accounting unit. So are the expansion of credit and consequently, the rise of personal and corporate debt to the present apparently unsustainable levels.

CACAMBO: You spoke on this already, but you still did not say anything on the way all this have come about, since 1971 but in the first place, I guess, since the Bretton Woods agreement in 1944?

PANGLOSS: Yes. After the end of WWII, the US had most of the world's supply of Gold and when it has been decided that the USD and the USD only, was redeemable in Gold, at first glance it, it did not seem that later on, something really new was about to happen. Bretton-Woods looked like a relocation of the Gold Standard, although in a somewhat different form, to a new destination, across the Atlantic.

CACAMBO: Have you forgotten than one currency before 1931 was as convertible to Gold as any other?

PANGLOSS: Would you let me finish first? We just said that the post Bretton-Woods Gold Standard was no longer the Gold Standard of 1822, since the access to Gold was restricted further and in practice the USD became the only real currency in circulation. Furthermore, under the gold exchange standard between 1925 and 1931, countries could hold gold or dollars or pounds as reserves, except for the United States and the United Kingdom, which held reserves only in gold. Nevertheless, however symbolic or nominal the reference to Gold may have become, it was still in place. Now, there is one question at this point. Was the establishment of an outright fiat money world financial system, the real finality of the whole thing right from 1944 or not? Had the whole development of the situation from 1944 to 1971 been an Intelligent Design plan, where Bretton-Woods is only the first stage of the play or on the opposite, a flow of blind economic forces conditioned by the circumstances of the day, and actually of all days throughout the whole period, for that matter?

CACAMBO: What? If you expect an answer, I will tell you that all this is mere history.

PANGLOSS: Yes. If you mean that, this is history in the making, I agree with you. Now, as we mentioned earlier on, should we compare the USD based system of fiat money to a Babel tower, on the first floors of this tower, where the offices of Banks, Investment Funds etc. are located, there is an insatiable appetite for banknotes, profits and therefore, a real competition. If we are to remain on the corporate or administrative level so to speak, there is simply no way of containing the flood of liquidity. Furthermore, from bird's-eye view, the ideal way of preserving one's position would be not a perfect equilibrium, but on the opposite, a sustained disequilibrium, created by a high level of credits and debts together with of a large variety of bubbles and a full-fledged financialisation of the whole society. Otherwise, there would be no way of exercising the power of finance in extra-economic matters, which both for the sake of the survival of the whole system of usury and for its own sake is the very reason for being of the whole thing. However, what counts at this point, is what is really meant be sustained disequilibrium. Should we make a compromise between the blind tension from the bottom of the tower and the self-conscious tension emanating from the top, a whole dynamic of change will come out of itself.

CACAMBO: Look at the Spirit! He just woke up and seems to be listening to your point!
PANGLOSS: We will pay a special attention to him later on, but for now, we will go further with the period between 1944 and 1971. They say, the US trade deficit with

Japan and Germany, a notable contribution to which had been brought by the one time, WW Beatle, as well as the Vietnam War eroded the position of the USD, since, as the mainstream version of these events asserts, the flight of Gold backed Greenbacks to foreign countries was undermining the whole US economy. At this point everything seems to be no less than great! Here is an apparently blind force or a mud like current flowing along the river of the never ending production line of the kind in Charlie Chaplin's 'Modern Times'. The implicit, encrypted real content of the whole message goes on something like this: 'Ladies and Gentleman, the present situation is absolutely beyond our control, since, as the Sun is rising and setting every day, so in the same way, the market is a reflection of the preferences of the consumer and what it happens at this point is that our US consumer buys foreign cars, foreign TV's etc. We scrupulously observe the freedom of entry and exit in our domestic market. However, as you can see, this is at our expense, since these foreigners, (in the 1960s mainly Germans, Japanese and the so called four Asian Tigers, Hong Kong, Singapore, South Korea and Taiwan.) have the upper hand in today's world economy.' Now, the expected result of the message in question, propagated in a concerted way and accompanied by a flood of apparently objective statistics by practically the totality of western's world media, and even reprinted in toto by Soviet and Eastern Bloc magazines,[18] was twofold: on one hand it helps sustaining in the public consciousness the illusion of the primacy of free market over anything and on the other hand, it projects an image of impotence of the US economy, at the very moment when the idea of scrapping Bretton-Woods by establishing the first ever, world standard of fiat money in recorded history was about to be put into practice. The City of London and Wall Street in reality were preparing a full-fledged attack on the world economy, of a kind that their forerunners such as Sir John Law in the 18th and others the 19th century could not even dream of.

Cacambo: Your fortune telling has taken an amazing turnaround. You put a hypothetical intent before the facts, without even making an allusion, however vague to the arguments that are allowing you of making a clear distinction between fact and fiction.

Pangloss: There is no better way of disguising a fact than eliminating the very possibility for the appearance of this same fact in consciousness altogether by the design of a specific state of mind or else a self-regulating mechanism of censorship. Here is a built-in epistemological myopia, both in the liberal and in the leftist rhetoric. When they say, 'capitalism' or 'socialism' or 'market forces', they imply abstract, amorphous, mechanically driven entities, where the interplay of live impulses, leaving their imprint on the process of production and exchange is obscured. Also, the natural drive for reflection is further repressed by the leveling effect brought by the empiricist dogma, substituting thinking with statistics.

Cacambo: Had the closing of the Golden Window in 1971, already been on the agenda back in 1944?

PANGLOSS: The conditions at the end of the Second World War, were not good enough for the outright implementation of a fiat money standard, not form a mere economic point of view, but from a cultural point of view as well. In 1944, the idea of a treaty for the establishment of one way system or the idea of giving something and taking nothing in return, sounded a bit like signing a formal agreement with a shoplifter for entering your shop and empting the content of your cash register at any time.

CACAMBO: Have I not told already that a visit to any $1 Dollar Store, may give you a precise account of what One USD bill can buy?

PANGLOSS: What we refer to here, is how much a One Dollar bill is worth at last resort. As for the goods you can buy at this very moment, the exact amount and composition of these goods, equivalent to One Dollar is a variable beyond your control, since at any time the real issuer of the bill can determine its price by the manipulation of the quantity of bills in circulation and nothing is hindering him in this, other than his own considerations. Therefore, if you think that you indeed possess your own bill for good, you are deceiving yourself.

CACAMBO: And who is the issuer?

PANGLOSS: Discretion is the sine qua non condition for the stability of the fiat money system.[19]

CACAMBO: Are you not going too far when you exclude the very possibility that the decision of closing the last reference to Gold in 1971 may have been taken at random or under a set of circumstances which could not have been predicted back in 1944? By the way, was not Nixon apparently preoccupied by the speculation with the USD, when he took this decision, known as the Nixon Shock?

PANGLOSS: The whole process leading in the end to the closing the Gold window in 1971 has been unfolding on two levels, a little like a detached house with a garden where those on the roof can see what is going on in the garden, but those in the garden may not even being aware that someone is watching them from the roof. When the outflow of Gold backed Dollars from the US increased, by the late 1950s, two opposite tendencies appeared on the scene: on one hand, those following the logic of the Gold Standard, based on the presumption of an ultimate equilibrium of the exchanges and therefore the necessity to keep most of the Gold inside one's own country,[20] and on the other hand, those following the logic of fiat money. The plan for the establishment of a world fiat currency, back in the late 1950s, may have had only three conceivable stages: Stage 1: Do your best to prevent, the US Dollars, spent abroad for imports and fuelling the trade deficit, from coming back to their home country. How is this to be done? A way for keeping all these, USD in circulation throughout the world and in practice beyond the jurisdiction of any country[21] has to be found out. And what is this way? The Eurodollar Market located in the City of London and growing each year in importance ever since the 1950s up to end of the period into consideration in 1971 and beyond.[22] By the way, it is precisely when the mainstream characterization of the UK as the 'Sick man of Europe' went into fashion, somewhere in the 1960s, that one bank after another was opening new branches in the City of London, and the Eurodollar market assumed a central role in world finance, as a prelude for the things to come. Stage 2: Increase public spending to unsustainable levels within the existing setting or within the arrangements for the convertibility of the USD to Gold: a target that had been reached, by the early 60s, thanks to the combined effect of Johnson's "Great Society" and the Vietnam War. Stage 3: Undo what you pretend to have done in 1944: demolish the last remnants of the Gold Standard as a house of cards by closing the Gold window, forever or may be even not forever, but only until the curtain will have already be fallen and the piece will have come to an end.

CACAMBO: All of the above has nothing to do with your intelligent design from the roof kind of thing. First, the Eurodollar market was based on the demand for the Gold backed USD as a reserve currency. Second, there was a Cold War, and both the Great Society and the Vietnam War are to be considered within the larger extra economic framework of the time. Third, the very expansion of the world economy was calling for a fiat money standard.

PANGLOSS: Suppose you are on board of a flying saucer right now, on your way to a distant planet and shortly before landing you are just reading a brochure about what is really going on in this place. Now, had the content of the brochure been the same content as the one, we presented, save the exclusive right of the USD and the USD only to be backed by Gold at the expense of the all other currencies in circulation, you would miss the overall picture of the place.

CACAMBO: Would Bretton-Woods still be called Bretton-Woods, if it had not been for this unique role, assigned to the USD? By the way, let me remind you that most of the others had almost no Gold after the end of the Second World War, save the USSR. So, would you just tell me, how is International Trade to expand if it were a return to the pre 1931 kind of Gold Standard?

PANGLOSS: I agree with your first question: what is really special about Bretton-Woods is the unique role of the USD without any precedent in recorded history. As for the expansion, before going any further, we have just to mention once again that the very idea of economic expansion is a feature of the modern and the modern economy only, since in the old view, well-being is not equivalent to quantitative expansion, quite the opposite, wealth is associated with harmony and the observance of the natural law, be it in China, India, Egypt, Greece etc. Now, should we consider the ways for a sustained expansion in these post war conditions, without making any judgment of value we may indeed, resort to a Gold backed USD, but only for a time. Once, say, a measured transfer of a portion of the Gold has been made from the US to the rest of the then non-communist world, provided you have no other ideas in mind as far as your ultimate goal is concerned, you will set a date and affix your signature for this date, already in the agreement of Bretton-Woods of 1944, so that a new Gold Standard, might be re-established. The potential disequilibrium, naturally following from a system where all want the Gold or the Gold backed Dollars out of the their country of origin, that is the US, save those defending the orthodox and in practice mercantilist view on Gold and International Trade, might have been easily predicted back in 1944.

CACAMBO: They say, this prevented the formation of trading blocs as in the 1930s...

PANGLOSS: This argument may be of any relevance, if there was no Cold War, which as you know has not been the case.

CACAMBO: You said: 'All want Gold backed Dollars'. Who are these 'All', after all?

PANGLOSS: There was a high demand for liquidity in the postwar world economy and the fact that countries such as Germany and Japan among others had been making efforts to earn as much US Dollars as possible, through exports is no less than self-evident. Furthermore, the Cold War rendered a great service to the advocates of the Eurodollar Market, starting from the Soviet apparatchiks, who found no better than depositing their US Dollar funds in the City of London.[23] It goes without saying that, had it not been for the Cold War and consequently the higher military spending, the ratio of printed Dollars to the Gold reserves would have been much smaller.

CACAMBO: Are you exposing in length all these abstractions simply to tell me, that there is out there a hidden, invisible center, from where, the real power is exercised by, say a branch of the so called 'Unknown Superiors'?[24] Do not you think that the millions of pages, throughout this electric kind of thing...how were they calling it? The Internet, I guess? Where all these theories of the Illuminati type have been reproduced are enough already so that you add still another semantic rearrangement of one and the same puzzle? Do not you remember the Rosicrucian Manifesto appearing a century before our own time, where a series of pamphlets that may have been written by anybody had been a matter of endless debates on just everything?

PANGLOSS: You are growing impatient to go back to the harbor and you did not let me finish my point. Had my intention been indeed as you say, you would be right to object, but as you will see in a moment, this has not been the case. The thing is that all these endless debates are an implicit denial of the only possible foundation that a genuine effort for insight may have. It is only reflection and mediation on the thing in itself or the intelligible essence that may give a consistent account of what is really going on and nothing else. Were all these fragments of, most of the time, dubiously selective pieces for a supposedly organized historical puzzle, assembled into a whole, without going in the first place, to their Metaphysical timeless background located in the deeper layers of Consciousness, all that would be left, might be nothing more than a list with a few names on it, whose eventual compilation would not advance the cause of transparency and Justice in a single iota. Once detached from their core, related to their Principle of manifestation, these pieces are subject, as we hinted it already, to all kinds of manipulation. This in turn, would become a fertile ground for the outpouring of grotesque narrow mindedness on a massive scale, since matters of dress, together with the transmission of pseudo-occult knowledge will naturally attract those who are predisposed to remain on the surface of reality. Even if it happens that somehow there has never been a single Illuminati walking on the surface of this planet, the relevance for what we said about the conscious design behind fiat money would remain no less than intact. The problem with Nominalism, whatever its disguise may be, is that the natural link between cause and effect is turned upside down, since in a such a reversed form of Consciousness the color of the ink with which a word has been written on a sheet of paper, being at its very opposite, is taken for the meaning of this word.

CACAMBO: Have you not said a short while ago that History is not a blind, anonymous force?

PANGLOSS: Yes. What is at stake here in no way contradicts the earlier point on the Monad and the deceptive nature of the concept of the Mass. Facts may be only an illustration of the primacy of the effort for insight over all the rest or the primacy of content over its form. Now, it goes without saying that there is a point where, the invisible does indeed, intersect with the visible, since the possibility for all these points exists a priori in Consciousness or in the Universe.

CACAMBO: It appears from what you said so far that the world actually came to an end already in 1971. Yet, we are in 2012 right now and things are still moving ahead. Is not today's world economy much more prosperous and complex even with or may be thanks to the piles of fiat money you oppose to all the time?

PANGLOSS: We have little time left on these island and that is why I reserve my answer to this for the end. As for 1971, in the mainstream view of the world economy, these events are known as the relative decline of the US and the stagnation or rather stagflation of the 1970s, apparently brought by the First Oil Shock. By the way, apart from, the USD backed Gold Standard, the World Bank and the International Monetary Fund the Bretton Woods conference established the GDP as the standard tool for sizing up a country's economy.[25] This measure appears in retrospect as a concerted onslaught on the last remnants of rational thinking on economic matters. Gradually the media throughout the world simply stopped reflecting on anything other than the GDP growth and the ways to expand this growth. Are you preoccupied by the future of your country? Gone are the boring and rather disturbing questions, of the kind raised by Plato, Joachim de Flore, Vico or even Montesquieu or Gibbon dealing with Cycles, Forms and more than anything with the impact of the Psyche on economic activity, which had been implicitly taken for granted in the pre-modern world. Just check the GDP growth. Are you concerned for the place of your continent in world politics? Gone are the historical events with all their covert dealings and the intricate issues on the unpredictability of the human nature or the never ending confrontation with the unknown, since all you have to do right now is just checking the GDP growth once again.

CACAMBO: You are going too far. The first pages of the newspapers and magazines of the time were literally covered with information on the OPEC embargo, the inflation, the unemployment.

PANGLOSS: Yes. What we said on the GNP fetishism in no way contradicts the diffusion of the information, you are referring to. The thing is that the constant preoccupation for quantity for its own sake is among other things a way to divert the attention from what is really going on literally before your eyes. However, it goes without saying that this is not enough to explain everything even in the most, so to speak nominalized form of consciousness. Now, there is one key reason above all the rest: this is the closing of the Gold window. The immediate reasons for this move, far from being opposed, are In reality complementary to the main reason.

CACAMBO: What is this main reason?

PANGLOSS: 1971 is the real start of the plan for the establishment of a global economy and for the hegemony of the issuers of the USD on the rest of the world.

CACAMBO: Why do not you make it simpler and just say the USA?

PANGLOSS: The issuers of last resort of the USD stand apart from the people of the US in the same way as they stand apart from the rest of the world. By the way, have you not noticed that the American Republic appears to be different today than back in our own time, when it had been founded?

CACAMBO: They say the reason for the War of Independence had been the Tea Act.

PANGLOSS: It was one of the reasons,[26] since from the very beginning a clear distinction was made between the pursuit of happiness in the New World and the pursuit of pleasure in the Old World. And another thing: When they speak of the US, in Europe and elsewhere, they take it for granted that it is a new country in a New World. Yet, here is a State based on a Constitution in the same way as the Cities of Antiquity used to be based on Sacred Laws and had a date of birth. In the Old World, different governments, different states come and go but the identity of those who stay around remains the same. France is no less France under Louis XIV than under Robespierre, Vichy or De Gaulle, whereas the US without the US Constitution would be somewhat like Sparta without the Laws of Lycurgus.

CACAMBO: Is not the printing of paper banknotes still part of the Constitution?

PANGLOSS: No. It is an exploitation of the Freedom given by the Constitution in the name of its opposite. The private monopoly for the printing of fiat money is an onslaught on Freedom, whose ultimate consequences are yet to be seen.

CACAMBO: Listen, I cannot stand it any longer. When are we to go back to the harbor? Is not all this beyond your subject of Foreign Exchange?

PANGLOSS: In the present world, there are essentially only two real opponents against the omnipresent invisible hand of Foreign Exchange, displaying freshly printed greenbacks like a pack a cards, throughout the four corners of the world at any point in time. These are the supporters of the US Constitution within the US and those in favor of a genuinely independent State in today's Russia.

CACAMBO: Have you not picked all this at random? I actually see these two opposed most of the time.

PANGLOSS: There is nothing unusual in this combination, since already in 1863 the North was supported by the Tsar against the colonially minded Confederation.[27]

CACAMBO: And what about the Cold War as they call it?

PANGLOSS: The Cold War helped the cause of an eventual Global Fiat Money Empire in a way that may be nothing else did.

CACAMBO: Here is another of you never ending riddles. Could you at least be more specific?

PANGLOSS: Should we put aside any, so to speak, dogmatic interpretation, of the UN Charter of State Sovereignty, some in no time, would appear as more equal than others. The reference to a supposed threat from the East acquired at some point a financially minded significance, where the Metropolis imposed its own version of how economic activity is to be carried out on its new de facto Colonies, now including most of West Europe. Even as late as the 1950 and 1960s, the idea of USD backed by nothing would seem grotesque to say the least. Do not you remember the uproar throughout Europe, mentioned among others by Goethe in his 'Faust', caused by Sir John Law with his Mississippi Bubble? Up to this very day, the apparently incomprehensible, for many foreigners, mistrust of the French toward money in general has a cryptic relation to these events of our own time, in the 18th century.

CACAMBO: Where is the exact location of the Metropolis, since it appears that this is not exactly the US?

PANGLOSS: As any military historian knows, a hidden enemy has over its overt counterpart the privilege of being everywhere and nowhere at the same time. The Metropolis in question is a little like the Flying Dutchman with the only difference that it is by no means a ghost, but a fast moving rocket leaving piles of banknotes along its zigzag type trajectory. It goes without saying that as any rocket, whatever its mode propulsion might be, needs fuel so is this one and therefore places such the City of London or Wall Street, right there on the harbor are among its preferred locations for refueling.

CACAMBO: What happened in the decade following 1971?

PANGLOSS: There are two different versions of the period, standing to each other as opposite poles. This is the version of the mainstream media on one hand and the original version of which the first is a reversed copy, on the other hand. First, let's start with the copy. So, in 1973 as the mainstream story goes, the OAPEC proclaimed an oil embargo in response to the US support for Israel during the Yom Kippur War. It goes without saying that in the immediate thereafter, a flood of comments, articles, books, statements by all kinds of public figures, both of the elected or the unelected variety, scholars, politicians etc. etc. poured out from all cracks of the now formally proclaimed permanently damaged seawall that the Western and US economy in particular has apparently become. The US, they said, were losing ground before the now formidable oil weapon of the oil producing countries, the balance of power was shifting away from the West etc.

CACAMBO: Your insistence on a supposedly parallel, so to speak, subtle reality is a groundless fantasy. The economic growth of the OCDE countries took a negative turn, since this had been the worst recession ever since 1929. This is a fact. As for the US, not only were they facing growing opposition from the Arab world, but by that time, it was already clear that the regime in Saigon had no chance of winning against the North and worse still, it appeared that, they were about to lose the arms race with the USSR as well. These are also facts. So would you be so kind as to tell me how much your preoccupation with fiat money is worth compared to all that?

Pangloss: Listen to me friend, if you want to go to the harbor for dinner rather sooner than later, let me finish my point, because we have very few time left. So, what you said is indeed so. However, it is so only from the point of view of the reversed copy, we just mentioned. However real it may seem, this reality is only a shadowy reality in the same way as a movie is real but only as a projection, since at any time those shooting this movie, may rearrange the sequences according to their own wishes and what is more, any movie is at last resort a copy of something other than itself or a copy of a given original. Now, should you attempt to see what is this movie in itself, you had better not losing you time with the projection that the copy is at last resort, but with the idea in the consciousness of those shooting the movie.

Cacambo: You can say all this of just anything. What is making you think that the facts, I mentioned are not simply what they are and nothing else?

Pangloss: Should we put aside for a second, the basic premise that at last resort nothing is what it appears to be at first glance, there is an event that rarely if ever appeared on the front page of any newspaper or magazine with a large circulation at the time. This is the already mentioned on several occasions Petrodollar, where Oil was to be exchanged only for USD. Now, the first question coming out of itself at this point is: why should you agree to exchange a commodity such as oil for pieces of paper, whose ultimate value is not in your own hands but in the hands of those to whom you ship your precious commodity? If the deal in question, dating by the way since 1973, or in another form may be even earlier, had been conducted on perfectly equal terms, according to the principles of UN Charta of State Sovereignty, it becomes utterly incomprehensible why agreeing to such a deal in the first place instead of requesting what the dealers of the place had been requesting as a mode of payment ever since the days of the silk trade, already in Biblical times? By the way, we could safely assume that there was no sand or paper in Ali Baba' cavern, since otherwise there would be simply no valuable reason to utter the magic words: Sesame Open up! Why saving the disgrace of requesting gold for oil to such an apparently waning power as the US at the time, if there is nothing else at stake?

Cacambo: Was not the rise of Oil prices enough?

Pangloss: You seem to forget that in the three dimensional space, any coin has two sides.

Cacambo: Where are your sources on all that?

PANGLOSS: Listen, have I not told you already, that time is running out? And another thing: there is one source above all other sources and this source is reflection. Should you insist, however, I will provide you one only other source and for no other reason than the following, quote: This is a Faustian Bargain.[28] By the way, have we not spoken on the Sahara desert already?

CACAMBO: Yes, but this was more than an hour ago and I do not remember why.

PANGLOSS: The exchange of Oil for paper made appear any grain in the desert as a piece of gold. However, this vision would last only for the time required so that one of these huge sand clocks that sometimes can be found in such places should complete a vast U turn on its dusty hands. Once the U turn is over and the Sun sets, the grains will lose their shine and will no longer appear as something other than what they have always been: grains of 100% pure sand. In such a context, Mephistopheles would not have any better to say than, the following, I guess: For a time all the mirages in the desert will be yours my dear friend Faustus provided you give me your oasis, the only possession you had, before I made the Sun rays projected on the sand look in your eyes like gold or just as good as gold. This has been the deal in question.

CACAMBO: Up to this point you have been describing your reverse copy. I guess. So, what is the original then?

PANGLOSS: Let's take for the sake of free reflection on the subject, one of the tales of 1001 Nights, which by the way, initially was not part of the original collection. This is the Lamp of Aladdin.

CACAMBO: Seriously, had it not been for my misfortune of having no access to your God damn Elixir, I would have gone to the harbor on my own a long time ago. As you very well know the potion you gave me extended my lifespan, but was not enough for taking advantage of the transmutation of metals and I became a wondering pauper as a result. Your tales are at best good for a children's book. Have I not told you already, that there is no better substance these days than the measured substance, no better evidence then the statistical evidence? For example, a text of the Ph.D variety devoted to the causes for which the color of the Greenback is no other than green with all the sources, references and other econometric equations leading to this solid fact has incomparably more scientific value than all of your metaphors combined.

PANGLOSS: My Elixir is just like Gold, it is in a limited quantity and as you also know it very well, it would be possible to give a portion of this Elixir only in a particular time frame and under the right set of circumstances. In the meantime, if you are so annoyed in my company, I could give you some cash and leave you alone.

Cacambo: Better not, right now, since there is one point at which I definitely agree with you. There is indeed no problem to print as much fiat money as you wish. The only problem is the accountability. How to account for the sudden appearance of trillions of USD out of nowhere, and at the same time sustain the illusion of the intrinsic value of fiat money on one hand and, and to make believe the public that there is a system of exchange, where in reality there is a system of distribution for some and appropriation for others. So, being an alien from another time, should you give me a large amount of cash, I will have to give an account for its origin to these 21 century people and this may be a problem at some point.

Pangloss: Yes. All the deficits of the current economic crisis, starting with the twin US deficits and ending with the Greek debt, may disappear with a stroke of a pen, since the cash may be printed and thrown out from helicopters in no time, but this would be at the expense of the present economic arrangements and at the price of a crisis of confidence that would be at last resort impossible to resolve, whereas with Gold there is a purely physical constraint, which, as we said it before, is in itself a limit to the emergence of bubbles. The size of a fiat money pyramid will always be much larger than the size of gold or silver backed pyramid. By the way, I was about to present my point on the lamp of Aladdin and the Petrodollar system.

Cacambo: Was not Aladdin an individual who went deep into the ground where he found out a kind of magic lamp?

Pangloss: Yes. Now, let's make the following rearrangement of the tale in question: The Sorcerer is the last resort issuer of fiat money or the USD and the trapped in the cave Aladdin is the last resort recipient of this same amount of fiat money, Petrodollars in particular. As for the magic lamp, let's equate the latter with the resources of the world economy as well as the natural resources of the whole planet.

Cacambo: That is really great, but this is not the whole plot of the tale.

Pangloss: Here is a rearrangement according to our subject. So, I suggest you to be more flexible with our version of the tale. .

Cacambo: What would you do if you were in the place of Aladdin?

Pangloss: Let's start with the Sorcerer, since it is he who made Aladdin to descend into the cave.

Cacambo: Is the Sorcerer in your version of the tale, in reality a banker?

Pangloss: No. He is who he is, that is a Sorcerer. So, let's say it again: what would you do in the place of the Sorcerer?

CACAMBO: I would take the lamp for myself and would leave Aladdin in the cave indefinitely.

PANGLOSS: Great! Now, I will tell you how such an event could indeed take place in the present context.

CACAMBO: Go ahead.

PANGLOSS: My first step as a Sorcerer will be to remain invisible on a permanent basis. So once in the shadow, without being a shadow myself, I will realize at some point that in the ever changing landscape all around me, I will be able to affect how things are going on by finding a way of flooding the world with grains of sand or fiat money. The more paper banknotes I put into circulation, the more power I have over those who detain them, since it is me and only me, who has the possibility of issuing these banknotes and nothing is standing in my way other than my own considerations as far as the exchange rate at last resort of my grains of sand is concerned. How should I maintain the proclaimed nominal value of these pieces of paper, so that their intrinsic worthlessness may not become manifest in a sequence of time, I do not desire but only when I think this would be suitable for me? There has to be something only I, the Sorcerer possess that others do not. This something is Oil. Once the monopoly of the USD is firmly established, there is no way to bypass the USD since Oil is denominated in USD only. Now, what shall I do to preserve this monopoly over time? There are political means but what are the purely economic means? This is the quantity of USD outside the US. The more this quantity is growing, the more secure is my position. Everything is good so that this might be going on without interruption: trade deficits, selling of securities primarily to foreigners and more than anything, a rise of the key commodity denominated in USD: Oil.

CACAMBO: But has not the price of Oil been falling at some point?

PANGLOSS: Yes, but when the whole system was established back in 1971, this process of flooding the world with USD was only beginning. That is why a sudden rise of the now USD denominated Oil was the condition 'sine qua non' of the new system. Once detached from gold the USD was in free fall by the way. So, the more the price of Oil was rising, the more my plan for global economic hegemony was in reality succeeding, since the dominance of my greenbacks was re-established once again in a new much more attractive footing. What only yesterday was causing trouble among the public figures concerned with the outflow of gold backed USD, now was a source of joy, if not for the profanes, at least for me, the Sorcerer. Up to now, everything is just fine. However, there has been something back in that time, the 1970s that was not going on the way I like it. According to my plan, once a transaction of Oil for USD has been completed, the USD now in global circulation had to be global indeed, but on the condition that, it is in line with Ford's saying about the color of his Ford T: 'Ford T, he stated is available in any color provided this color is black.' The Petrodollar had to be located exclusively in my own territory and nowhere else. Once sent back to me, these Petrodollars had to multiply a little like an image in a labyrinth reflected by thousands of mirrors and be sent back to world markets in the forms of credits, securities, purchases of the most extravagant goods and services etc. By the way, the whole process was described in very realistic terms, since the expression, 'Recycling of Petrodollars' came about in that time. You cannot indeed recycle gold, the way you can recycle plastic bags. What in reality was hindering to some extent my full-fledged onslaught on the world economy was not the USSR, China, Germany or Japan or France with all the theoretical commitment of De Gaulle to gold, but a small, Lilliputian like country by the name of Lebanon.

CACAMBO: What? Was not this the place, where the present version of the 1001 Nights came into the West, a century before our own time?

PANGLOSS: Yes. As for the thing about the Petrodollars, it is the following: when I provoked the first Oil Shock in 1973 and expected as a result, already at that point to flood the world economy with USD in equal proportion to the rise of the Oil price, some of the USD did not come back right away to my own places, on both sides of the Atlantic, but remained instead in the Lebanese banks. And there is more to come: this used to be in reality a way to subvert the closing of the Gold Window, since the holders of USD from the Gulf States rushed to deposit their assets in Beirut. And worse still: the then Lebanese Pound had the largest percentage of gold backing by its central bank.[29] Do not forget that, after the USD had been detached from Gold in 1971, the price of Gold skyrocketed, since my move created a crisis of confidence.[30] So an eventual under the counter agreement for the covert gold backing of the Lebanese Pound in exchange for the flood of Petrodollars was giving me a real headache at that point. In October 1974, the Lebanese Pound had reached a record high value, standing at 1.2.22 against the USD.[31]

CACAMBO: Did not a civil war, apparently coming out of nowhere suddenly brake out a few months later, in April 1975?

PANGLOSS: Yes. By the way, the prototype for the macrocosmic rearrangement of the main narrative, as they say these days, in reality came out of the microcosmic conditions, brought forth by this same civil war,[32] which lasted for 15 years, up to 1990. Now, would you just let me go on further with my role playing of the 1001 Nights type Sorcerer?

CACAMBO: What happened to the piles of USD entering other places, for example Japan and Germany?

PANGLOSS: At the very moment back in the 1970s, when I was handing, to my various contributors and other valets, their pay checks for ringing the alarm bells about the growing US trade deficit with these countries, I was delighted to see all these BMW's Toyota's, Sony TV sets and other things of this sort flooding the highways and the markets of the US. Not only, was this a real bargain, since all these items were coming in exchange for the few words inscribed on my Greenbacks and other Treasuries, just like the words: Sesame Open up! Whose uttering was enough for entering the Ali Baba's cavern, but at the same time the recipients of my banknotes were now supporting in their turn, the very illusion that I had created in the first place: the illusion of taking my grains of sand for gold. So, the more the deficits were growing, the better my plan for globalization was working. I do care about these piles only in respect to their impact on, the actions I intent to undertake at last resort and that is why what is really of concern to me is that the way for channeling a constant flow of USD in foreign recipients might be cleared out on a permanent basis.

CACAMBO: Are you not sacrificing the productive basis of the US economy with all these imported goods?

PANGLOSS: Beyond any doubt. But what is a mere manufacturing compared to my ultimate design for a Global Fiat Money Empire? Had it not been for the twin US deficits, and needless to say for the closing of the Gold Window, the process of globalization would not have taken place on such a massive scale. It goes without saying that a number of USD driven bubbles, have already taken place in the process, appearing in retrospect as no more than a repetition of the ultimate bubble which is yet to come. The first bubble on my post Bretton-Woods record, has been the Oil Shock of 1973, and all its aftershocks ever since, the next one on my list, was the Latin American Debt Crisis in the 1980s, caused by the excess of liquidity or the piles of Petrodollars, further on, the 1986 Japan Asset Price Bubble, and now the bubble that is about to burst in China in the next 2-3 years at the latest.

CACAMBO: Did you not miss the Internet Bubble, the 2007, US Real Estate Bubble and the present Sovereign Debt crisis?

PANGLOSS: No. The bubbles I just mentioned are primarily driven by the ever growing Petrodollar and Eurodollar denominated liquidity. Here is the key weapon in the whole of my arsenal. The other Bubbles are somewhat different since, these are due to the excess of a still USD denominated liquidity, and exported overseas, but only after the whole thing started in the US in the first place.

CACAMBO: After all you have said on the USD and the built-in excess instilled in the very idea of fiat money and private central banking, I still do not see how it happened that the 2008 crisis was contained and the worst avoided, at least up to now?

PANGLOSS: Have you not asked this question before?

CACAMBO: Maybe, but if I raise the issue once more, it is because now you are not exactly what you are, since you play the role of the Sorcerer from the tale of the Lamp of Aladdin, right?

PANGLOSS: This crisis irrupted suddenly as a volcano. It has been caused by the ghostlike expansion of the fiat money supply, whose present day expression in the form of derivatives, debt swaps and the like came as a surprise even to me, a little like a clock with so many buttons and hands that at some point its very owner has no clue any more, where to press so that the alarm of the clock might be set. Now, what really counts here is that, the system simply passed away in 2008, but this has not been noticed in a tangible way yet. Had it not been for the process of distribution or baling out, the banking system would have ceased to function already more than 3 years ago. If it is still here, however, it is at the price of the explicit denial of the very principles by which a system of exchange is distinguished from a system of distribution. Had the humans been as mechanically driven as this clock, it would have been possible to throw fiat money from helicopters indefinitely. But the thing is that this is not so and a terminal crisis of confidence is already on the horizon, as a result.

CACAMBO: Is the crisis of the Euro already the beginning of the end?

PANGLOSS: The confection of the Euro as a fiat currency backed by no more and nor less than the value of the office furniture at the disposal of a few individuals, sitting in their Brussels based, armchairs has nothing to do with economic activity whatsoever.

CACAMBO: Who put into circulation the Euro?

PANGLOSS: Me, the Sorcerer from the tale of Aladdin and Magic Lamp.

CACAMBO: Why?

PANGLOSS: I love order or my own version of order in particular, to be more precise, including the idea of correctness, but being not that stupid as *Big Brother* from '1984', I do not support the one neither the other, for its own sake, since this is only an end to a mean. All these European states were giving me a headache with their pretensions for sovereignty from a by-gone era. Many elements in these places were simply not enlightened enough to realize that ever since the end WWII, Europe, save for two or at best three countries, is in the same position as India used to be at the time when the East India Company was at its height. So, I had to waste my precious time by posing as an equal partner to some whereas, the others, those I had real dealings with, knew very well that some are definitely more equal than others. The resulting confusion was putting me in real trouble sometimes. For example, I had to deal with dozens of different central banks, financial institutions and the like at the same time. The Euro brought an end to this confusion. From now on, I could dictate my own terms in a much more efficient way. Furthermore, the Euro is a repetition for the time when I shall come back on the scene with a new global currency. Since I have not been successful of shattering the last remnants of sovereignty that these countries had, by purely political means, I decided to act accordingly, by means of economic pressure from below. Now, if the reason for being of the Euro, as I said it already has nothing to do with rational thinking neither with the simplest common sense, there must be a price to pay for all this. So, as you shall see later on, I made them pay this price. In the past, the Mediterranean economies, used to be highly efficient, but in their own terms, not on my terms. By the way I dislike these people, because they still hide cash and gold in the basements of their houses instead of handing them to me and realizing once and for all that their most precious asset for the rest of their lives on this planet is their credit card. There is a real mistrust toward the State and any central power for that matter in these places, inherited from a complex past, and as result the citizens of these countries are richer and much less corrupt in their own traditional terms than their respective governments. Also, do not forget that it is me and me only, who is setting the correct standard of what corruption is all about these days. Once their main tools of affecting economic activity through competitive devaluations, and interest rates appropriate to their own conditions, not to the conditions of a whole continent, were no longer there, their debts grew on a much higher level. Something that I knew it was going to happen right from the beginning, in 1999 when the Euro was introduced. And at this very moment I started firing without interruption at what had remained of the now dwindling economic credibility of these places. I charged a double digit interest on their bonds. I made my best to show them that they must hand to me the last remnants of their sovereignty. The present Sovereign debt crisis is my creation. Once I extracted funds from the States to pay for my insolvent banks and then I made a profit from these same funds taken from the taxpayer by raising the interest rate for a risk that I had caused in the first place. This task of mine is really stressful and that is why sometimes I am just relaxing by watching on TV the latest, so to speak, advices of these so called, credit rating agencies, a little in the same way as they watched the performances of gnomes and other clowns in medieval castles or at the carnival of the onetime Venice.

CACAMBO: They say the Euro is a rival to the USD. What do you think?

PANGLOSS: When I provoked the first Oil Shock, back in 1973, my valets of various kinds and other pen friends throughout the world, either in full consciousness, in half consciousness or without any consciousness at all, spread the rumor of the decline of the US economy and respectively, the rise of these same places that I was entangling in my dense, intricate web of Petro and Eurodollars at that very moment. The same happened in the 1980s with Japan, when there was hardly a page in any self-respecting publication without at least one reference to the so called Japanese miracle, and all this was going on up to the point at which I tightened the knot by bursting the asset bubble that I had caused indirectly with the US trade deficit and respectively the influx of USD used for giving a pyramid shaped form to the Tokyo real estate and stock market. The same is happening right now to China. I exploit the blind impulses of the now virtualized world public and respectively its ingrained tendency to fetishism or the worship of quantity by presenting China as a threat to the west, as a rising titan, propelled to global hegemony, somewhat like the yellow peril stuff, a century ago. At the same time, I am repeating the old story of the 1970s and 1980s but this time on a much larger scale, in accordance with the size of the place. Each second, millions of soldiers from my Greenback army penetrate the Great Wall in total impunity.

CACAMBO: Great! Yet, are they not buying up your own assets with your own banknotes, and what is more, cannot they just stop accepting them at any time?

PANGLOSS: No. The whole system of production and export along the coastal cities, in particular, through the very influx of USD, now already more than a trillion, conditions on one hand the willingness to preserve the nominal value of these USD and on the other hand causes a rising dependency on Oil and now, food, due to the adoption of a McDonald's style diet. Should they refuse my Greenbacks, they will in a sense destroy the value of their own labor, and then the whole of their export oriented system, since the USD will plummet in no time. Furthermore, have I not told you a number of times already that you cannot buy a single barrel of Oil on the International market if you have no USD? It goes without saying that such an arrangement is not based on mutual consent. It is based on Realpolitik, including its military expression. As for the assets bought with USD, these assets are only a credit, that is, by no means a debit for me. As far as I have the monopoly to print my Greenbacks, whoever uses them is objectively, so to speak, on my side. Why should I object to someone who has no better to do than coming to London and buying up one of these stores of the Harrods' variety that no self-respecting 'Nouveau Riche' can afford to ignore these days? By the way, even when they buy property in Belgravia or around Hyde Park and elsewhere, they own this property on very limited terms since they do not own the land and only have a long term lease, which simply may not be renewed at some point.

CACAMBO: Do not you have to change your USD for Pounds Sterling there?

PANGLOSS: This is a trifle detail. Do not forget that my real base is invisible and the current role played by the US as the UN, just as any role is only temporary. Should you not make a distinction between the US Constitution and the realm of fiat money, you are only adding to the general confusion that is indeed my only real capital. Had it not been for the peculiar mixture of this same confusion with Realpolitik, my Greenbacks will in no time revert to their natural condition of grains of pure Sahara like sand. You should never forget that all this complex equations on the money supply, official statements and the like objectively have one only purpose: sustaining the on-going process of systematic self-delusion and making appear my system of fiat money in the eyes of the general public as reliable and more than anything as complex, and hence finding a pretext to shut the door on any semblance of real inquiry, let alone an audit of the whole thing. As I told you already, this is not like the old system based on the Gold and Silver. I can print as much banknotes as I desire in no time. The problem is how to account for the whole thing, first in the eyes of the public and second in the eyes of those who play an active role in the system. The thing is that I know what I am doing, but others should not know. Otherwise my fiat money empire will crumble. Once more: there is a visible accountability and an invisible accountability, the former is for sustaining the confidence of the public and the latter is for me and those few around me. The first is based on delusion, the second on the effort for understanding my own moves, since reality is complex, before being simple, and as a result, all the effects of a given cause are not always easily predictable.

CACAMBO: You were talking about astronomy, I mean one of these metaphors that you happen to use all the time. So, you said something about the Swiss National Bank and you did not go any further.

PANGLOSS: Yes. The recent move of the SNB of fixing a ceiling of 1.20 CHF for 1 Euro indicates in its own way, the sand like nature of fiat money. Why should the CHF be so high in the first place? In the pre-fiat money past, the safety of a given place, and hence its magnet like attraction for investors used to be based on purely physical considerations. A fortress had to be untouchable, preferably located on a high mountain such as the Mount Ararat, which was not flooded by the waters of the Deluge or in a dense forest or its walls had to be at least as solid as those built by Justinian in Constantinople. This was even more so, when a place for a store of value had to be found out, since basically nobody other than a chosen few were supposed to know the magic words: Sesame open up! In the case of Switzerland, its atomic shelters apart, none of these things apply. The CHF is not even gold backed, nor is there gold in Switzerland, as you shall see later on. The answer is that the safe haven status of Switzerland, located in the one of the most densely populated and militarized areas on the planet is as virtual as any of my scriptural money signs can be. Further on, the rush to the CHF following the 2008 crisis reveals, that in today's economic environment, the allocation of resources is in reality no different from a mere shift of nominal values, denominated in fiat computer clicks. Gone are the last remnants of the tangible reality, such the level of material production, productivity etc. that still played a role in the incomes of the then industrialized economies, compared to the mainly rural economies of Asia or Africa. Today, I can wipe out the wealth of any place in a few hours, provided I decide to do so. My only problem in reality is that I am not able to do one thing, without affecting at the same time many other things. For example, shall I raise the CHF against other currencies in a global speculative move for higher virtual profits, I have to sacrifice also the productive base of the whole place, since the Swiss exporters will no longer be still there, if the 1 CHF reaches 1 Euro at some point. Thus, in a few months, I will be in a position to destroy an industrial basis, behind whish lurk centuries of craftsmanship. By the way, provided that I am basically everywhere and nowhere, I always have this problem, as in the US or the UK, whose manufacturing industries have been sacrificed in the name of my plan for a global fiat money empire.

CACAMBO: You did no answer my question about the Euro.

PANGLOSS: Listen to me, my friend I am not that confused to rival my own self, so to speak. As far as Oil is on my side, the demand for my USD is assured, whereas the demand for the Euro is driven by the terms of trade just as any other vulgar commodity. Furthermore, any hint on the eventual replacement of the USD by something else, automatically triggers the question: what to do with the trillions of USD already in circulation for half a century throughout the world? The world economy is a hostage suffering from the Stockholm syndrome. Ever since 2003, I decided that the Euro should rise against the USD simply because the USD denominated debt, and deficits have been growing too fast and at that stage a mild devaluation was required. If you still remember, back in 2001, the USD was higher than the Euro and later on there was a parity for a year or two. Now, when by the end of 2004, the Euro reached something like 1.23 or 1.24 for the USD, a concerted outcry was raised by various politicians in Europe. 'If we are less competitive right now etc. they said this is because of the USD.' There was a deep concern by the media etc. for the future of the world economy and the future of the USD as a reserve currency. The conclusion that was reached goes on something like this: 'Ladies and Gentlemen, the Dollar should not fall any more. Something has to be done about it or else the world and the European economy in particular will be in deep trouble etc. etc.' But what happened later on? The USD fell as low as 1.60 against the Euro in 2008 and yet, ever after, the big talk on the apparently intolerable fall of the USD simply went out of fashion and as a result was no longer heard of back again. Why? As I hinted already, I had decided for a mild devaluation of the Greenback, which needless to say had been at the expense of the European economy. The overvalued Euro is the best recipe for a sustained economic downturn in Europe, since the export oriented German economy will be focused more on the other countries of the Euro zone at the expense of the rest of the world, which in turn will create deficits and a larger imbalance with the south of Europe, that cannot be resolved through competitive devaluations as it was the case in the past.

Cacambo: Since 2001-2012 the USD lost more than 50% of its value against currencies other than the Euro such as the CHF, the CAD, the AUD or the Yen, except the Pound Sterling and you still call this 'mild' devaluation?

Pangloss: At this stage, nobody knows for sure, not even me the Sorcerer, the exact amount of USD in circulation nor the real level of debt, including corporate and personal debt. The so called Subprime crisis is only the tip of the iceberg, indicating that the still invisible tower of scriptural money signs is of a size that only a few years ago, let alone decades was unconceivable. An earthquake is looming on the horizon. At some point it will become obvious that all previous obligations or debts will have to be cleared, since otherwise the system will simply stop functioning. So, I will have no better option than starting from scratch once again. The USD will cease to exist in its present form.

Cacambo: And what will you be doing, then?

Pangloss: I may revert to Gold for a time.

Cacambo: What? Are you mad? You will go back to something that you have been denying all the time? You must be kidding!

Pangloss: Do you remember the Tulip Mania, a century before our own time? Later on, there was Sir John Law with the Mississippi Bubble and the most stunning of all, the Cacique of the Principality of Poais, who sent would be colonists to a non-existent country in the Americas.[33] And then, if I skip some less impressive events comes out the 1931 Gold default and all the rest up to now. What do all of these have in common? It is always the same story: at the beginning there is a grain of truth. Then, someone comes along and distorts this truth, for example, there was indeed a place by the name of America in the 19th century, but not a place by the name of Poyais; there was indeed Gold in the vault of the Bank of England in 1931, but not as much as people believed etc. The things do not stop here, however, since the distorted truth temporarily assumes the role of an original, on whose behalf copies are made or printed up to the point when there is nothing to print any more. This is a sign that it is time for a new beginning. We will get back to the harbor in a minute, and after the dinner I will bring to the vault of New York, which up to this point is still a tourist attraction.

Cacambo: How come a tourist attraction?

Pangloss: Yes. There are tours in the vault of New York where is kept most of the world's stock of gold.[34]

Cacambo: I heard that the gold reserve of Germany is kept in the New-York vault, although there seems to be a controversy on the subject.[35] But at least that of Switzerland must be in Zurich, where a large part of the gold bullion trading is going on, I guess.

PANGLOSS: No. The Swiss gold is also kept in the New York vault.[36] As for the controversy in Germany, it reveals among other things the level of transparency on these matters, since the Bundesbank claims that at least most of the gold is in Germany, but it does not say where this gold is located, in the same way as the on-going debate on the amount of gold, stored at Fort Knox does not seem to be on the point of reaching a consensus. Present day gold is like the Flying Dutchman for some while for others it is a hard rock, since for them, its intrinsic solidity is beyond any doubt.

CACAMBO: And what about the US gold reserves?

PANGLOSS: The gold reserves of the US amount to 8.133.50 tones out of a world total of 29, 634 tones and are the world's largest.[37] Should we add the gold reserves of the 36 countries and other international organizations such the IMF, stored in the New York vault, into the account, the percentage of the world's gold physically located in the US may be much higher than these figures suggest.

CACAMBO: Listen, you have been talking about a fiat money empire and now it happens that you turn to gold. Furthermore, it appears to me that your role playing of The Sorcerer from the tale of Aladdin is only adding to the general confusion on the matter. Would you at least revert back to the individual by the name of Pangloss, the one I already knew back in the 18th century?

******

PANGLOSS: Okay. I am back to my own soul of Pangloss right now. As for the confusion, the only confusing thing I have seen so far is not the apparent contradiction between fiat money and gold, since the one is versus the other as the original is toward its copy or the concept of a limited entity is toward its opposite or unlimited entity. What seems to be confusing for me in reality is the finality of the Sorcerer's design.

CACAMBO: Look at the Spirit in the bottle!

THE SPIRIT: You woke me up for good this time! Let me on the loose and I will tell you what is this all about.

PANGLOSS: Okay. So be it. I do not a have a corkscrew and I will have to push the cork into the bottle, if you do not mind.

THE SPIRIT: Please open it now! I have a mountain of gold for you! Believe me, Ali Baba's cavern is a small change in comparison!

Pangloss takes the bottle from the table and opens it. Suddenly, the silhouette of the Spirit vanishes. A strong noise combined with a dense fog of exhilarating vapors pervades the surrounding area.

CACAMBO: What is going on?

The huge figure of a several meters tall giant like creature is making his appearance at this very moment. A loud laughter of the like of a bullet shot from a cannon is flowing in huge waves out of the head of the monster.

THE SPIRIT: I will tell you now, what is going on! Listen, my dear tiny rats, if you think that I did stay for nothing in this god damn bottle you are definitely wrong! So, a little patience and I will throw both of you deep into the sea!

CACAMBO: No! No! Look, why should you throw me? I did nothing wrong to you!

PANGLOSS: As I see you learnt nothing in this bottle! By the way, do take notice that if you still persist in misbehaving, I intent to react!

THE SPIRIT: Look at yourself small rat! You are so funny! If you say only a word I will throw you into the sea right away!

PANGLOSS: Okay. Try.

The Spirit approaches Pangloss and makes an attempt to lift him in the air, but to his dismay the small human like Pangloss proves to be no less solid than a rock and as a result the action attempted by the giant turns into an outright fiasco. At this point The Spirit hits Pangloss once again, but the latter remains unaffected, as if nothing really happened.

THE SPIRIT: Who are you?

PANGLOSS: I may tell you, but not right now because in a moment I have to go to the harbor with my friend Cacambo. So, you had better join our debate on the Forex and fiat money.

CACAMBO: Why were you locked in this bottle for so long?

THE SPIRIT: It is the Sorcerer, that your friend has been representing who exploited me and then threw me out into the sea.

Pangloss: How come that you entered the bottle in the first place?

The Spirit: I used to be a beggar and I saw this god damn Sorcerer passing by and asked him for a small change. 'I will give you big change, he said, provided you bring some change to the things all around us.' I said, 'Fine. Better getting big change than small change, but you did not make it clear, how will I be able to change everything all around me in the first place?' 'Do not worry about that, he said, you will do it by making yourself small.' 'But how can I get small?' I asked, 'Just take this pill and enter this bottle.' He replied. So I did just that and after I had become small enough, I entered the bottle for real. At that point, the Sorcerer closed the bottle and threw it into the sea.'

Pangloss: Have you not skipped many sequences? Did he not give you this pill because he wanted you to prove your integrity to the cause of change? Furthermore, did you not bring some changes for good, after all?

The Spirit: Yes. How do you know?

Cacambo:(to Pangloss) What do you really mean by 'Change' here? Is it the 'Change' by which is designated the act of changing one currency for another that at this very moment is performed countless of times by the legions of money changers throughout the world or an ontological, historical, political or social change?

Pangloss: Both, but in a reversed order. The act of money changing is usually performed in the open whereas the other 'Changes', those you just mentioned take place in the invisible plane in the first place. Here, the former is covert whereas the latter is overt. Furthermore, there is no such thing as ontological change, there is only ontological awareness.

The Spirit: Yes, in a sense, I indeed got some 'change' in order to bring change to the then social and political setting. I was operating on an ontological level, whatever you friend might say on the matter. Also, I was operating on other levels.

Cacambo: Could you be more specific?

The Spirit: The ontological level for me is located, if not in the ultimate, at least in the inner layers of the Psyche. I had introduced there, the idea of sameness, the most unnatural, inverted form of self-delusion, based on a combination of 33.3% pure barbarity, 33.3% pure envy and 33.3% pure greed or as they say, 'ôtes de là, que je m'y mette!' (Fr.) and then, I packed the whole thing, a little as one of these financial instruments of the subprime stuff, and thus hid its real highly toxic content by renaming it: 'Equality'.

CACAMBO: But this is a blind force. What really does count right now is where did you pour the whole liquid?

THE SPIRIT: It is a very long story. Should I compress the whole thing to its outmost limits, however, I will pass to the lower, ideological level where, my intent has been to disguise what was really going on through vague words. So I blurred the picture by referring to anonymous, formless entities such as the 'classes', 'the class struggle' etc., and then fabricated a whole team of marionette like dolls, along the lines of mechanical determinism. Now, I was not stupid to the point of believing my own stuff, otherwise I would not have been able to pursue the task whatsoever.

CACAMBO: Were you not against fiat money and all kind of money for that matter?

THE SPIRIT: What counted was bringing changes to the then world. Do not forget that up to 1914, various players dating from the Middle-Ages and still earlier were standing in my way. I was supposed to destroy theses antiques in the first place and hence paving the way for fiat money, although on the level of ontology I am opposed to money, but to real money only. On the historical level I am in favor of fiat money for a time, whereas at last resort I stand for the suppression of all forms of exchange, since in any form of exchange, there is still a degree of freedom. Now, between fiat money and collectivism there is a natural connivance. As a representation of a hidden and therefore unknown original, fiat money is only a virtual expression of property, including the very notion of personal responsibility. However that may be the thing is that after 1989, I went out of fashion and as a result started floating on the surface of the oceans locked in this god damn bottle.

PANGLOSS: How come you went out of fashion? You just receded with the tide, only to reappear later on with the new storm.

THE SPIRIT: You guessed right this time. The very fact that I am already on the loose is speaking for itself.

CACAMBO: When are we leaving for the harbor?

PANGLOSS: Right now. And you, where are you going?

THE SPIRIT: I do not know yet. However, from now on, wherever I go, you will be seeing my traces. So, have a nice day!

PANGLOSS: Do you know that you happen to be on a place by the name of Liberty Island, right now? So, what is freedom is all about according to you?

The Spirit suddenly dissolves into the air apparently a moment before Pangloss has uttered the whole of his question.

CACAMBO: As you can see, he just vanished. Would you answer the same question in your turn, before we leave the place?

PANGLOSS: Freedom is a coherent whole, where the invisible intersect with the visible. From a visible perspective this is the lack of an outward constraint and that is already half of the way to the end. Also, there is no such thing as desecrated freedom, since freedom is either sacred or it is nothing. Provided the goal is the same, any way to attain this goal is as good as any other and therefore, each of these ways is unique in its own way. The place where we are right now is no exception, since things that elsewhere are a matter of particular concern, here are associated with the very core of freedom. Following this, we have enough grounds to assume that the day when the First Amendment and the Second Amendment of the US Constitution are abolished this Statue right there will be reduced to ashes out of itself and the very idea of exchange will be obscured, for a time and at a cost that I have no time to calculate right now.

NOTES

[1]Robert Sobel - *Dangerous Dreamers: The Financial Innovators from Charles Merrill to Michael Milken* (1993), (ISBN 0-471-57734-0).

[2]Special Drawing Rights, September 13, 2011 www.imf.org.

[3]Peter Harrison (historian). "Was Newton a Voluntarist?" (pp. 39-64). *Newton and Newtonianism: new studies.* James E. Force, Sarah Hutton.

[4]'Le Péché Monétaire de l'Occident' Plon 1971 Jacques Rueff ('The Monetary Sin of the West').

[5]'Trade in perspective' by Richard Eliot, Valore International www.florin.com.

[6]About the immediate effect of the 1931 default, see Bank of England Report 21 January 1932 Sunday June 21, 2009 *Report entitled 'The suspension of the Gold Standard in Great Britain and its effect on the countries of Europe'.* This report in the Bank's internal archives traces some of the consequences of the suspension of the gold standard in the United Kingdom. Foreign central banks which held sterling suffered substantial losses due to Britain's effective devaluation. These losses placed some of their currencies under speculative pressure. *After the Gold Standard,* Volume III 1931-1999.

21 January 1932

It was not to be expected that such a momentous step as the suspension of the Gold Standard by Great Britain, after six years of imperfect and difficult working, would be without grave and far-reaching repercussions on the rest of Europe. [...] Sterling held by the Bank of France was estimated at £62 million and the loss on this through devaluation at 2½ milliards of francs (£20 million), a sum well in excess of the capital reserves. [...]

In Italy, as in France, Belgium and Holland, the adhesion to the gold standard resulted in heavy losses on all sterling balances, especially as the Italian currency was stabilised in 1927 on a gold exchange standard and the largest proportion of the Banca d'Italia reserves was in £s. [...]

Immediately after Britain's suspension, the Banque Nationale de Belgique exchanged all visible foreign exchange for gold (according to the return of 24th September 1931). In fact, Belgium was responsible for the greater part of the earmarking of gold in New York during the eight days ending 24th September, when gold to the value of $184 million (£36 million) was set aside for foreign account. Balances held at the Bank of England have increased slightly. The depreciation in the value of sterling gave rise to severe loss in Holland, since a large part of the foreign bill portfolio of the Nederlandsche Bank consisted of sterling bills. [...]

The dollar has replaced the £ as the basis for calculating the value of the Greek drachma in foreign currencies. Balances held by the Bank of Greece at the Bank of England have fallen by £1.2 million since the 19th September 1931. [...]

Bulgaria has suffered serious dislocation of her export trade as the great majority of exports have always been contracted in pounds. There has been a heavy drop in exports and a restriction of credit. [...]

Switzerland followed the general tendency and strengthened its position by the withdrawal of funds from abroad and by the conversion of foreign exchange into gold. The gold reserve on Banque Nationale Suisse was only £28 million on 31st December 1930, [but] by the end of September 1931 it was £68 million and had risen to £93 million by the 31st December 1931. Sterling held at the Bank of England was entirely liquidated, but gold held has risen 19th September to over £6 million.

Source: *Bank of England Archives*, OV48/9, 1538/4, no. 86.

[7]Between 1815 and 1832 the value of Indian cotton goods exported fell from £1.3 million to below £100,000. By the middle of the 19th century, India was importing a quarter of all British cotton goods. Teresa Hayter, The Creation of World Poverty (Pluto 1990, 2nd edition) p. 45; From Nick Robin's The Corporation that Changed the World: how the East India Company shaped the modern multinational (Pluto 2006):

After Robert Clive's victory at Palashi (Plassey) in 1757, the company literally looted Bengal's treasury. It loaded gold and silver onto a fleet of more than 100 boats and sent it down river to Calcutta. In one stroke, Clive netted a cool £2.5 million (more than £200m today) for the company and £234,000 (£20m today) for himself. Palashi was the company's most successful business deal...

It was the unrivalled quality and cheapness of textiles that had lured the East India Company to Bengal, and it would be Bengal's weavers who felt the full force of the company's newfound market power. Never rich, the weavers nevertheless had a better standard of living than their counterparts in 18th-century England. At a time when the British state was intervening on the side of the employer--for example, to set maximum levels for wages--India's weavers were able to act collectively, aiding their ability to negotiate favourable prices. But the East India Company eliminated the weavers' freedom to sell to other merchants, and so crushed their limited but important market autonomy. It imposed prices 40 per cent below the market rate, and enforced them with violence and imprisonment. Many weavers were driven to despair. One account reports that, among the winders of raw silk, "instances have been known of cutting off their thumbs to prevent their being forced to wind silk".

[8]See Jacques Rueff, *De l'Aube au Crépuscule*, p 302.

[9]See *The Wizard of Oz* by L. Frank Baum, 1900.

[10]See,Luca Einaudi, *Money and Politics: European Monetary Unification and the International Gold Standard (1865-1873)*. Oxford: Oxford University Press, 2001. xiii + 241 pp. $100 (cloth), ISBN: 0-19-924366-2.

[11]The Bland-Ellison Act of 1878 had required the US president to invite foreign governments to an international conference on restoring bimetallism.

[12]Following the Yellow Brick Road: How the US adopted the Gold Standard, Francois R.Velde. 2Q/ Economic Perspectives, www.chicagofed.org.

[13]Ibid, p.47.

[14]See *Gold Standard = Fiat In Disguise* , Copyright 2002 J.N. Tlaga, www.gold-eagle.com.

[15]In 1793 King George III dispatched Lord George Macartney to seek an audience with the Qianlong Emperor. Macartney was able to access the Emperor and their meeting was cordial despite Macartney's famous refusal to perform the koutou, a bowing ritual customarily required for those paying tribute at the Chinese court. Despite the outward cordiality, Macartney was unable to secure formal diplomatic relations or any additional trading privileges. The Qianlong Emperor issued two edicts that he sent home with Macartney. The edicts are often quoted as a summation of China's view of its place in the world order, and its opinion on the prospects of European trade:*"Our dynasty's majestic virtue has penetrated unto every country under Heaven, and Kings of all nations have offered their costly tribute by land and sea. As your Ambassador can see for himself, we possess all things. I set no value on objects strange or ingenious, and have no use for your country's manufactures."*
(Two Edicts From the Qianlong Emperor on the Occasion of Lord Macartney's Mission to China, September 1793).

Retrieved from Asia for Educators Columbia University http://afe. easia columbia.edu).

Although the language was lofty, it does it fact appear to be true that China had little use for what England was selling – tin, lead, copper, wool, and cotton. Europe on the other hand had a tremendous appetite for China's exports of silk, porcelain, and especially tea. By the year 1800 the English East India Company was shipping more than 23 million pounds of tea annually. Since the Chinese were not interested in English goods, a terrible trade imbalance existed. The Company was able to mitigate this imbalance somewhat by establishing a trade circuit which facilitated trade between India and China, but the net effect of the deficit was nonetheless a flow of silver bullion out of England and into China. 'The Canton system of trade' www. thepeacefulsea.com.

[16]See 'How the Great Recession was brought to an end' July 27, 2010 Alan S. Blinder and Mark Zandi p.2 www.economy.com.

[17]See, Gary Gorton, "Haircuts." Also, 'The (sizable) role of Rehypothecation in the Shadow Banking System.' Manmohan Singh and James Aitken, 2010 International Monetary Fund (IMF Working Paper) www.imf.org.

[18]For example, the journal *Mirovaya Ekonomika i Mezhdunarodnye Otnosheniya*, MEiMO, (World Economy and International Relations) issued since 1957 by The Institute of World Economy and International Relations (IMEMO), back in the 60s, reprinted this view of the then world economy from the mainstream western media practically in its integral version, since the semantic differences brought by the Marxist-Leninist discourse, here, are of no significance. According to the Soviet view, the so called three centers of capitalism, the USA, Western Europe and Japan were characterized by an uneven development, where the USA was lagging behind the other two centers. Here, as elsewhere, we see the methodological limits of the unreserved acceptance of statistical fetishism as a tool for the comprehension of economic reality.

[19]A Bloomberg News story published Feb. 9 said the Treasury Department, Federal Deposit Insurance Corporation and Fed have lent or spent almost $3 trillion over the past two years and pledged up to $5.7 trillion more. A March 31 article raised the total amount committed or disbursed to $12.8 trillion...A statement e-mailed by Coleman's office yesterday said the Fed board's inspector general doesn't have legal authority to investigate the transactions that have swelled the central bank's balance sheet. YouTube Clip of Lawmaker, Fed Official Draws 166,000 (Update1). *By Timothy R. Homan - May 12, 2009 10:16 EDT www.bloomberg.com.*

[20]The United States Interest Equalization Tax, Robert A. Butterworth, Jr. *Lawyer of the Americas*, Vol. 2, No. 2 (Jun., 1970), pp. 164-172, Published by: University of Miami Inter-American Law Review, Article Stable URL: http://www.jstor.org/stable/40175358. See also Voluntary Foreign Credit Restraint and the Nonbank Financial Institutions Rachel Strauber *Financial Analysts Journal* Vol. 26, No. 3 (May - Jun., 1970), pp. 10-12+87-89 Published by: CFA Institute Article Stable URL: http://www.jstor.org/stable/4470672.

[21]See City of London Corporation.

[22]F. Klopstock, The Euro-dollar Market: Some Unresolved Issues, PEIF, no. 65, 1968.

[23]Fred Hirsch, 'Money International' London Penguin 1969 quoted by Paul Painchaud, in 'De Mackenzie King a Pierre Trudeau, p164:' Supreme irony the Soviet controlled Moscow Narodny Bank was an initiator of the Eurodollar market. The Soviet Union sold Gold in the Zurich market, to pay for wheat to pay for imports of western wheat; the proceeds of the sale were paid in dollars…'

[24]See *Beasts, Men and Gods* by F.Ossendowski; *Le Roi du Monde* R.Guenon, *A Secret History of Consciousness* (2003, ISBN 1-58420-011-1) by Gary Lachman.

[25]The extraordinary tale of a false statistic, 7 October 2011, Alasdair Macleod, www. financeandeconomics.org ; GDP: a brief history. By Elizabeth Dickinson |January/February 2011 Foreign Policy, www.foreignpolicy.com.

[26]See, H. Graham Lowry's *How The Nation Was Won--America's Untold Story, 1630-1754*. At Gettysburg, Abraham Lincoln spoke of Franklin and the other American founders as ``our fathers," who ``brought forth on this continent a new nation, *conceived in liberty,* and dedicated to the proposition that all men are created equal," and, ``that this nation, under God, shall have a *new birth of freedom*..." *The Gettysburg Address*, Gettysburg,Pennsylvania November 19, 1863.

[27]See "*The Tsar and the President: Alexander II and Abraham Lincoln – Liberator and Emancipator,*" published by The American-Russian Cultural Cooperation Foundation John A. Bernbaum, Russian-American Christian Institute/US Office, P.O. Box 2007, Wheaton, MD, 20915, www. russianamericaninstitute.org.

[28]Petrodollars, War, Peace, and Economics, Part 1, May 12, 2011 Terry A. Hurlbut www. conservativenewsandviews.com.

[29]"I remember reading a book in the 1970's by gold bug Harry Brown where he advocated investing in the Lebanese pound because it had the largest percentage of gold backing by its Central Bank. Unfortunately Lebanon soon suffered a devastating civil war followed by a foreign invasion, so the currency was damaged.' *Will the dollar be devalued: independent investment advice*' Posted by Don Martin on Mon, Mar 14, 2011 @ 04:00 PM www.mayflowercaiptal.com See also *The Gold Standard, What it means+ how it affects Lebanon*, Maria Frangieh, 12th January 2012 in Ragged Highlights, You and Your Country, Ragged Features www.ragmag.co.

[30]By the end of 1974, Gold had soared from US $35 to US $195 an ounce. (The 1970s gold bull market).

[31]See *The Middle East and North Africa*, Volume 50, Europa Publications Limited, Routledge, 2003-10-30-1370p; pp.749.

[32]See *The Clash of Civilizations* by S.P. Huntington.

[33]His Highness, Gregor, the Cacique of Poynais, actually a Scotsman named Gregor McGregor

who made a killing in 1821 selling Londoners the bonds of a make- believe country. Charles R. Morris *"Beyond The Bubbles"*. Commonweal. FindArticles.com. 28 Mar, 2012.

[34]The gold you see in the vault of the Federal Reserve Bank of New York attracts more than 25,000 visitors a year. It is the world's largest accumulation of gold and belongs to 36 foreign governments, central banks and official international organizations. Only a very small portion of this gold belongs to the U.S. government. The Federal Reserve Bank does not own the precious metal but serves as guardian for the nations and international organizations that choose to leave their monetary gold reserves in the Bank's custody. It is estimated that the gold in the vault represents a significant portion of all the monetary gold that has ever been mined. 24 April 2010 www.crypton.org.

[35]Restore national sovereignty: Repatriate all gold reserves, Submitted by cpowell on Thu, 2012-03-29 04:16. Section: Daily Dispatches www.gata.org

[36]Four members of the Swiss parliament presented a "Gold Initiative" and they intend to collect the required signatures to allow the Swiss people to vote on securing the Nation's gold reserves, specifically, on the following issues:
- Storing all Swiss National Bank gold physically in Switzerland
- Prohibiting the Swiss National Bank from selling its gold
- Requiring the Swiss National Bank to hold at least 20 percent of its assets in gold

Switzerland, Germany Fret about Their Gold Reserves March 12, 2012 www.seekingalpha.com.

[37] *The World's Biggest Gold Reserves*, October 20, 2009 www.seekingalpha.com.

TALE XIX

Freedom And The Free Market

Pangloss and Cacambo leave Liberty Island and after a dinner in a Manhattan restaurant, take a walk along Broadway Avenue. They pass by a Radio Shack store.

Cacambo: Look at the devices on the window!

Pangloss: As far as I can see, these are mobile phones.

Cacambo: Is this not the present day version of your crystal ball?

Pangloss: My crystal ball is based on the subtle currents of energy permeating the forms in their way to each consecutive rearrangement of the cosmic puzzle. By the way, the orb that the Monarchs were holding together with the scepter in their hands up until recently is no else but a representation, a remote souvenir, precisely of this same kind of crystal ball dating from the time of the antediluvian Magician Kings. However, the devices you see up there on the window are indeed a copy of my crystal ball in the same was as electricity is only a reflection of its all present ultimate source.

Cacambo: I did not know you are such a sophisticate, who happens to hold all the secrets of the Universe in his pocket.

Pangloss: The Monad is infinite in the same way as the knowledge of its sufficient reason is also infinite. My only secret, by the way, is that I do not own any secret whatsoever. A patented secret is an empty shell, since the grains of truth wherein leave it at his very moment.

Cacambo: Okay. I agree. Let's enter the shop. I want to give a closer look at these devices.

Pangloss: Which ones in particular?

Cacambo: Let's see that thing on the shelf.

Pangloss: This appears to be a mobile phone to me.

CACAMBO: A phone? How come a phone? Where is its rotary dial?

PANGLOSS: What? Do not you know that the thing you are referring to has been replaced by a push button version, already in the early sixties?

CACAMBO: Yes. I forgot it. But there are no buttons either.

PANGLOSS: No, press. Press the small button below! This is a touch screen phone.

CACAMBO: Okay. This phone of yours has so many features! I am definitely lost.

PANGLOSS: Why do not you just buy one? I gave you a thick pile of cash only a short while ago.

CACAMBO: Better not, right now. I prefer to know more about the whole thing before making up my mind.

PANGLOSS: So, are you not telling me that your choice would not have been free if you were ignorant on the nature of the thing you intent to buy?

CACAMBO: Yes, in a sense.

PANGLOSS: A free choice is a conscious choice and therefore there is no such thing as a blind choice, since this would not have been a choice whatsoever.

CACAMBO: Are you saying that a choice is in reality possible only in a transparent environment? But do not they say an invisible hand is guiding your choices in the best interest of all?

PANGLOSS: Yes, suppose that any statement may somehow become a true, valid statement provided we repeat it long enough.

CACAMBO: What?

PANGLOSS: What I mean here is that for the time being, we will take the inherited, from our own time, issue on the Invisible Hand of the Market for granted. So, we will proceed further on, under the famous 'ceteris paribus' conditions. Now, let's get back to the previous point on transparency and free choice. The phone you happen to hold in your hands right now has so many different features, right?

CACAMBO: Yes, it has.

PANGLOSS: And what about, say the red pork chops on the shelves of the supermarket where our friend the rabbit in all probability is still competing with the turtle?

CACAMBO: Have you not paid enough attention to these animals already?

PANGLOSS: There is more to come. Do you still remember that we used to speak already before going to Liberty Island, on the way present day industrial bread is produced? We said that the original technology dating back from the early 1960s is publicly known only in the U.K. but not in the U.S. since over there this happens to be a professional secret, a little like the formula of Coca Cola. Here is another illustration that secrecy is something relative, for the time being at least, since what is a secret in one place may not be a secret in another and vice versa. The thing is that present day buyers have no clue what they happen to consume every day. For example, they have no idea what does the chemical composition of the dye used for preserving the original red color of the pork chops consist of, neither do they know what kind of bread do they eat, in the same way as you do not know what are the features of the touch tone phone right there on the shelf in front of you. The picture gets still darker when you enter the pharmacy next door, where the on – going global experience with newly licensed medications is taking its toll at any hour of the day. The concept of the Invisible Hand from our own time had in reality a visible expression in the mind of those exchanging goods on the marketplace. And this used to be so, simply because the commodities they were buying were made in accordance with custom. The then buyers had much more extensive knowledge on the substance of what they were buying than their modern counterparts, as a result.

CACAMBO: And where was the choice, then? Did they not simply follow a pre-established pattern?

PANLGLOSS: No. The pattern in question was not imposed by anyone. It was based on experience. For example, in the case of an Invisible Hand stretching from the counters of an 18th century European food market, most to the items, save for those imported in the 16 the century after the discovery of the New World, were coming straight from the pre-historical past, when some allusions on the origin of agriculture had been encrypted in various myths, including the Mysteries of Eleusis etc. So, the buyers and the sellers in such a market were not following a pre-established pattern. They were following an inherited pattern, fragments of whose real nutritional and cognitive value are in the process of being rediscovered only recently by present day ecology. The freedom of choice in this market is no less than complete. In our own time there used to be real choice, whereas today there is only virtual choice. Such a choice rests on self-delusion and manipulation. The buyers in a 2012 food market are deceived buyers and the ultimate effect of the on-going process of deception on the health of these buyers and the environment will only be seen, judging from the speed with which the whole thing is going on, in a not very distant future. Should we measure, the degree of knowledge the ancient buyers had in comparison with the new ones, you can just go to the traditional markets still in operation in various, so called 'Third World'[1] countries, and ask the people there about the quality of the items they buy and then go to any 'First world' supermarket of the Safeway variety and just do the same.

CACAMBO: Ok, ok! But they had no mobile phones, in our own time, did they?

PANGLOSS: We said already at the beginning that our point on the freedom of choice within the context of an 18[th]century Invisible Hand versus its 21th century counterpart is to be considered under 'Ceteris Paribus' conditions, right? Furthermore, the origin of the devices you seem to you like so much is at the very opposite end on all that the virtual world of Postmodernity stands for.

CACAMBO: What?

PANGLOSS: Have we not presented the epistemological framework of modern versus ancient science already? Had it not been for the insight of Tesla, based on Metaphysics and the Spiritual nature of the world within and around us, all these devices would simply not be available.

CACAMBO: These days the Invisible Hand of the market is presented as a self-regulatory mechanism. They say, the only difference between the Sun and the supposedly free market is that you cannot intervene in the rising and the setting of the Sun, and as a result the latter is always turning along its trajectory, whereas in the case of the market, this same movement may be prevented. The market is in a sense, like a Sun which is rising and setting on demand.

PANGLOSS: The market rhetoric is no different from the basic message of postmodern philosophy, since the good philosopher these days is the one denying the very foundation of Philosophy, going to the point of literally excusing himself for engaging in such an exercise of futility.

CACAMBO: Where are you getting at this time?

PANGLOSS: I am getting to the point of substance. Substance is a love and hate kind of thing. For example, any self-respecting ruler needs, on one hand thinking figures, spending their time in reflecting on the way of preserving or better still, strengthening his position of power. If you happen to be, say a president of a Fortune 500 company or a brigadier general or whatever, you cannot get away with thinking, since otherwise you may simply lose the reins of your power in no time. On the other hand, these same rulers or usurpers or usurers of whatever variety have toward thinking the same attitude as their heirs had toward alchemy. Not only want, they to expropriate all the gold for themselves, but they want also to expropriate all the thinking for themselves too. At this point, these stumble on a seemingly unsolvable riddle: how to preserve the substance of thinking and emptying it at the same time of its essentially free essence? At best, they cling to the ideal of the clever white hamster reflecting on the things that are yet to come within the narrow confines of the wheel, where he is turning on with his tiny legs. Yet, this solution is only a half solution, since in matters of thinking the smartest hamster is no match to any free reflecting human being.

CACAMBO: If the substance of yours is to depart from your subject, at the slightest occasion, we would better stop somewhere for a rest, since I am so full and tired right now. By the way, if you happen to have on you say, a cigar of the Cohiba variety, I will be listening to anything you say with the utmost attention.

PANGLOSS: We could go later on to the Carnegie Club. There is a smoking lounge over there. So, I hope you will not be fined for lighting up a cigar in this place.

CACAMBO: Great! Were you not talking of a kind of think tanking creature, a short while ago?

PANGLOSS: I was presenting a point on the substance of the whole thing.

CACAMBO: What thing?

PANGLOSS: The thing we have been talking about is the market and the invisible hand behind all that is going on in such a place.

CACAMBO: And what is the conclusion?

PANGLOSS: It is that the market has been taken by present day pseudo liberal rhetoric for what it has never been, that is a substance.

CACAMBO: What is it, then?

PANGLOSS: It is a mean to an end, not an end in itself.

CACAMBO: Is it not an efficient means, though?

PANGLOSS: Have we not referred to the Ceteris Paribus conditions only a minute ago? We will get there later on. Now, let me go on further with the market as a mean toward a given end. You can conduct activities that are detrimental to the whole economy and society by relying on the market for their realization. The market is perfectly indifferent to the quality of what you do, provided, this quality has the propensity of being reduced to its representations or quantified by the Invisible Hand through the formation of a competitive market price. By the way, would the Opium Trade be more efficient, if the East India Company had been broken into smaller competing units? Should we start from the presumption that competition is always better than the lack of competition, we have to say 'Yes' without any hesitation. Yet, this is not as obvious as it may seem at first glance. Remember what we said on the point of virtual versus real choice? In our case, the Opium addicts have an essentially deceitful picture on the thing they crave for, on one hand and being under the categorical imperative of compulsive demand for their dose, on the other hand, they are very likely to accept any or almost any substitute of the original standard on which the production of opium had been originally based. Now, most if not all standards for better or for worse are not the result of the interplay of market forces, but are set beforehand. Should we leave the market competition to itself, the quality of what is on offer will be debased in no time, just like coinage had been debased when gold and silver were still in circulation. And the more virtual is the choice of the buyers, the faster the existing standards will be reduced by the competing sellers on the market. However, as we will see later on, in other situations the free market price, set by competing producers may indeed be much more efficient than a monopoly, be it a State Monopoly, a Royal Charter or a de facto monopoly of the Standard Oil type.

CACAMBO: I am tired of walking. Where is this place?

PANGLOSS: We can take the Ford T to get there faster.

CACAMBO: No, I want to have a smoke right now. If it happens that I will be fined, you will pay.

PANGLOSS: We had better going somewhere else. I see a place around the corner.

CACAMBO: Are you sure I can have a smoke there.

PANGLOSS: I think so.

They enter the place in question, sit on a table and order some tea. Pangloss takes out of his pocket a Cuban cigar and offers it to Cacambo.

CACAMBO: That is really great! In my view the first puff, is always the best. By the way, is not this the kind of stuff that is enjoyed by both capitalists and revolutionaries alike?

PANGLOSS: I should have asked the Spirit, since he seemed to be rather well versed on these matters.

Cacambo: It is too late now, he is gone. However that may be I am ready to listen to your next point on the market and this invisible kind of thing…

Pangloss: The Invisible Hand. We do not have much time left, as we have to leave this city and the whole continent of America very soon. So, I will go on with another point, related to the functioning of any market.

Cacambo: What is this?

Pangloss: It is profit or the famous profit motive that has been strolling on the pages of the books devoted to the subject ever since our own time.

Cacambo: Wait a minute. Why 'on the books' and not on what the books are supposed to represent?

Pangloss: Because, the reason behind the pursuit of profit, quoted in all these writings has never had any semblance of existence outside of the realm of printed paper.

Cacambo: Come on! Is not everyone running after profit these days?

Pangloss: They say, the reason for the pursuit of profit is greed.

Cacambo: Is not indeed so?

Pangloss: No. It is not.

Cacambo: Why?

Pangloss: Greed is only a half truth, which is definitely worse than an outright, blatant lie. The thing is that economic activity as a whole, including production and manufacturing, is conducted in the same way as the ever present metaphysical forces at work, behind the Foreign Exchange or the Stock Market. These forces are nothing else but another expression of the law of polarity operating throughout the Manifested Universe as a whole. It is the combination of greed and fear in any particular moment in time that leads to the relative inner equilibrium which in turn makes possible any form of economic activity. Now, greed versus fear, do indeed describe the fundamental operation that is taking place from the cellular level up to the broadest macroeconomic configuration of any system of production and exchange. However, the precise meaning of these same terms is misleading. Portrayed as greed and fear, economic, including Stock market activity appears as a reversed triangle. Why? Greed is in reality a passive state of being and not the active driving force portrayed in this context. Again, as a primeval life force greed may be represented in mathematics by minus (---) since greed as such has no ultimate existence whatsoever, although it may have a relative one. Greed as an expression of passive desire, crosses the Rubicon from semantics to reality only in combination with its opposite.

Cacambo: It should be fear, I guess?

Pangloss: If it were fear, this would imply that the active side of reality, be it cosmic reality or economic reality, since the latter in contained in the former, is somehow passive, which is a contradiction in terms, an absurdity. No, my friend the fear, they say is in the mind of any Stock Market or Foreign Exchange trader may indeed become a free fall kind of fear only if the effort to sustain the price of the currency or the stock at a certain level happens not to be enough. The passive desire embodied in greed is in reality the opposite double of effort. As there is the flux and the reflux of the sea or inspiration and expiration in breathing, so there is greed and the effort to overcome greed in economic activity at any point in time and in any place. Therefore, we can keep the first term 'greed' but we cannot keep the second, 'fear'. Let's replace it with 'freedom'. Further on, fear and greed imply blindness and this is not so. The relative equilibrium without which there would be simply nothing whatsoever, including any form of economic activity is made possible in full consciousness only, although as time goes by, the spider web of economic links of the present system makes this consciousness to be more fragmentary by the day. As in the one-time Venice, there used to be a carnival and the wearing of masks was taken very seriously indeed, so today the actors on the world economic scene are either of the active or the passive variety. On one side there are those looking for an easy way out of any effort, with a natural preference for the shadow over its substance and on the other side, those making efforts to go in the opposite direction.

Cacambo: You talk of self-delusion all the time and now you just said that economic activity is conducted in full consciousness. How come that both may be valid?

Pangloss: This is full consciousness in respect to the immediate circumstances together with the effort for conducting a given form of economic activity. Yet, this same consciousness which in its immediacy is a full consciousness indeed turns into a self-delusion when the perception of economic reality as a whole is concerned. However, the degree of self-delusion is not the same, since it is conditioned by the effort to look beyond one's immediate surroundings, where some have been given lenses whereas others observe the play with naked eyes.

Cacambo: This 'Cohiba' kind of thing is really great! I made a number of puffs already and I feel somewhat dizzy, but not to the point of being unable to take notice of your extravagance reaching its utmost limit! And what is profit, then? Is not profit the very essence of greed?

PANGLOSS: No, not at all. Have we not talked about substance already? Now, the thing is the following: in some spheres of social activity profit is the undisputable proof of success or a victory over the ever playing and apparently chaotic four elements, as well as a valuable contribution to the public good, whereas in other spheres profit is exactly the opposite: a harmful activity detrimental to society and ultimately to those conducting such an activity. All this is related to the substance of the activity, and as it has been demonstrated already this substance cannot be provided by the mechanism of the market alone, since the market is a mean to an end and consequently not an end in itself. On the positive side, profit is realized through the right effort in the same way as in other spheres this same effort is directed to meditation or asceticism, since in both cases the containment of desire and fear is the sine qua non condition for success.

CACAMBO: Your substance happens to be quite vague, by the way. What is this all about?

PANGLOSS: We have no time to talk about this right now, since we have to leave the place. There is a boat waiting for us at the Port of New York for a transatlantic crossing. Once we are in the open sea, I will go further on with all this.

NOTES

[1] www.thirdworldtraveler.com. The French demographer Alfred Sauvy coined the expression ("tiers monde" in French) in 1952 by analogy with the "third estate", the commoners of France before and during the French Revolution-as opposed to priests and nobles, comprising the first and second estates respectively. Like the third estate, wrote Sauvy, the third world is nothing, and it "wants to be something."

TALE XX

The Crossing Of The Sea

Pangloss and Cacambo are on board of a Cunard ocean liner sailing away from New York harbor. It is late afternoon. They have taken a sit outside, on the side deck and are having a tea.

Cacambo: Whenever I have tea I think of the rabbit from Alice in Wonderland being in a hurry for an appointment and always rising from his seat only to sit back again in the next moment. So, are we not supposed to come back to this place one day, are we?

Pangloss: We have talked about this already. This may be so indeed, but never in the same way and still less to the utmost detail.

Cacambo: Okay. By the way have you heard of the Dutch child finding a solution to the euro crisis using pizza plan?[1]

Pangloss: This crisis has been created on the presumption that there will be no way of turning the clock back. So, if the Euro is to break up, it will be within a larger context, not the smaller context of the recent past. The Drachmas or the Liras with all their competitive devaluations are du Déjà Vu. So, the child has basically missed the point.

Cacambo: Is not your Déjà Vu about to make a tremendous come-back, where the talk of a return to the Drachma in Greece is getting more serious by the day?

Pangloss: The Euro is a step further toward a third solution, beyond both the USD and the Euro. If it happens that this does not work at this point, they will step down, but not from the whole ladder, just from the next incremental step, only to step up later on. In the meantime, they will resort to Dollarization of the whole place. Remember my friend: as long as Oil is on the side of the Sorcerer from the tale of Aladdin and the on-going Dollar based, Stockholm syndrome[2] epidemic is still spreading throughout the four corners of the world, the firm position of our acrobat playing on the global ladder is assured.

Cacambo: Judging from Argentina in 2001, you Dollarization kind of thing does not inspire much confidence?

PANGLOSS: These futurologists do not thrive on confidence alone. What does relay count in the way to globalization is their ability to cause earthquakes of various magnitudes at will, on one hand, and getting the exclusive right for repairing the resulting damage, on the other hand.

CACAMBO: Okay. Yet you still did not make it clear what is your own solution to the problem?

PANGLOSS: I do not own the Universal Natural Law no more than I own the rays of the Sun. And least of all do I own the effort for insight into the way this same Natural Law is operating on this planet.

CACAMBO: There is nothing to be done, then.

PANGLOSS: The postmodern economy is like a racing car running over a steep and tight mountain road along the sea, where instead of slowing down when approaching the next hairpin turn the driver is accelerating to the utmost limit.

CACAMBO: How come that this driver is doing the opposite of what he is supposed to do?

PANGLOSS: He is dizzy. The speed for such a driver is no longer a mean to an end. It is an end in itself. The initial goal of winning the race and thus reaching the shore of peace is supplanted by the means to attain it.

CACAMBO: I heard of this already. You are hammering once more the same kind of thing that you have been presenting right from the beginning.

PANGLOSS: The effort required for taking part in the race is not material. There is no such thing as material effort, since any effort is spiritual in its very essence. Once you become aware of the spiritual nature of economic activity, the distinction between sacred and profane is dissolved right away. The shore of peace is the right effort to attain the state of economic equilibrium. As a part of the global, social, political equilibrium this effort has been the distinctive feature of civilization and indeed of humanity itself from the dawn of history and beyond.

CACAMBO: Great! But how is this to be attained in a way other than in words?

PANGLOSS: The insight in question is not a word and has never been a word. It is the core of reality and therefore of the postmodern economy.

CACAMBO: You still did not make it clear what is to be done in the present context?

PANGLOSS: We started with the right effort. Now, we will be gradually going down to the interplay of the elements along the lines of production and exchange.

CACAMBO: An economy reflecting the Universal Natural Order from its positive side is to be based on the Sacred Primacy of Quality over its representations or quantitative expressions. This is the First point.

CACAMBO: And what is the Second?

PANGLOSS: The evaluation and respectively the organization of economic activity according to its substance.

CACAMBO: Is there a third point?

PANGLOSS: Yes. These two Sacred Principles are not to be put into question under no circumstances, since these are the bridge between what is below and what is above.

CACAMBO: As I see, you just solved the whole problem in a few short sentences. Is your representation over?

PANGLOSS: The above referred substance of different spheres of economic activity may be divided in two parts. The first part will include what is not moving and the second what is does.

CACAMBO: What do you mean?

PANGLOSS: There are sectors where the allocation of resources is efficient if it is conducted through a real competitive market price, provided it is not a fake one, as it is the case today, and others where it is the opposite.

CACAMBO: What are these sectors?

PANGLOSS: What is essentially the reason for being of the nearby Post Office?

CACAMBO: According to *Encyclopedia Britannica* this is the institution—almost invariably under the control of a government or quasi-government agency—that makes it possible for any person to send a letter, packet, or parcel to any addressee, in the same country or abroad, in the expectation that it will be conveyed according to certain established standards of regularity, speed, and security.[3]

PANGLOSS: Have you noticed the words: 'established standard of regularity'?

Cacambo: Why do not you also ask me to make a public reading of the instructions on the fire extinguisher right there?

Pangloss: Is not the term 'established' rather interchangeable with 'fixed' and the latter in turn with unmovable or motionless?

Cacambo: Okay. Following this, there must be a propensity of any form of economic activity whose, 'substance' is 'fixed' to turn into a monopoly, be it private or a state monopoly, I guess.

Pangloss: Yes. Should we examine these 'fixed' activities under the 'ceteris paribus' conditions, by the way, a method in the absence of which, there is simply no way of treating economic reality, a natural tendency for concentration of both property and decision making or responsibility will come out of itself. The very 'substance' of a 'fixed' activity calls for a centralization, where the better the administration of this same activity, the higher the efficiency.

Cacambo: Why? Is not this another of your assortment of preconceived dogmas, of the best in the best of all possible worlds, kind of thing!

Pangloss: This cup of tea does not seem to be your cup of tea indeed, since it is making you quite nervous. Would you like to have some Scotch?

Cacambo: Scotch whisky? Why not, but of you do not mind, of the Black Label type and with another 'Cohiba'.

Pangloss: Yes, sure. Just call the waiter, when you see him.

Cacambo: Great! So, why is there such a tendency?

Pangloss: Your Whisky is coming.

The waiter brings two glasses of Scotch and a third one with ice cubes on the small table, in front of the sea where Pangloss and Cacambo have taken place. Pangloss grabs three cubes of ice with the ice tongs and puts them in his glass.

Pangloss: What have I just done?

Cacambo: One of these illusionist night club kind tricks of yours.

Pangloss: Have I not put three cubes of ice in my glass only a few seconds ago?

CACAMBO: And so what?

PANGLOSS: Now, what in reality did take place is the following: Me or my consciousness directed my right hand to the ice tongs and then took three cubes of ice and put them in the glass. This act has been an act that I executed in full consciousness and without the slightest degree of hesitation, since I have been repeating the same gestures for thousands and thousands of times throughout all the years I happened to spent on this planet. The information on the way this same act is to be performed, stored in my consciousness, is no less than perfect. Nobody has interfered in its execution. Transposed to the sphere of production and exchange of material goods and services, either on the Macroeconomic or Microeconomic level, the act in question is equivalent to direct allocation of resources.

CACAMBO: Wait a minute. Is not your 'direct' allocation of resources in reality the same kind of thing as the command economy of the recent past or the temple of absurdity that the so called central planning turned out to be?

PANGLOSS: No.

CACAMBO: What is it, then?

PANGLOSS: Have we not said that the allocation of resources is to be done according to the substance or the intrinsic quality of the different types of economic activity? What we referred to as 'fixed' activities, using the terms, borrowed from the mainstream definition of what a Post Office is all about may be best performed through administrative regulation, characteristic of the State. Apart from the Post these 'fixed' activities include, electricity and water supply, telecommunication services etc.

CACAMBO: Are you not, by the way, one of these disguised statists, if not an outright tot...tota...total...

PANGLOSS: Totalitarian, I guess? Look left!

CACAMBO: Why? Is there a whale or something?

PANGLOSS: No. 'Look left' is an inscription that you can read at the edge of any sidewalk in the London's city center.

CACAMBO: What is this all about?

PANGLOSS: If you want to get a precise account of all activities that should be under public scrutiny and consequently beyond any form of competition, just take a look on the privatized public monopolies in this same place, back in the 1980s. Nothing is further from economic rationality and more arbitrary than a private monopoly, be it formal or a de facto monopoly, on a 'fixed' activity, where under the Trojan horse type rhetoric of liberalism, all check and balances are suppressed and consequently costs are socialized and profits privatized. However, it goes without saying that in comparison with the global fiat money scheme starting already in the 19th century with the Gold Standard pyramid, this is definitely a small hat. We mention it here, only as an interesting case study of a particularly clear-cut policy, characterizing the attempt of rolling back the last remnants of rationality and common sense, a little like the backwards running sections in a reversed movie.

CACAMBO: Is not fiat money related to the dismantlement of public activities in the name of easy profits or rather in the name an outright de facto expropriation, a process which accelerated its pace ever since the 1980s throughout the world and whose matrix goes back to the reversed movie taking place on the London sidewalks?

PANGLOSS: Yes, but this is only an effect, and by no means the only effect, of a cause that initiated it in the first place and which already before WWI used to be beyond the sphere of formal politics.

CACAMBO: Now, if the State appears to be sometimes still more inefficient than even these monopolists looking say from an ontological point of view, for an easy way out of this world, this is not the state under the ceteris paribus conditions that we are taking into consideration here, but the bureaucratic tentacles of an octopus. This is not a real state. This is only a state like apparatus, precisely in the same way as fiat money is not real money.

CACAMBO: How come 'out of this world'? Are they not precisely the agents of this same world?

PANGLOSS: This appears to be so at first glance, following centuries of ontological dichotomy with the corresponding atrophy of the intuitive, intellective side of human self-perception, where the subtle currents at work bring forward superficial amateurs of the Machiavelli or the Marquis de Sade type, initiating yet another rising tide of confusion and blindness. Fiat money and its social, cultural etc. crystallization is the most explicit flight from reality on record. Here is a display of methodical illusionism, where economic activity, before its last stage of final dissolution comes out on the horizon, still appears as a bad joke, as an exercise in futility.

CACAMBO: Do not you see that everything is shaking around here. There is a sea storm.

PANGLOSS: Look at the replica of this storm in your own glass of Scotch.

CACAMBO: What the hell my glass has to do with all this?

PANGLOSS: The uncertain position of the cubes inside the glass is what really counts at this point.

CACAMBO: Why did I embark on this boat, with all these electric bulbs and polished plastic components? The boats of our own time were better! The storm is getting worse by the second! There is a wave coming up! It is just in front of us! It is coming!!!

PANGLOSS: It will not rise to the level of the deck, whose height is the same as the one of a several stories building, after all. Just keep your glass in your hands and take a look at the ice cubes inside.

CACAMBO: Go to hell with your ice cubes!

PANGLOSS: Would you only tell me if it would be possible for you to stop these ice cubes from moving around the glass?

CACAMBO: Of course I cannot stop them from moving. It is beyond my control. The storm makes the boat shaky and moves the ice cubes in the glass and that is it!

PANGLOSS: Yes, indeed. I agree with you. If you were a central planner right now and the ice cubes were the resources you are supposed to allocate, you would be lost, would not you? Your hands or your tools of central planning would have been helpless in the face of the storm, since it goes without saying that the conditions that brought this storm in the first place are simply out of your reach. Now, this does not mean however that the knowledge on the duration, the strength of the storm or the height of the waves brought forth by this storm is beyond anyone's reach. This knowledge is available, although it is a disseminated, diffused knowledge throughout the consciousness of several players or rather in our case observers of the whole phenomenon. Furthermore, it is a relative knowledge, since, for example the height of the sea waves lasts only for the duration of the storm, where each wave is rising and falling only in a few seconds.

CACAMBO: Great! The storm is about to pass. The ice cubes in my glass do not move around any longer. You seem to be right, after all!

PANGLOSS: So, we got at the second part of economic activity or the substance which by its very nature is designed to move.[4] Here everything is turned upside down. The decision making process is decentralized. Private property reigns supreme. There is one only price and this price is the competitive market price.

CACAMBO: What are the constituent parts of this second movable substance?

Pangloss: All that is relative, transitory and unpredictable by its very nature, just as fashion is, calls for decentralization, personal responsibility and market resource allocation. The production of consumer goods along with Trade, including International Trade, among other things is within the sphere of the second part. You will never allocate resources efficiently if you confuse these two opposite doubles, in the same way as the sea will never obey your central planning type commands to stop the storm, so that the ice cubes cease moving around in your glass of Scotch. A profit earned through fair competition is no greed. It is a contribution to the public good and the effort for such a contribution is no less spiritual than any effort, including those in science or art.

Cacambo: How come that you speak of private property but you do not show any concern for what they call ever after the 19thcentury, 'capitalism'? Is not your fiat money system the very core of the capitalist kind of thing?

Pangloss: Capitalism as an idea or as a specific perception of reality is based on the presumption for the implicit primacy of the form over its content or the object over its subject. There is no human nature in such a perception. There is only a piranha or a shark like greed assumed to be a constant. The containment of greed or the natural propensity for equilibrium of both the subject and its object, assumed to be the very core of the concept of rationality since the dawn of civilization, here is turned upside down, since the outpouring of blind greed is equated with rationality. On the level of the Psyche the picture in question led to thick smog of self-delusion, where the propelling force of economic activity or the sufficient reasons for the right effort in any given circumstances has been associated precisely with its opposite. The reality portrayed by the notion of capitalism, both in its liberal and collectivist versions is a false reality.

Cacambo: Are then private property and personal responsibility also false values?

Pangloss: No, since these are the last remnants of economic rationality in the today's world.

Cacambo: The last remnants? And you Pangloss are also taking yourself for one of the last Romans, I guess?

Pangloss: There is no place for anything personal in the ultimate design of the fiat money system, be it freedom, responsibility or property, since by definition ghosts can pass through any wall. As for the Romans, they are essentially new comers to a scene, where the traditions inherited from the Etruscans, including the Vestals and the Gladiators were already transmitted for a long time. By the way, the Etruscans seemed to know how to store electricity, but they did not pass this knowledge to the Romans.

CACAMBO: Listen, I wonder how is it that you, who are basically committed to the best in the best of all possible world staff are at the same time, what appears to me, a convinced catastrophist.

PANGLOSS: Catastrophism either in its mild Neo-Platonist form or in its harsher Gnostic variety is always Dualism in one way or another. So, had you been less distracted by the surface of the sea, you would already have noticed that there is no such thing as a broken Monad, since the latter has no windows, and as a result the very idea of catastrophe, in the realm of substance, is excluded both in potency and in act.

CACAMBO: Okay. So, what would be the place of money in the Monad of Quality, then?

PANGLOSS: Money exists by proxy only. It is a reflection of quality. If you look at yourself in the water just like Narcissus did, the closer you are to its surface, the better you see your face. So is the case with money. The further the copy is moving away from its original, the closer it is to the point of no return or to its own demise.

CACAMBO: If you go any further with your metaphors, I insist for still another Cuban cigar.

PANGLOSS: The quality of money may be kept intact if there comes out a new Bi Metallic Standard. Gold alone is nothing but the introductory level course for a future fiat system. It is only in combination with silver that gold may preserve the real value of money. Thus the ghostlike world of bubbles, Ponzi schemes, together with the waste of natural and human resources, the debasement of money and the corresponding debasement of the human condition, all of these will disappear without leaving any trace other than a remote souvenir of a bad dream. The very existence of bubbles with their inevitable bursting, illustrate the absolute validity of the intrinsic nature of money. At last resort, the value of any commodity is equal to what it is in itself and not what it appears to be in the eyes of the public or the wishful thinking of those who happen to deceive this public. A tulip will always be a tulip, whatever the value you happen to place on it.

CACAMBO: Was not the world on a kind of tacit Bimetallic Standard for millennia? Yet, this did prevent poverty and brutality from reigning supreme throughout all this time?

PANGLOSS: The present day picture of the past is distorted to the point that should any soul of the pre-modern times, and antiquity in particular, resurrect for a few brief moments only to read all the clichés imprinted on the consciousness of epistemological self-delusion behind this picture, he will hardly be able to recognize even his own name let alone the immediate surroundings of his previous life. The economy of ancient India or China or the Mediterranean during the Greco-Roman period and earlier used to be based on the natural law of equilibrium. The ultimate origin of Agriculture, Building, Natural Medicine and Clothing, including Purple are shrouded in a mystery, whose deciphering is the sine qua non condition for real economic advancement. The few scattered fragments of this legacy in the present are often enough to unveil vast horizons of knowledge. There are no theatres like ancient theatres today. There are no buildings as massive and solid as the temple of Baalbek, the Sphinx or the Pyramids. There are no roads today like Appian Way still in use, more than twenty centuries after it had been built. As for ancient pharmacology, the extent of the in-depth knowledge of nature, including human nature, is revealed in the legacy of traditional medicine, despite its alteration with the passage of time and the classifying of its likely achievements such as the Elixir of Life as legends. There are also periods of time and places, however, where primitive conditions were indeed prevailing. The world of the pre-modern past used to be a diverse world. Furthermore, following the traditional view of the cycles, the knowledge in the Iron Age is only a remote souvenir, a collection of scattered fragments from a whole, hidden within the potential of the universal cyclical causality, where nothing is ultimately lost, but only forgotten. What appears to be a progress today, and which in some areas is indeed so rests on the present misuse of some sudden flashes of insight into the cognitive pool of eternity by such figures as N. Tesla, since nothing ever has been discovered in a consciousness veiled by materialistic obscurantism, other than self-delusion, greed, envy and frustration.

Cacambo: I finished my cigar already. Why do not you call the waiter for another one, until you get again to the main point of money?

Pangloss: Although built on a sound ontological basis the Bimetallism of the pre-modern past, had a limited impact, since trade as a whole was only seldom exceeding 5-10% of the size of the overall economy, essentially based on self-sufficiency and agriculture. Furthermore, the old Bimetallism appears as a spontaneous, even chaotic and yet still, rational reaction to the general conditions of insecurity, blindness and brutality prevailing in the Iron Age.

Cacambo: What will a present day version of Bimetallism look like?

Pangloss: The amount of gold and silver in circulation will be under the close scrutiny of a state owned central bank resting on absolute transparency. Hoarding will be a matter of the utmost concern, since otherwise the restraint of credit resulting from hoarding and hiding as well will be hindering economic activity.

Cacambo: Is there a place other than in words for economic freedom in such conditions, where each piece of gold and silver is to be accounted and deposited in the banking system?

PANGLOSS: The system of checks and balances of the supply of gold and silver is the sine qua non condition for freedom and harmony, since it is precisely hoarding that would create a favorable climate for price instability and consequently for bubbles.

CACAMBO: How will you respond when some persist in hoarding and hiding to the point of creating a separate black market price for gold and silver? Will you put them behind bars for life or confiscate their belongings?

PANGLOSS: I will adopt two separate prices of precious metals, the one being the market price, where each coin and its corresponding expression in paper money will be stamped with a special mark, attesting its presence within the banking system or its origin accounted by this same system. Those who succeed in hiding and hoarding a certain amount of the precious metals will still be able to use the gold and silver in their possession but at a price determined by the state, designed to discourage the expansion of these activities. By the way, ancient Bimetallism prevented the likely expansion of trade precisely because of hoarding. During the Middle-Ages most of the gold and silver used to be concentrated in the hands of Venetians, the Florentines and the Genoese, who manipulated the price of gold and silver and thus were effectively able to buy up the Crowns of a number of Monarchs, by acquiring monopolies such as, for example, the Florentine monopoly on the production of wool in England, acquired by the 14th century.[5]

CACAMBO: And how about the banking system? Is it movable or immovable according to your scheme?

PANGLOSS: There is an immovable as well as a movable part. The former includes the provision for a state owned central bank, whose operations are to be as transparent as the National Debt Clock displayed on Time Square. Once set, these provisions may be no less sacred than the constitutions or the symbols of ancient city states, from where originate the Meta historical roots of Europe and America. The latter or the movable part rests on the total freedom of a private banking sector set up along the lines of a real market competition for loans and clients.

CACAMBO: Would you specify what total freedom is all about?

PANGLOSS: Here is the freedom from outer constraint other than the limits of a real market competition. This applies both for those inside any given entity of the system as well as for those outside. To put in another way, no bank and no lender will be operating at the expense of state coffers. There will be one only place for today's bailing out kind of thing and this place will be the shelves of the libraries with books devoted to financial history.

CACAMBO: How is this to be achieved in reality?

PANGLOSS: You start with the delimitation of the sacred boundaries between the State and the private sector and you end…

CACAMBO: …You end where?

PAMGLOSS: You end the whole thing with these same boundaries.

CACAMBO: If do not bother to specify what do these boundaries look like, this is surely because, here is another free quotation of the wishful thinking on the integrity of the state, against cronyism etc. written in the constitution of practically all states, currently members of the UN and therefore printed at least as much as the instructions, inscribed on the fire extinguisher right there on the deck, and those on all other fire extinguishers throughout the world for that matter.

PANGLOSS: These boundaries are the same invisible boundaries separating what is movable from what is immovable in the same way as in the Emerald Tablet of Hermes, what is above is like what is below. The activities appropriate to the state are to remain in the domain of the state and vice versa, those appropriate to the market are to remain in the sphere of the market. Now, within the boundary of the State the allocation of resources is to be done primarily In Natura i.e. In-Kind whereas within the sphere of the market this would be respectively In-Vivo or in Cash.

CACAMBO: That is definitely great! Would you be just kind enough to tell me what the tax collection of such a state will look like?

PANGLOSS: The tax collection is also to be mainly in kind.

CACAMBO: What?

PANGLOSS: Yes. You heard it right. The tax collection is to be mainly, although not exclusively, in kind. The present VAT and the like, may be abolished and replaced by a tax, where a portion of the working hours of those exercising activities, whose nature is within the confines of what a Sacred Code may stipulate as being within the sphere of the public good, is to be collected in kind. Now, goods and only goods that cannot be distributed in kind to those outside of the private sector, such as the elderly are to be collected in cash. In this way, the State will preserve its real independence on one hand and on the other hand, there will be a strong stimulus for a diversified productive base and for the development of local production. International Trade will lose its spectral nature and will be confined to the boundaries of Reason and the concern for Harmony and Freedom. The rabbit we have talked about earlier on, will no longer be making speedy U-turns around the shelves of the supermarket in the search for discounted pre-packed toxic items but will slow down to the pace of rationality. By the way, the present oppression of the elderly in the name of the so called state budget cuts apart for being a human catastrophe, is arguably also the most articulate and consistent display of economic absurdity on record.

CACAMBO: Why?

PANGLOSS: The on-going global expansion of fiat money is, on a material plane, what the consciousness of self-delusion is on a spiritual plane. Such a perception of reality takes the copy for the original and as a result, the physical side of economic activity is put on the back stage at the expense of the ghost like accounting or financial side. From the point of view of accounting, the activities of a drug dealer are a positive contribution to the economy, since the profit generated by these activities appear to be a creation of wealth and consequently has a potential for redistribution, either in the form of taxes, or in the form of donations. Accounting takes for real only what has been accounted already and therefore excludes what it is to be accounted in the future and hence the long term diffusion effect of harmful activities such as the drug trade, which far from being a credit is in reality an enormous debit, to society as a whole is not, and worse still, cannot be adequately evaluated, if there is not a larger point of reference, beyond quantity i.e. quality. In today's economic environment, there is no intrinsic need for labor as in our own time or still earlier, when the slave market used to be the most important market in Rome. From a purely physical perspective, the goods required for the maintenance of decent living conditions for the elderly may be produced with a relatively small effort, especially in a place such as the one we just left, the US. The problem is not physical, as by the way, it has been the case in our own time, nor is it technical. The problem is with accounting. And the sand like nature of fiat money exacerbates this problem still further by compelling the debtors to give out of themselves for real, what is only virtual for the creditors or for specifically for the last resort creditors. Once again, backed essentially by nothing really consistent, paper and now plastic money is nominal for its creator or issuer, but real for the debtor and the holder of assets denominated in what appears to be of some value for a time, but later on inevitably ends in revealing its real sand like nature. To say that there are too many old people creating an economic imbalance is the same as you said, for example that the US will collapse because food is now produced by only 2-3% of the working force, sustaining the other 95-7%, whereas in the past more than a half of the working population used to be employed in agriculture and food processing.

CACAMBO: The question of State debt, in this 21 the century is everywhere, starting with the Debt Clock right there in the city of New York. By the way, what will happen to the world bond market in your planet of Quality?

PANGLOSS: There will be none.

CACAMBO: How come?

PANGLOSS: A genuinely sovereign State is to have debts only to itself or to its own citizens. The part of State revenue which cannot be collected in kind is to be evaluated in cash backed by gold and silver or by a special provision of the publicly owned central bank for a limited emission of paper money.

CACAMBO: Did I hear you right? Listen to me my friend are you not transgressing your own principles in the most abject manner, right now?

PANGLOSS: Should you see the waiter passing by, just raise your hand again. I will order whisky once more and still another 'Cohiba' for you, so that you may calm down. Gold is indeed no barbaric relic. In combination with its natural counterpart, silver this is, as we saw it before in more detail, the only universal and timeless medium of exchange, ever since the meteors had deposited it on this planet. In times of distress or when the fundamental macroeconomic equilibrium is to be restored through a scheme of economic expansion, fiat money may be temporarily issued on condition that the last printed $1 bill is accounted as precisely as the US debt is displayed on Time Square right now. By the way, paradoxically enough, not only the Lincoln Greenbacks, were not the starting point for a Ponzi scheme, but on the opposite, objectively so to speak, they used to stand against the ultimately fake gold standard of the 19th century, since once detached from silver, gold becomes like the Flying Dutchman and it is only a matter of time before, it is suppressed altogether and replaced by sand like fiat money. It goes without saying that such a measure may be nothing else than a temporary measure and should a limited edition of paper money be issued, a date for the re-establishment of Bimetallism is to be set.

CACAMBO: And what is the place for the private sector on the planet of Quality? You did not go any further after your ice cubes kind of thing?

PANGLOSS: A real private sector is to be kept as far away as possible from the potential of corruption provided by the State with its lucrative monopolies of the easy life type. By the way, this is not our own time and the reintroduction of guilds may not be really a good thing, since the world around us is moving very fast. Further on, the corporation is to be abolished and the very idea of limited responsibility is to be studied for a long time to come as the best example for the worse in the worst of all possible worlds.

CACAMBO: The say the corporation, by achieving these...I forgot it...

PANGLOSS: Economies of scale, I guess?

CACAMBO: Yes.

PANGLOSS: These economies of scale play the same role at last resort as the debasement of coinage used to play ever since the first coins were minted by the Phoenicians, several millennia ago. The only difference is a difference in degree, since the scale of ancient debasement and its impact on the society as a whole is no match to the present corporate inspired debasement of just everything, starting, from any item on the shelves of the supermarket, where, our friend the rabbit is making U turns, since his uncompleted attempt for outpacing his rival, the turtle may still be going on at this very moment. Let's take the following example, so that we may shed some light on the on-going display of global corporate efficiency. So, suppose the distinguished chemist, M-r Newborn Patent a likely heir of the Nobel Laureate Paul Sabatier comes along with a new recipe of artificial fats[6] and still another one for the latest variety of hydrogenated oil and knocks at the door of the expanding Multinational Corporation, 'Correct Foods Inc.' Following a brief introductory presentation to the president of the corporation, the venerable M-r Margarine, our fellow gets an A+ for his recipe and in the very next day, the text of this same recipe is already circulating from the top down to the ground floor of the entire building, where the successive steps of the corporate ladder climbed by experts on human resources, natural resources, management and the like, along with some fine connoisseurs of the latest amendments in the *Codex Alimentarius,*[7] happen to be located. Great! Say those on the roof 'The recipe is great!' Add the chartered accountants from the middle floors of the whole corporate structure. Thanks to the new recipe, the manufacturing process that is taking place at this very moment, somewhere along the shores of Vietnam, being le dernier cri of delocalization, will be going on still faster and the dividend per share of 'Correct Foods' is to increase by more than 10% in the process. And this is only the beginning of all that is to follow, since a lucrative chain reaction has been initiated and a speculative frenzy around the 'Correct Foods' stock has taken place already. In the meantime, a number of Hedge funds, ranging from the Caiman Islands up to the shores of the Lake Leman have included 'Correct Foods' in their portfolios. Mortgages, credits and other default swaps, backed with 'Correct Foods' stock guarantee are about to flood the world financial markets for one moment to the next.

CACAMBO: So, what? Is not this the best in the best of all possible worlds, kind of thing?

PANGLOSS: Do you know the story of Hansel and Gretel?

CACAMBO: What?

PANGLOSS: This is one of the Grimm Brothers fairy tales, authors from a little later time than our own time. So, both Hansel and his sister Gretel are supposed to get fat in this tale. It is the same with the consumers of artificial trans fats, with the only difference that they get fat for good, whereas Hansel stretched out a little bone instead of his finger to the old witch, who could not make the difference with her red dim eyes.

CACAMBO: Your tale seems to be just fine, although you had better spare me the details and go a little further with the whole thing.

PANGLOSS: Now, the very idea of corporate efficiency requires that the likely cause and effect relationship between the artificial trans fats and the on-going obesity epidemic is to be obscured or so to speak, it is to be shelved by a huge army of corporate lawyers and other figures through the propagation of an assortment of alternative explanations, such as the lack of physical exercise, too much calories, hereditary disorders and so forth.

CACAMBO: But this may be so! How do you know?

PANGLOSS: As we said it earlier, this is the most likely cause, and any subsequent research on the subject will show that here is something in the right direction. There were no fat people in our own time, but only overweight people and without today's accompanying disorders such as diabetes, cancer, muscular dystrophy etc. It is highly probable that the cause which is usually advanced to explain the whole phenomenon that is the intake of too much calories is simply utterly wrong. And this might be so, because the human organism cannot be reduced to a sum of atoms or granules or genomes or God knows what else, for the simple reason that the Monad has no windows, and as a result nothing in the manifested reality is ever reduced to anything other than itself, no more than the cards constituting a pack of cards may be reduced to a single card, without altering the whole game. The manifested Universe is like this pack of cards, with the only difference that, contrary to the pack of cards, which is only a copy, the Universe is its original and therefore nothing can ever be altered, since this is the only possible game. On the subtle level, here as elsewhere, we are in the face of collectivist, nihilistic dogmatic obscurantism, standing in the way of reason and in the way of knowledge itself. Once more, following the very idea of substance, which is no other, than Plato's Forms or the Buddhist Two Truths doctrine, the human organism is a substance, i.e. a quality, in the first place and if we do not know how this quality is operating on all levels, which is indeed the case ever since the beginning of the Kali Yuga or the Iron Age, we had better follow the course of nature and leaving natural fats in the food ingredients instead of substituting them with plastic like, toxic imitations in the name of a still another incremental rise of the printed paper by the name of money, in circulation. If natural fats are to be reintroduced and artificial ones banned once and for all, the chances of reducing obesity to the levels of the pre-industrial food diet may be very high indeed. Now, provided this very likely reason is indeed the reason and nothing is done to prevent what appears to be an on-going process of physical self-mutilation on a scale never seen before, for each gained corporate dollar, future generations will have to pay, may be 100 may be 1000 dollars, who knows? In the face of the intrinsic nature of things or quality per se, accounting of fiat money is like a blind unicellular organism lost in the sand dunes of Sahara. Now, what will happen if all that has been said, on artificial Trans Fats so far tomorrow is somehow proven to be the truth and the whole truth? Who will pay the price?

CACAMBO: The members of the corporation and those on the top in the first place, I guess?

PANGLOSS: Nobody will pay anything.

CACAMBO: Why?

PANGLOSS: The Corporation ever since its appearance on the scene, in the second half of the 19th century is a legal and a conceptual puzzle. This is an entity acting for real on the scene but considered to be only half real and respectively half unreal, since the corporation is based on the utterly incomprehensible, odd concept of limited responsibility. Here is a child who has rights, such as the right to contract debts, for example, making it the ideal match for the fiat money creditors, but who has no real obligations. And another thing, when they say that capitalism appeared for good in a time which happens to be simultaneously also the time when the corporation was born, by the middle of the 19th century, they show in the most unambiguous way that here is catchphrase for something utterly different. The very concept of capitalism is in reality a bad joke. The corporation is a form of diluted property and as such is at the very opposite end of private property and the corresponding notion of personal responsibility. If the concept of capitalism means anything at all, there used to be much more capitalism, for example in the city states of antiquity and in the independent medieval cities of Italy and Germany than in the 19th let alone the 20th and the 21st centuries. So, fiat money together with the corporation is bringing forward a kind of communalism which, by the way, is only the prelude for the things to come.

CACAMBO: Has not the time for my gold come already?

PANGLOSS: Let me see my crystal ball first. You guessed right. In one hour, you will find out the tablet with the formula for the transmutation on the table of your cabin.

CACAMBO: Great! That is really great! I waited for so long to get this formula. From now on, I will be just like you or this man by the name of… one of whose houses is still standing in the Ile de la Cite[8]…I will have at my disposal not only the elixir of long life but gold also.

PANGLOSS: Yes, so our journey is coming to an end I guess. We will arrive at

Southampton, if I am right in only five days. By the way, if you are bored with all these discussions, you can very well spent the rest of the transatlantic crossing alone or in the company of one of these charming Ladies who are strolling around and just looking for a good time, provided that you do not tell them how old you really are.

CACAMBO: Yes, why not, after all. Yet with your permission I will be glad to come from time to time and debating on you never ending points on this and that.

PANGLOSS: I would be happy to see you again and yet I am somewhat surprised by your reaction, since you did not really agree with what I have been presenting so far.

CACAMBO: Maybe, but there was a discussion at least. I have traveled a lot before we met at the Geneva railroad station, but I was seldom discussing anything because wherever I was going, there were as many different truths as different people. That is why, I overslept myself at some point and as you had the occasion to see, I missed many things in the process, including the precise location of the UN. Truth these days is treated in reality somewhat like the items on the shelves of your supermarket, where the enchanted rabbit is still making U turns, I guess. Everyone is told to believe in mutually exclusive truths, whose sum may be just anything except the truth, by the way. I was quite bored to wander in such a soap bubble like universe.

PANGLOSS: Great! So, this journey to Europe appears to be only the first among still many others.

NOTES

[1] *A Dutch Child's Solution to the Euro Crisis*, Diane Ellis, Ed. · Apr 3 at 4:18pm, www. ricochet. com.

[2] "*Understanding Stockholm Syndrome*" (pdf, page 10), Federal Bureau of Investigation (FBI)
[3] Postal System www.britannica.com.

[4] See *The Cambridge Companion to Hayek*, Edited by: Edward Feser, Pasadena City College, California.

[5] See Frederic C. Lane, "*Money and Banking in Mediaeval and Renaissance Venice*".

[6] See *Trans Fat: What the Food Industry Wants to Hide From You* October 5th, 2009 www.naturalbias. com, *Ban the Trans: These Sorry Lipids Should Go Away*, Rob Fursiewicz, Volume 20 Issue 17 2012-05-04 www.voicemagazine.org.

[7] See www.codexalimentarius.org.

[8]See *The Philosopher's Stone: A Quest for the Secrets of Alchemy*, 2001, Peter Marshall; *Also The Secret History of the World and How to Get Out Alive*, p43 by Laura Knight-Jadczyk.

www.ingramcontent.com/pod-product-compliance
Lightning Source LLC
LaVergne TN
LVHW011221080426
835509LV00005B/258